The Lord Is My Husband

by

Janet Lash

JANET LASH
MINISTRIES
A FRIEND WITH FAITH

The Lord Is My Husband

Trilogy Christian Publishers A Wholly Owned Subsidary of Trinity Broadcasting Network

2442 Michelle Drive Tustin, CA 92780

Rights Department, 2442 Michelle Drive, Tustin, CA 92780.

Trilogy Christian Publishing/TBN and colophon are trademarks of Trinity Broadcasting Network.

Cover design by: Natalee Dunning

For information about special discounts for bulk purchases, please contact Trilogy Christian Publishing.

Trilogy Disclaimer: The views and content expressed in this book are those of the author and may not necessarily reflect the views and doctrine of Trilogy Christian Publishing or the Trinity Broadcasting Network.

Manufactured in the United States of America

10 9 8 7 6 5 4 3 2 1

Library of Congress Cataloging-in-Publication Data is available.

ISBN: 978-1-63769-756-6

E-ISBN: 978-1-63769-757-3

ACKNOWLEDGMENTS

For my parents, Noble and Caris Kendall, my grandparents Rev. Leslie and Isabelle VanInwegen, and Merle and Ruby Kendall, I am grateful for their example of a love that lasts the tests of time;

For the many leaders, teachers, and pastors over the years who have sown into my life the truths found herein that will hopefully continue to bear fruit in the lives of many more;

For my mentor and friend, my spiritual mother Vicki Kendrick, thank you for your love, compassion, and truth;

For my friends and family who walked this journey with me, I am grateful for the lessons we learn, the encouragement and joy we share;

For Debbie Hester, my prayer partner and worshipper, that shared in this word with me, thank you;

And finally, for the design team and editors who helped with this;

May God bless each one and be glorified in this.

DEDICATION

The following journey is dedicated first to my true love, the Lord my Husband, for His tender mercy and great grace with which He persistently pursues loving me through times of single life, marriage, divorce, single parenting, remarriage, and now widowhood, while leading me into His presence.

Then, to the man He chose to reveal Himself through, my loving husband, Ken Lash, who, after twenty years together, has gone on to be with the Lord, leaving a legacy of love in me, our family, friends, and associates that I pray bears fruit eternally.

And then, to you, my friend, may you be encouraged with hope to know the Lord is coming for you. I invite you to the altar where love is waiting; may your response be "I Do" as well.

Wherefore, my brethren, ye also are become dead to the law by the body of Christ; that ye should be married to another, even to him who is raised from the dead, that we should bring forth fruit unto God.

Romans 7:4 (KJV)

For I am jealous over you with godly jealousy: for I have espoused you to one husband, that I may present you as a chaste virgin to Christ.

2 Corinthians11:2 (KJV)

Introduction

As I have observed, it seems many women struggle today, experiencing fulfillment or peace. Whether they are dating, single, divorced, widowed, or married, it does not seem to matter. The ones that have a mate don't want one, and the ones that don't have one do! At the core of our projected social paradigm, we hope for or imagine the dream of love living "happily ever after." But it seems the dream is only possible for others, at least by their Facebook posts, but illusive to us. Somehow, in the meantime, we train ourselves to be self-preservationists. In one sense, we protect our hearts by an aloofness or even coldness instead of opening up. Yet, on the other hand, we may act out in an aggressive, angry, or even predatorial flirtatious, "party girl" way. In the one, we stand off. In the other, we "get them before they get us," or so we think. Maybe you have been there, as have I. Oftentimes through no fault of our own, we act out of the pain of past hurts. Whether through abuses, abandonment, fears, lies, or insecurities of our own or those we have observed in others, we are trapped in cycles of defeat. With our expectations dashed, we no longer hold out hope for relational success. Here we are resigned to simply survive.

Yes, it is true; as a result, many women today stay single longer. Some wait to marry later in life, possibly in hopes of better choices. Some choose not to make such a binding commitment, while others settle for "friends with benefits." Like making a pact with ourselves, we leave an escape route open. Hoping to leave our options open, establish a career, or at least maintain an independent identity, we avoid such relational decisions. This accounts for the probability of multiple significant relationships outside of marriage. Add to that the probability of multiple marriages; we can quickly understand the heartbreak condition so much experience and the vows made out of that, like "I'll never marry!" Here you may find yourself "in-between" relationships or maybe "in" a meaningful relationship, dating or married, but still feeling confused, lost, dead, hopeless, and yes, even lifeless. You may be wondering if it is even possible to experience deep satisfying joy, fulfillment, and intimacy in a relationship. If so, can it last? On the other hand, you may be wondering, "Why would God leave me alone, and for so long? Why do 'I' have to wait?" You may even wonder, "Why He (God) gave me 'this' man? Oh yes, of course, I love him, but I just don't like him a lot! Of course, I'll stay married to him. I know divorce is wrong, but I don't have to like it!"

Have you ever found yourself asking these questions or even just entertaining the thought for the briefest of moments? Maybe you or someone you know talks this way: your daughter, step-daughter, sister, mother, friend, or coworker. If so, I understand and came to tell you there is hope. There is a life of joy you can have and share. God has given me a word that I believe will change your life and your world. It did mine. If you will open your heart and ask God to give you His spirit of understanding, I believe confidently that He will lead you into all the revelation and fullness He has planned for you. God wants us whole. He is coming back for the love of His life, His beautiful bride, you! He wants our heart so He can fill it with His joy. He has come for it, and He is asking you to take His hand and go on this journey to find your true love, your forever soulmate! He is "lovesick" waiting for you!

Would you join me in this prayer:

Lord, thank you for your love, thank you for loving me, for hearing my cry and seeing my pain. I believe you sent your word and healed them and that you have sent your word to heal me. I open my heart to you, Lord, flood me with your light, open my ears to hear your voice, and my eyes to see you. Please take me on this journey to discover your heart, to find the true intimacy I desire. Please give me a spirit of faith to believe and a spirit of wisdom to understand. Thank you, God; I love you in Jesus' name, amen.

TABLE OF CONTENTS

ENDORSEMENTS

"How can I comment intelligently on a marriage book? What does a comedian know about marriage? Well. I have been happily married for over thirty-five years, and those years were served consecutively. Secondly, I have known the author for many years. She was married to my best friend. In the later years of my friend's life, he was a pastor; nevertheless, he was no saint. To live with him, she must have known something about marriage and how to survive it.

Janet is a strong woman who knows what it is like to have all her strength knocked out. But, she also knows how to find her strength renewed. She knows how to come back swinging—but not swinging in anger or vengeance, but swinging a well-crafted sling of David, with stones of God. So, join her on a journey that will may change your life and the life of those you love.

This book will help you find healing if you need healing from a tragic relational pastor, find transformation in your marital present, or find joy and inspiration in your marital future."

—Mike Williams
Author of *Men Moved to Mars When Women
Started Killing the Ones on Venus*

"One might ask the question if the Lord is Janet's husband, where does that leave you as her earthly husband. How can you compare with the Almighty? The reality is I wouldn't have it any other way. What you have in this book is, in essence, a survival manual that my wife used to keep her sanity while she attempted to be a godly wife to a man who wasn't what she thought. Little self helps, or patent quotes wouldn't allow her to get her physical and emotional needs met. The answers could only be found in the Holy Scriptures. As she lay stone upon stone, precept upon precept, the answer became apparent only God could meet her needs. Her earthly husband, no matter how he would try, could not and would not meet the deepest needs in her life. I have observed Janet not only espouse these truths but practice them. Paul tells us the weapons of our warfare are not carnal but spiritual. Personally, I have seen the victory won in the supernatural and enjoyed the peace that came into our lives and our home when the Lord became her husband. If your husband isn't what you thought he would be and you know that God has more for you than just existing, this book is for you. For my beautiful bride whom I love and adore,"

Yours always,
Ken Lash

CHAPTER 1.
CHOOSE YOUR RABBI

He continued, "I am a good Jew, born in Tarsus in the province of Cilicia, but educated here in Jerusalem under the exacting eye of Rabbi Gamaliel, thoroughly instructed in our religious traditions."

Acts 22:2 (MSG)

"Let him go!" How could this be God? Here, in my quiet time, spent reading the Bible and praying, I sensed the Lord speak to my heart to let him go. The questions were there, yes, but the need to hold on was gone. This was not about me. Sometimes, letting go of what we hold so tight is the best offering. Within three days, he left, and this time, I let him go. This time, however, I did not question him or even resist. The Lord had shown me through scriptures His divine perspective, so when he left, I was not surprised. But I was surprised by the overwhelming peace of God. Here I was, with a hundred dollars in hand, the blessing of our three-year-old son, a suitcase of clothes, and the peace of God. Where would I go, and what would I do now? I found myself abandoned, homeless, and jobless. Our world was turned inside out. Now I knew the sudden loss of something held dear.

But God!

We would not see or hear from him again for six months. Oh, but for the goodness and grace of God, His great plan unfolded! God was so amazing. My friend Mary prayed for peace over me, and during those next six months, I experienced such supernatural favor and blessing of God. With no place to call my own, my grandparents took us in for a couple weeks. Then after church the next Sunday, my friend recommended I apply for the job he just left, and within a few short weeks, I had a job and a car. Then, through a friend, a gracious sister from church took us in until we saved enough to get a place. Another family watched Matthew for me and even fed me dinner after work too many times to count. Between Goodwill, Salvation Army, and many generous gifts from friends, I had more than enough clothes until I could retrieve my belongings from storage in another state. God's hand was so evident; everywhere I turned, He was there with provision and favor. A couple of guys from church offered to drive a rental truck to North Carolina to bring back all my belongings. Then before you know it, thanks to the surprise help of some total strangers and their truck, we moved into our own little apartment, a home, a place to call our own, all within six months. Wow, what an awesome God!

Temptation to Turn Back

Then he called. What, he wanted to come back? Yes! That was all I wanted for Christmas, so I thought, little did I know. In my spirit, I knew something was wrong, though. I said no initially upon the advice of my friend. Then, he called again, you guessed it! I caved. I did not heed the voice of reason. And yes, after only three months, I found myself alone again. Oh, this time I was mad! I lost not just my peace but time, energy, and money as well. Sin takes you further than you wanted to go and costs you more than you wanted to pay! How would I ever get over this feeling of hatred? It overwhelmed me like never before; I did not know you could feel this bad toward someone, but especially mad at yourself for trusting again. The emotional roller coaster began; feelings of anger turned into hatred and then confusion. *Where was God in all of this*, I thought. Every day I went before the Lord and asked God to help me. All I wanted was my peace back.

Finally, God spoke to my heart. He told me that I got in the way that I tried to play "Savior." By bringing him home on my own, I stepped in as the rescuer. Oh my...I messed up. I was not the "Savior" and could not save him. But, even worse, I actually got in God's way. I am not born of a virgin, nor am I the Son of God, definitely not sinless, and did not go to the cross for him. My salvation was futile and could only fail. I came up short. I would find out later this is otherwise known as a "perverted mercy gift." I thought I knew better how to love him more than God. However, bringing him back then only served to meet his fleshly needs, not his spiritual need. Now, this only served to delay the plan of God. Whoops, how could I be mad now? I did it to myself.

My supposed needs got in the way of God's work. I wanted to try to save my marriage to no avail. *Why didn't someone counsel me better?* I thought. However, someone was; I was just not listening to what God was saying. The trouble is we think we know what we need and want, but oftentimes to our own detriment. So many people were silent, perhaps not knowing how to counsel, what to counsel, or if I would listen. I get it; been there. I wondered, though, where they were and why we could not seem to get help. For that, I felt hurt; and unknowingly allowed bitterness to enter my heart. I did not want to be another divorce statistic. How could people really be glad he was gone? What a seeming disgrace to our family. I just did not understand. I didn't know what I didn't know. All I knew at the time was confusion, loneliness, and pain. No one in my immediate circle of family and friends could relate.

Prayer

I asked God to help me learn what I needed to know so I would not have to pass this way again. Over the next six years, God opened my eyes, ears, and heart to really learn and understand what it is to live by faith, whether I was single or married. God was about to open my eyes to a faith that trusts Him in every situation, for every need, and with every relationship. If this finds you hurting and alone in a relationship disaster, help is on the way. Just keep reading and be comforted; you are not alone. Thank God He has brought you to this place that I may share with you and, hopefully, save you time, heartache, money, separation, or divorce.

School Begins

God took me to school or to "task," you might say. He began to show me through the Word and retrospect what I did not know about the faith of God that works in love. Maybe you have been dumped on more than once; I understand what you are feeling. I had never felt such anger before. What an oppressive feeling. Anger at myself first and foremost, for not listening to my friend, for believing the lie, and for the lost time, money, and heartache. God, however, would not allow me to go on without dealing with this. Every day in my devotions, He began taking me to the Book of Job. For the next three months, He taught me the simple yet profound truths found in the oldest story in the Bible. This lesson changed everything, and once practiced, then I could move on. What follows is how God began to open my understanding as to how I and others find ourselves in these broken states. Only there can we begin adjusting our vision to see the true love waiting for us. Get ready to be surprised by love!

The book of Job is an interesting story of blessing and favor, of trial and testing, of truth and error, of rebuke and repentance, and finally of restoration in abundance. We can look at Job's experience and learn much. God revealed to me two specific principles and one underlying truth: the power of ungodly counsel, the power of forgiveness, and the expanse of His sovereignty. Look with me into this story and let God speak to you:

> *There was a man in the land of Uz whose name was Job; and that man was blameless and upright, and one who [reverently] feared God and abstained from and shunned evil [because it was wrong]. ...so that this man was the greatest of all the men of the East.*

> Job 1:1-3b (AMPC)

Job, blessed and favored personally and financially by the hand of God, had a reputation as a good man. Then, the unthinkable happened; a "hedge of protection" surrounding him by God was lifted upon Satan's request. Satan was now allowed a free course to test Job, but he was not allowed to touch him. Upon losing all his livestock, servants, and children, Job responds:

> *Then Job arose and rent his robe and shaved his head and fell down upon the ground and worshiped And said, "Naked (without possessions) came I [into this world] from my mother's womb, and naked (without possessions) shall I depart. The Lord gave and the Lord has taken away; blessed (praised and magnified in worship) be the name of the Lord!" In all this (testing), Job sinned not nor charged God foolishly.*

> Job 1:20-22 (AMPC)

Imagine, God was so proud of Job that He bragged about Him to Satan! After all this tragic loss and disaster, Job continued to fear God and maintain his integrity by worshipping the Lord. However, that was not good enough; Satan, challenging God, asked Him for permission to attack Job physically. Surely, he thought, Job would curse God then. He just had to push him. God allowed him, but only to a point, he could not slay Job. Seeing Job covered in boils from his head to his toes, his wife, angry with God, told Job:

> *Do you still hold fast your blameless uprightness? Renounce God and die! But he said to her, You speak as one of the impious and foolish women would speak. What? Shall we accept [only] good at the hand of God and shall we not accept [also] misfortune and what is of a bad nature? In [spite of] all this, Job did not sin with his lips.*
>
> Job 2:9-10 (AMPC)

How amazing! He did not sin with his lips? What a lesson, through incredible loss, destruction, and disease, he spoke rightly of God. We could stop right there until we learn that lesson! Not until Job's "friends" Eliphaz, Bildad, and Zophar came to comfort him, however, did Job sin. He started to look at his life and began to curse the day he was born and to speak against God. He said, "Therefore I will *not* restrain my mouth; I will speak in the anguish of my spirit, I will *complain* in the bitterness of my soul [O Lord]!" (Job 7:11, AMPC) (emphasis added)

He said, "I will *not* restrain, I will complain," or we might say, "Let me give you a piece of my mind!" Or "I will say whatever I want." And so he began to indulge himself by letting the complaints roll. Looking at his own goodness and not the goodness of God, he started down the dangerous road of "justification," thus essentially putting God on trial. Why are we so quick to blame God? If we could just remember, God is good, all the time, He can be trusted! "If I called and He answered me, yet would I not believe that He listened to my voice? When [His] scourge slays suddenly, He mocks at the calamity and trial of the innocent" (Job 9:16, 23, AMPC).

After more than thirty chapters of Job and his friends going back and forth, God had enough. God was listening, and, not liking what He heard, He interrupted the conversation: "Who is this that darkeneth counsel by words without knowledge? Gird up now thy loins like a man; for I will demand of thee, and answer thou me" (Job 38:2-3, KJV).

God did not like or appreciate what He heard, essentially calling them "stupid" or "clueless." As God then began to point out and itemize His provision and control of all creation, Job concluded he had talked way too much; and realized he best just "shut up and listen" (Job 40:5, MSG). What a great decision! When God begins to ask rhetorical questions, you know you are in trouble. After four chapters of God waxing eloquent with questions like, "Where were you when I laid the foundations of the earth? Did you tell the waves where to stop," or maybe, "Did you give the peacocks their wings and feathers to the ostrich?" Job got a clue, "no" being the obvious answer! God asked, "Will you instruct me?" To which Job responded rightly, "I am vile, I will lay my hand upon my mouth and not answer thee" (Job 40:4, 5, NKJV). The message translation actually quotes Job as saying, "I've talked way too much. I'm ready to shut up and listen." He had overlooked the omnipotent, omniscience of God, known as His sovereignty and His kingdom, His right to rule and reign as He pleases. He is God: big, big lesson! He is the creator and sustainer of all living.

As God continued, Job finally repented. This repentance must have been heartfelt because God accepted it. Interestingly, though, God told Job's friends they must go to Job and ask him to pray for them. Why? The possibility of offense rested with Job. They had not spoken of God rightly to Job. He had the power to release and forgive his friends or not. Even though they may have spoken some truth, Job was provoked by them to speak against God. So Job humbled himself and prayed for his friends. When he did, God turned his captivity and gave him double for his trouble. In so doing, Job released himself from the trap of Satan. This bait of offense lures us into the trap of bitterness and unforgiveness. Satan then uses this to keep us from fulfilling our destiny, the will of God. With our hearts in his trap, held captive to hatred through unforgiveness, we surrender our freedom to love. Now Satan can easily fire away his attacks of fear, doubt, and unbelief in our minds and cause our hearts to grow cold. One simple act of worship, the prayer of forgiveness, released Job from Satan's trap by the grace of God. Immediately he sent the devil packing, positioning himself to once again receive all God had for him. When he let go of anger, bitterness, and unforgiveness, the supply of heaven flowed. Little did he know that God would give him double what he had possessed before, along with the most beautiful daughters in the land!

Every day I read this until it resonated in me, "When Job prayed for his friends, God turned his captivity." Wow, so simple yet so powerful prayer, a prayer of forgiveness. God had accepted Job's repentance, but it was not until he forgave and prayed for his friends that God turned his captivity. Not just any prayer will do, though. A heartfelt prayer for mercy and blessing on his friends brought God on the scene. Obedience to God through the simple act of humility and love all wrapped up with a prayer of forgiveness, what a great gift! A prayer of letting go set the captive free. I wanted this gift for myself and for the others who had hurt me.

I knew then what I had to do. Now I would accept God's sovereign plan, forgive, and pray a blessing. These prayers of blessing were not only for my spouse but for anyone I may have put undo expectations on for help and or advice. This was not just forgiveness; this was a proactive prayer of blessing that kept my prayer life busy. My heart changed, and after three months, I suddenly realized I was free. I mean, I experienced a physical, tangible release. No longer was I carrying or harboring any ill will towards anyone, whether known or unknown to me. Oh, what a relief! Sweet peace returned, and now I could go on. The love of God was flowing again, and as it flowed, the healing began in my heart. Oh, the powerful love of God, oh, how He loves you so. Receive Jesus' instruction in: "But I say to you, *love* your enemies, *bless* those who curse you, do *good* to those who hate you, and *pray* for those who spitefully use you and persecute you" (Matthew 5:44, NKJV) (emphasis added).

Love, bless, do good, and, finally, pray. In order to heal, we must first deal. Deal with the hurt in prayer. This is evidence of a child of God; we forgive as He forgives us. Prayer is an act of forgiveness. Job forgave as God had forgiven him. The prayer of forgiveness and blessing opens up the heart for the healing to begin. Through the healing, the "feels" will come again! Job felt loved and blessed again with physical healing, children, and provision all restored.

Why is this important? For this reason, ask yourself, "What kind of counsel am I receiving?" Does it edify and encourage me to walk in the ways of forgiveness and prayer, or of justifying myself and condemning God? Maybe my heart is too hard to hear the truth. Often we only listen to those who say what we want to hear, those who "tickle our ears," as the Bible calls it. To whom am I listening? Usually, the ways of man seem like the "easy way" out. What way you choose leads to either freedom or to continued bondage. Maybe you do not even realize you are being wound up by the "advise" of so-called "friends." When thinking of someone who has offended you with hurts or abuse or by leading you down the wrong path with his or her counsel or advice, does a name come to mind? Your circle of people may have good intentions, but somehow, you are angry and hurt. Or, maybe you are giving counsel, advice, or opinions that have hurt or offended someone. As the text in Job shows us, we are to go to them and ask them to forgive us. Their freedom may rest in praying for you.

> *Blessed is the man who walks not in the counsel of the ungodly, nor stands in the path of sinners, nor sits in the seat of the scornful; But his delight is in the law of the LORD, and in His law he meditates day and night. ...and whatever he does shall prosper.*

> Psalm 1:1-3b (NKJV)

Blessing comes when we give weight, value, and delight to God's word over the counsel of the ungodly or scornful man. That is someone who is insulting, rude, and disrespectful. The amplified version calls the blessed person "happy, fortunate, prosperous, and enviable." When we take time to see what God has to say about a matter and follow Him, we go in a direction that leads to life. Blessing came to Job as he humbled himself in repentance and obedience to the Lord. He lived one hundred and forty more blessed years, seeing four generations of children, "old and full of days" (Job 42:17, NKJV).

This lesson started me in the right direction. From this time on, not only would I seek godly counsel, but also I would forgive and release those who hurt me or did not give me godly counsel.

What a wonderful day when I realized I was set free to love again. I, too, would endeavor and commit myself to giving godly counsel whenever and wherever God led me. The devil would not get the victory. God hates divorce, and I would hate it just as much. Is the advice or counsel you're hearing provoking you to love or stirring you up to anger? Do you feel justified, like you're "right" and you have rights and deserve better? On the other hand, maybe what you are hearing is causing you to feel sorry for yourself—to get even, to get him before he gets you—to protect yourself and keep an escape route ready. Or, maybe you are having a pity party, just giving in to feelings of guilt, shame, condemnation, or justification. That is always the "easy" way, the way of our flesh. Job went that way for thirty chapters. A lesson on what *not* to say.

If you are feeling this way, follow Job's example: repent, acknowledging God's sovereign right to rule His creation, then forgive yourself and others, and finally, pray for your "friends/advisors," anyone who has hurt you. Now you can thank God for bringing you to this book. You are reading this "for such a time as this." What abundance of blessing God could be waiting to pour out in your life when you forgive and pray for those who have misled you or hurt you? One simple act of obedience done in sincerity could turn your captivity, your situation around immediately. You may not know, like Job, how God will respond. That's faith! Your loving obedience to the Almighty will change everything. He said in Isaiah 1:19 (NKJV), "If you are willing and obedient, you shall eat the good of the land." So pray, pray now! Now is the best time to pray, forgive and love. "When Job prayed for his friends…God turned his captivity." The power of the simple act of prayer will change lives, beginning with your own.

Now, if it is your counsel that is stirring up either yourself, your spouse, or your friends, stop immediately! Before you give another word of advice, check to see if it lines up with scripture first. Then determine if it confirms the Word of God or the word of the enemy. The enemy destroys relationships. Jesus, the great Rabbi, said, "The thief comes to kill, steal, and destroy, but I come to give life and life more abundantly." That is what God wants for us, an abundant life, full and overflowing! If the advice of your counselor, or as the Hebrews call their master teacher "rabbi," directs you to follow the path of truth, this will lead to life. If not, you have a destiny of death awaiting you. It may look and sound easier, but it will only get worse. I have seen it happen repeatedly; the price is always higher than one thinks. You may look back with regrets and say, "If only I would have, could have, should have…" Now is the time to give it your all and say, "Not me!" Why wait for tomorrow to forgive when you can start living free today?

In order to receive God's best, we cannot straddle the fence between the world's way of thinking and God's way of thinking. There is only one truth, the Word of God. He will confirm His Word, not man's word. Make a commitment now to seek only godly counsel and remove any counsel that is not the truth of God; a faith-filled life of love. We must choose who we will listen to, who will be our "rabbi," our teacher. "Rabbi" is a Hebrew word meaning "my teacher or my master." When a Hebrew Rabbi chose his Jewish disciples, they were to follow him, learning literally every step of the way in order to emulate him. Jesus, our Rabbi, now invites us to come and follow Him; He is the way, the truth, and the life. We are His students called talmidim, the learners that hopefully learn something new every day. Since Jesus has gone to the Father, He sent the gift of His Spirit to lead us through pastors and teachers. They help to guide and teach us, confirming the words of Christ. Jesus calls them shepherds and Himself the Great Shepherd. He says my sheep hear my voice, and the voice of a stranger they will not follow. He has specific teachers and/or counselors for you who you can trust. Ask God who that is, and He will show you. Then, trust God, and bring yourself under their covering for teaching, encouraging, and protection.

One woman I counseled separated from her husband at the advice of a professional marriage counselor. Now how could I counsel someone who is acting on the counsel of someone else? At our second visit, I asked her if I was to disciple her, to prayerfully consider a change. Following the scripture that encourages couples not to be apart except for prayer and fasting, I asked her to invite her husband back home. In a few short weeks, she did. Within a year, they found the underlying cause of their issues, started marriage counseling, settled into the church, and worked their way back together. Through continued commitment to discipleship, the pastor's marriage counseling, and a body of believers that loved them, they experienced healing in their marriage and their family. In turn, they became a blessing to many others, teaching and leading small groups in their home. The key here is following the counsel found in the Word of God.

The example of Job is clear. Job forgave. In turn, we must forgive, pray, release, and go with God. Jesus forgave us first, and He is calling us to forgive. Remember, we were not asking Jesus to forgive us. He simply said, hanging from the cross, "Father, forgive them, for they know not what they do" (Luke 23:34a, KJV). This is the first step. You cannot go any further until you start here. This was my first step. Not only did I have to forgive and release myself, but also my spouse and all those who I felt gave either no counsel or bad counsel. Day after day, I prayed for them, asking God to bless them. Yes, bless. And, after praying for salvation and blessing, one day, I realized the anger, bitterness, and hatred were gone. I did not feel any animosity toward him or the others and never would again. I was truly free. Forgiveness is a choice, not a feeling; it is a commandment of God. It is obedience, an act of faith. If I desire to receive forgiveness, then I first must forgive. Jesus said to pray like this: "And forgive us our debts, as we also have forgiven (left, remitted, and let go of the debts, and have given up resentment against) our debtors" (Matthew 6:12, AMPC).

He goes on to explain further in the Message translation:

> *In prayer there is a connection between what God does and what you do. You can't get forgiveness from God, for instance, without also forgiving others. If you refuse to do your part, you cut yourself off from God's part.*
>
> Matthew 6:14-15 (MSG)

My part is to give the gift of love without any animosity, bitterness, or hatred. When I do, I position myself to receive the forgiveness of God through His son, Jesus Christ. For all those who have given their ungodly opinions and/or hurt you, I ask you to forgive them now, including your spouse. Renounce any of the advice you have taken that is ungodly. Furthermore, renounce any agreement you have made with this ungodly counsel. Breaking any agreement you have made for separation and/or divorce will break the power of the enemy, Satan. I renounce when I repent and declare no, it isn't so! Then, I bring the power of God to bear on the circumstance when I agree and decree what He says. For example, "I forgive and release all those (list them by name) that have hurt me, lied to me, stolen from me, or abused me in any way." You hereby disannul any vow you have spoken in agreement with divorce and cancel Satan's right to attack you and carry this out. You kick him out and shut the door on him. The very atmosphere in your house will change. Confess and repent, and healing begins. Ask God to forgive you for sitting in the seat of the counsel of the ungodly and to help you embrace truth. Then, ask God to forgive them and bless them. I decree blessing upon them and upon my marriage or life. It may be hard at first, but remember, God determines what a blessing looks like; we can trust God with that. Forgiveness gives room for God to now deal with the offenders. Here, we are actually encouraged to stay out of God's way:

> Beloved, never avenge yourselves, but leave the way open for [God's] wrath; for it is written, Vengeance is Mine, I will repay (requite), says the Lord (Deuteronomy 32:35).
>
> But if your enemy is hungry, feed him; if he is thirsty, give him drink; for by so doing you will heap burning coals upon his head (Proverbs 25:21-22).
>
> Do not let yourself be overcome by evil, but overcome (master) evil with good.
>
> Romans 12:19-21 (AMPC)
(emphasis added) (parentheses added for clarity)

God deals out the justice; we deal out service. May God give you His comfort, counsel, and courage to do good. Then as you do, you find that in the "doing is the ungluing." When you boldly and lovingly serve, you literally physically detach and overcome the evil of the hurt in your heart and mind. Like me, you will suddenly realize one day, the pain and hurt are all gone. The doing releases you from the trap. The truth sets you free! It did me, and it will you too.

Do not fear or be afraid, be strong in the Lord. He will never leave you or forsake you. He will heal your heart as you walk in forgiveness and love. This call to a life of faith pleases God and is one He rewards. Exercise faith as a living love, one that brings life to those around you. As Jesus forgave us, so we, too, forgive others. He loved us first and gave us life; now, we love Him by loving others, especially the unlovable, to life.

This is the beginning of God turning your captivity. Set yourself to shun "ungodly counsel." Reject and refuse the desire to justify yourself. Seek, pursue, and hear the truth. Mix that truth with faith that you might receive it from your head to your heart and back again, meditating on God's word.

> But his delight is in the law of the LORD, And in His law he meditates day and night. He shall be like a tree planted by the rivers of water, That brings forth its fruit in its season, Whose leaf also shall not wither; And whatever he does shall prosper.

Psalm 1:2-3 (NKJV) (emphasis added)

When you reflect and think on the many ways God shows His love and reveals Himself in the Word, you are meditating. As you do this, you will be like a tree by the water, standing still, flourishing, and seeing the salvation of the Lord!

This may be a major adjustment. You may have to change some numbers on your speed dial or start having lunch with someone else or maybe even by yourself. Nevertheless, whatever "cost" or "adjustment" you must now make to carry out your commitment, it is critical to fulfill God's plans. His plans are the best plans; they raise your hopes up! "For I know the thoughts and plans that I have for you, says the Lord, thoughts and plans for welfare and peace and not for evil, to give you *hope* in your final outcome" (Jeremiah 29:11, AMPC) (emphasis added). A hope in God that never makes you ashamed. This hope is an anchor to your soul that holds steady through the toughest storms of life. A confident expectation that God is working all things together for your good, to those that love Him, and are the called according to His purpose (Romans 8:28, KJV). This is true biblical hope. Hope placed in God alone and not man brings security and stability to your mind, your will, and your emotions. No need to numb the pain because we are not alone, God is with us, and His words anchor us. He is holding you right now, whatever your storm may be.

Ask the Lord what adjustments He would have you make—ask Him who is your "rabbi." Who is that one individual teacher, counselor, mentor, or pastor to whom you could willingly submit, open up, and receive biblical guidance? God has a trusted individual with wisdom and discernment who will gladly encourage you on your way. Your mission is to obey quickly and willingly through faith in His Word. Adjust. Make the changes necessary to set yourself up for victory, accepting no defeat. This person will feed your faith, challenge you in the ways of God, and encourage you when the going gets tough. You cannot do it alone; you are part of the body, get connected, get under the covering of a godly leader, and stay in your place.

For now, I want to be that person for you. Here in this book, take from my mistakes, my struggles and save yourself some time. I am endeavoring to feed your faith, to give you hope. Things *do* change, and so do people. If it ever changed before, it can change again! If it went from good to bad, then it can go from bad to good again! Nothing is impossible with God! God can cause people to "will and to do of His good pleasure." He responds to faith. When He sees you, He sees your spouse. (That is, if you are married!) You are one. He is a just God, looking for a legal right through an invitation to move on your behalf. God says ask! Position yourself through forgiveness to ask God for His will in your life and marriage. Release everything in your life to the light of His word, let Him give you discernment to see if it fills you with faith and hope or if it feeds your fear of failing, pain, or more hurt.

God encouraged me in the same way to take this very important initial step. I found my church "plugged in," meaning I started serving, even if just for accountability, and then submitted myself to some godly spiritual parents, my "rabbis," by attending their small group. From that point of connection and safety, God began the teaching, stretching, growing process for which I am so grateful. Several different people tried to get me out from under this covering, even well-meaning family, but I knew God had put me there, so I could not move. Thank God!

These adjustments, made one by one, may seem uncomfortable or even painful at first. Gradually though, as you experience the presence of God from each act of obedience, faith in action, you will find a renewed sense of purpose and direction. When you don't have any answers, you will feel a sense of stability. Your life will seem brighter and brighter. He is right there beside you, holding your hand. Go with Him; the adventure is worth it! From faith to faith, each step, you will see more of His glorious grace. You will sense a new beginning of the romance of His love like never before. The simple humility of obedience positions you for an abundant outpouring of His immeasurable, amazing grace.

> But he giveth more grace. Wherefore he saith, God re-sisteth the proud, but giveth grace unto the humble. Submit yourselves therefore to God. Resist the devil, and he will flee from you.
>
> James 4:6-7 (KJV)

Grace, the power of God, raises you above your circumstances into the glory of His presence. Through humility, we receive His amazing grace to pardon, perfect, and preserve us. Receive His grace today, and in humility through obedience, trust Him. Others may not have proven themselves as trustworthy, but He has! He has never failed you and will never let you go. He is faithful and true and keeps His word. The adjustments you make may include changes in time spent with friends, family members, jobs, or even church. I do not know, but He does. Please, will you trust Him and ask Him to show you today?

Prayer ~

Lord, You know how I have looked to things and others, even my children, and to myself to fulfill my life. Forgive me of fear and unbelief in falling for the illusion of control, rebellion, and stubborn pride. I forgive all those who have hurt me in any way, releasing them to your will. I ask your mercy and blessing on them now and trust You, Lord, with their life. I now know to find my life, I must lose it to You—take my life, rearrange it to be every bit in order with Your will for me, I submit to Your authority. I trust Your plans are good for me and not for evil. Show me Yourself, help me to know You and see who You really are, then strengthen me to release anything that is not of faith and to make the adjustments necessary to experience

You and the abundant life You give. Help me to find and know my rabbi, the mentor, teacher, or pastor You desire to set over me. Most importantly, Lord, help me to stay and willingly obey. I love You, Lord, and commit my trust to You, giving You complete Lordship of my life, in the name of Jesus, amen.

Before long, you will be amazed at how your heart heals and, once again, is full of a renewed love for God. Keep your eyes wide open on the lookout for your rabbi, the covering, mentor, teacher, or shepherd He has for you. Trust God to lead you and show you whom He has just for you. This person, you will recognize as one who lives their love for God.

CHAPTER 2.
THIS IS THE MAN?

Now that I was free in forgiveness and found under the authority of my spiritual parents, God had a new word, a new lesson. Time has passed, dates have come and gone, and now the Lord has a new command, "no more dating." What? I had been dating seemingly good eligible bachelors, but none approved or sent by God. He wanted me to stop, wait, and sit still. He comforted my questioning concerned heart with the promise in: "Search from the book of the LORD, and read: Not one of these shall fail; *Not one shall lack her mate.* For My mouth has commanded it, and His Spirit has gathered them" (Isaiah 34:16, NKJV) (emphasis added).

He promised I would not lack my mate, it is His command, and He, God (not me), would gather him. My job was to stay right where God put me. God takes sole responsibility for giving me His man if I will simply trust Him and be still. I was twenty-nine years old the first time, and by now, I was thirty-seven. Even still, now it was up to God how long I would wait. These words provided relief actually and brought much comfort and rest. Now I knew the man I would marry was up to God. I did not have to look for him. I just had to do, be, and go what and where God wanted me, so simple!

The days and weeks ahead were very peaceful. More and more, I wanted to spend time with the Lord. Then one evening, my friend Debbie and I were praying and worshipping the Lord when God gave us a very special word. She read: "For your Maker is your *husband*, The LORD of hosts is His name; and your Redeemer is the Holy One of Israel; He is called the God of the whole earth" (Isaiah 54:5, NKJV) (emphasis added).

Hmmm, my Maker is my Husband; the *Lord* of hosts is His name, my Redeemer, the God of the whole earth? At that moment, this word was so comforting and yet powerful, "the LORD is my Husband." God of creation, my Maker, took me as His bride. I was not alone. He declared His relationship with me. This was so much more personal than I could have ever imagined. He is my husband! I am married to the *Lord* of hosts? What a divine revelation that was. We so rejoiced in that word. I could stop looking for love—I was loved! Days turned into weeks, and weeks into months as I settled in my heart that the Lord was now my husband. I was a married woman! I would never walk anywhere alone. Then it made sense when the scripture says, "He who finds a wife finds a good thing, and obtains favor from the LORD" (Proverbs 18:22, NKJV). Since I am now a covenant woman in a covenant relationship with the Lord as my husband, then, when a man finds me, he finds a wife, a good thing. A faithful, covenant woman of God, a "good thing" because she brings the favor of God with her into the new relationship.

What a beautiful picture the scriptures paint of the bride of Christ. Even Paul confirms this in 2 Corinthians 11:2b (KJV), speaking to the church when he says, "I have espoused you to one husband, that I may present you as a chaste virgin to Christ." And then again, in Ephesians 5, he compares the Lord loving and laying down His life for the church as a husband doing the same for his wife. The most powerful word, however, Paul reiterates from Genesis 2:24 (KJV), "and the two shall become one flesh."

I am one with the Lord, my husband. You, too, can receive this word and accept the proposal to make the vow or renew your vow with the Lord. He desires and longs to be your Husband as well.

Now, with the Lord as my Husband, I could trust God completely, finally, rest. God would help my mate "find" me; no need to go on a "man-hunt!" God allows man to enter into an already existing covenantal relationship. No wonder God said He would gather up my mate for me. He was not just going to let anyone into our relationship. Wow, this was awesome! Talk about a renewed sense of value. The God of all creation, the Lord of hosts, was calling me His wife, His bride. Now, He would gather my husband, His man, for me and bring us together. The waiting and watching became such an adventure as I continued to worship and walk out my faith with the Lord as my Husband.

Then it happened, after almost a year and a half of waiting, I was found. While visiting with some mutual friends on a sweet summer Sunday afternoon, we met. A mutual friend introduced us and walked away. I really was not in the mood and did not even give him any eye contact. Although this first interaction was brief, he called the next day. You guessed it, a date. Really, was this the man? Was this God? A couple nights later, the Lord woke me up and confirmed through His word in the story of Esther that, sure enough, this man was sent and approved by God. God showed me he had the heart of Mordecai. That would prove to be a marker we would never forget. God gave him a reference. Who can argue with that? Then my mentor, a few days later, confirmed the same word God told me. That settled it; I could date him with confidence.

Although there was some common ground in our faith, there were many differences. Little did I know he was still rebounding from his previous relationship. This was of enough concern that I backed out of the relationship for a season. However, neither he nor God gave up. After all the time of waiting, this was the man. No matter what I saw or questioned, this was still the man. After eleven months, we were married on a beautiful summer evening with friends and family at the Lake Mirror promenade. Our lovely daughter Jeanette played the trumpet as my dad walked me down the stairs front and center. We both took comfort and joy in knowing God brought us together. I rejoiced in God's choice, at least through the honeymoon.

Then it happened; here I was in my long-awaited marriage only to find myself in a state of shock and disillusionment. *Wait,* I thought, *this is the man? This is the marriage I waited for?* I was overwhelmed; *this is the life I signed up for?* So many demands and adjustments all at once left me feeling confused. I felt like I lost myself and my son in this unknown, unfamiliar world. It came in more like a whirlwind. With little understanding and patience for adapting from him, disillusionment settled into my heart. Just the idea alone of having a gourmet dinner on the table at 5:00 sharp was almost enough to break up our marriage. I mean, he did make fun of me because I just used to eat tuna from a can for dinner, and now all this cooking? And look out if he didn't like it! Okay, let me just say we bought more than one glass tabletop! I was a working girl; now, at forty years old, I'm going to stay at home when my son is now ten? Then worse was the feeling that the Lord had turned me over to this man and left me. We had different ideas of almost everything, including parenting. Not to mention the still underlying hurts from not being completely healed from his divorce, which seemingly brought a dark cloud of emotional fear hovering over us. Oh, I was so disenchanted, and now I felt myself drifting and shutting down. How could God, and why did God put me here, with him?

How could the Lord, my husband, call me out of a peaceful single life into a marriage with such demands? Where did God go? Was He still the Lord my husband? Then after about a year into the marriage, my friend Debbie called and said the Lord had put me on her heart for about a week. She said, "The Lord told me to tell you, 'He is still the Lord, your husband!'" There I was, piled in a heap on the floor, crying. Now, I just did not understand, talk about feeling lost. Even though I was now married and ministering, something was very wrong. Funny thing is, we think we are so ready for the next chapter or season, but when it comes, we realize, maybe we weren't as ready as we thought; only God knows, though. Sometimes I think God just says, "Ready or not, here we go!" A demanding, controlling man now challenged the intimacy I had with God. How could I feel so abandoned by God in this relationship? We're Christians, after all; we love each other! If He, the Lord, is still my husband and I'm supposed to be so happy and "in love," then what's wrong? I was confused and wanted answers. Maybe you find yourself in a similar situation, wondering what God is doing. Mostly I wondered if God led me here, where is He? I hope to help you find the answers God gave me.

Thus, it began. God was about to take me back to school. What I learned, I believe and trust will not only bless you as it has me, but save you heartache, and maybe even save your marriage, or someone's you know. Only now would I fully understand what God truly meant when He said, "I am the Lord, your husband." I pray you will join me on this most intimate journey to find Him. Follow me, and let me take you to your Lover.

The Lord took me to a very powerful story that opened my eyes and helped me learn and understand what God was saying and doing. Oh, how this story helped me realize the power I was overlooking in these special words, "The Lord is my Husband." He was about to show me the depths of what He meant. Whether you are single or married, this is for you, even if you are male or female. As I sit here writing, I am burdened and sharing this story with a sixteen-year-old young woman. At her young age, she sadly has given herself to men who care little to nothing about her. God, however, is using this word to bless her. This message has no age, gender, or geographical limit, no color or socio-economic limitations either. No matter who you are or where you find yourself, this word has no barriers or limitations; it is for you.

The Prophet and the Prostitute

Go with me to the book of Hosea, where we discover in an amazing story the depths of what the *Lord* is saying and doing in the silence:

> *The beginning of the word of the LORD by Hosea. And the LORD said to Hosea, Go, take unto thee a wife of whoredoms and children of whoredoms: for the land hath committed great whoredom, departing from the LORD.*

Hosea 1:2 (KJV)

Wow, talk about an adjustment! A prophet of the Lord, holy, upright, "clean" is to bond with the "unclean." Specifically, Hosea marries a whore, simply put, a prostitute, a worldly woman. God speaks to this faithful servant, a holy man who has set himself aside for the purposes of God, in order that he might be a physical demonstration of the immeasurable love of God for this woman. Why? What has this to do with me, you might ask. God wants to answer this question and our deepest questions and deepest needs. Through this prostitute Gomer, God put on display the depths of His jealousy, the deceptions of life, and the power of His love and mercy for not only Israel but for you and me. "So he went and took Gomer the daughter of Diblaim; which conceived, and bare him a son" (Hosea 1:3, KJV).

God chose and called Israel out and set His love upon her. Although, in all His goodness, God's people shunned Him and sought love elsewhere, crediting their blessings and provisions to other gods. God was angry and jealous, and Gomer's life would serve as a mirror to expose their wanderings. Here, Hosea, the husband, as the picture of a loving God, acts in complete trust and obedience, quickly and willingly takes Gomer as his wife, and proceeds to begin his family. Imagine how he approached her and try to imagine what she is thinking. Here is the resident prophet/preacher going into the local whorehouse, and he asks for Gomer. "Hello, Gomer, would you marry me? God told me you were to marry me." I imagine it might be a little like a *Cinderella* story. "Why would this prophet of Israel want to marry me? Doesn't he know I'm a wild woman?" She obviously figures this is a good deal! Not only would she get a husband, one man, but also a home, a name, status, and provision; she might as well go along with it! What a deal, or so she thought. So they marry and immediately begin to bear children.

These children would become very significant. The names given the first three children prophesy of God's feelings of jealousy: the first, a son "Jezreel," means "God scatters," the second, a daughter, "Lo-ruhamah," means "no more mercy," and the third, a boy "Lo-ammi," means "not my people." God declares to Israel, "I will scatter you, not have mercy on you, and disown you." He was mad and done with them for cheating on him, for leaving him, and speaking ill of his blessings. He loved them deeply and affectionately and lavished his love on them through protection and provision under the reign of Jeroboam II. Yet, they turned away from Him to adulterous relationships with other gods.

He was about to withdraw himself, his mercy, and scatter them but gave them one last picture, or drama if you will, to show them their ways. He was showing them they were not His people but rather nothing more than a "whorehouse." Why would He go to such great lengths? Even in His anger and jealousy, He gives them an opportunity to see and turn before He actually fulfills the prophecy declared in these children. What patience, what mercy, imagine, after running after other gods and giving them credit for His blessings, He still pleads.

> *My people are destroyed for lack of knowledge: because thou hast rejected knowledge, I will also reject thee, that thou shalt be no priest to me: seeing thou hast forgotten the law of thy God, I will also forget thy children.*

Hosea 4:6 (KJV) (emphasis added)

God is directing and producing a real-life drama through the lives of the prophet Hosea and his wife of harlotry, Gomer. A strange name we don't often hear. It means "the completion or filling up of the measure of idolatry." As the inspiration for this allegory, Israel is portrayed by the adulteress, the prostitute Gomer, and God, the faithful, loving husband, is portrayed by Hosea. They are so far deceived in "rejecting knowledge" and "forgetting God" that God plays out this biographical drama in front of them in order to shine light on their darkness. Imagine the ways of God in using our lives to teach others. May my life, good and bad, bring Him glory! Even while revealing His disdain, He still plays out this drama. It begs the question, "Why?" Was this only to justify Himself? Why would He go to such great lengths to show them their sin if He was about to scatter them, remove His mercy, and renounce them?

As we will see, Hosea is preeminently the prophet of love, but unlike some teachers today, he does not minimize the holiness of God. We are told that "God is love" in 1 John 4:8 (KJV), but we're also reminded that "God is light, and in Him is no darkness at all" (1 John 1:5, KJV). God's love is a holy love, not a sentimental feeling that condones sin and pampers sinners. In His holiness, He calls us to "be holy, for I am Holy" (Leviticus 19:2, KJV). Therefore, Hosea is presenting God's case.

> For rebellion is as the sin of witchcraft, and stubbornness is as iniquity and idolatry. Because thou hast rejected the word of the LORD, he hath also rejected thee from being king.
>
> 1 Samuel 15:23 (KJV)

God sees the stubbornness of their ways and their choices as the sin of idolatry. They are worshipping themselves—what they want to do, their agenda, their ideas, going their own way, and doing their own thing. They are first and foremost rejecting God's love, but then His word. The word He gives is to serve Him only and to obey Him. Their stubbornness, in turn, became the idol worship of self. They forgot God. Forgetting His love and blessings, they became ungrateful, giving themselves credit. Moreover, in doing so, they were saying they did not need God.

> Because that, when they knew God, they glorified him not as God, neither were thankful; but became vain in their imaginations, and their foolish heart was darkened. Professing themselves to be wise, they became fools... Who

changed the truth of God into a lie, and worshipped and served the creature more than the Creator, who is blessed for ever. Amen.

Romans 1:21-22, 25 (KJV)

They were ungrateful for all God's blessings on their lives, so much so, they were taking the credit, not giving glory to God, thus refusing to recognize Him as the true source of their blessing and favor. They began to worship any idol they could make, including themselves. In the Old Testament, prostitution, or whoredom, is symbolic of idolatry and unfaithfulness to God.

Before you ask what this has to do with me, let's continue. If you already feel a heart pull, stay with me. Israel certainly would not want to think of herself as an adulterer or a whore, or as a bad example. But God, through Gomer, was showing them their stubborn heart was no different from that of a "loose woman" who sold herself out for nothing. We may not like to think like this, but this is how God sees it. God has not changed. He is the same, yesterday, today, and forever. His commandments still stand true through time: "Thou shalt have no other gods before me..." (Exodus 20:3, KJV)

Jesus replied, "'Love the Lord your God with all your heart, soul, and mind.' This is the first and greatest commandment. The second most important is similar: 'Love your neighbor as much as you love yourself.' All the other commandments and all the demands of the prophets stem from these two laws and are fulfilled if you obey them. Keep only these and you will find that you are obeying all the others."

Matthew 22:37-40 (TLB)

God commanded then, and now, we are to love and worship Him alone as God, our true lover. We do this when we recognize and acknowledge that He loved us first and best. We give God thanks and praise for His unfailing love, forgiveness, and grace. When we look at ourselves in the mirror of Gomer, how do we look? All too often, we look the same. We, too, ignorantly or knowingly, forget or ignore God, His love, and His blessings when we choose our own way. "I got this," we say, or maybe, "forget you!" Attempting to satisfy the longings for love in our flesh or soul, we indulge in personal comforts and provisions. God gave us a soul so large that only He, the Creator of it, can fill. Like Gomer, we trust ourselves, not the Lord, our husband. Our comforts are familiar and safe, so we think. Just like Israel, we have rejected knowledge and forgotten God in our ways, leaving the true worship of the one true living God. In this, we sell out, and remember, for nothing in return! We become adulterers, worshipping and giving credit to what our own hands, mind, beauty, or strength can seemingly provide. Like Gomer grieved Hosea, we grieve our husband, the Lord, as we give ourselves to imitations posing as lovers. Absolutely lovesick, He hurts deeply as He watches us fail. Yet, we wonder why our life is empty and meaningless.

Deceived by our views of God and self, we fall into a state of confusion, fear, and worry, posing as victims. Or, as in this case, we take over control and act like the "life of the party." Maybe afraid of the pain of authenticity, we pretend. Running here and there to other things or people, we try to hide from ourselves and God. We forget all too quickly who we are and where we are going. The temptation is great. People have failed us, and we feel vulnerable. How could we ever trust again after what we've been through? I'm in control; it's my body, my life; I'll do what I want. We are not so far from Gomer after all. Have you ever taken matters into your own hands? Often we feel the disappointment of people, or even God, like they are holding out on us, so we had better get things under our control. We think we know what love is and what life is. Yet, this is the very idolatry God is addressing, our unfaithfulness to trust Him first, and then our ungratefulness in not acknowledging Him as our source. We act as if He does not know, see, or care. That is easy to do; trusting requires surrender.

Let us learn from Gomer and Hosea, and let Israel be the example. In all their success and prosperity, with the favor and blessing of the Lord upon them, Israel gave thanks to the gods of their own hands, serving themselves. They thought they knew more about love and life than the one who made them, the Creator. Oops! Big mistake! They forgot God. Ever been forgotten? That is a sad feeling. We have come along so much, though, and we think we know so much more now. But God is still our only source today of life as He was theirs. He is not some imposter like "Santa Clause" or the "Easter Bunny." He is still the first, the one, and the only giver of love and life. They must have thought God did not really mean "thou shalt have no other gods before me." Or, crediting themselves, they said, "We've got a lot on the ball! We are sharp! Look what we've done!" Oh my! God disowned them, saying they were to Him, "nobody's," when really He wanted them more than anything, all to Himself.

Back to our story, we pick up where Gomer has had three children and then leaves. She has probably had enough of this by now and is ready to return to her old life. A wild life of parties and a revolving door of lovers; her supposed identity, comfort zone, and source of life. Imagine going from doing it your way, leading a life of parties and men, to the service of a husband and three babies who are there to show some people you do not even know the error of their ways. She could not get out of there fast enough. What kind of life was that, certainly not for her? Now Hosea is fiercely upset and tells the children:

> *Plead with your mother, plead: for she is not my wife, neither am I her husband: let her therefore put away her whoredoms out of her sight, and her adulteries from between her breasts; Lest I strip her naked, and set her as in the day that she was born, and make her as a wilderness, and set her like a dry land, and slay her with thirst. And I will not have mercy upon her children; for they be the children of whoredoms. For their mother hath played the harlot: she that conceived them hath done shamefully: for she said, I will go after my lovers that give me my bread and my water, my wool and my flax, mine oil and my drink.*

> Hosea 2:2-5 (KJV)

Hosea, like God, is mad, angry, upset, and jealous! He wanted Gomer to himself. All He gave she spurned. Now he knew all too well how God felt. If you want to show yourself around, he says, "I will help you, I will strip you naked." God wants us to Himself. God feels the same way today; He is a jealous God. Did you ever think about the fact that God has feelings and can be hurt? He is a very passionate lover who grieves when His church, His "bride," walks away.

Why did Gomer go back to the streets after being given a husband, one man, a father to her children, a name, a position, protection, and provision? See what she said in verse 5: "I will go after my lovers that give me my bread and my water, my wool and my flax, my oil and my drink" (Hosea 2:5, KJV).

She looks back longingly to the wrong people with *wrong* thinking. She says her life, her needs, her provision are all filled by these other lovers—idols. Looking back is a very dangerous thing to do. The Israelites had done this before in the wilderness after their deliverance from Egypt's bondage; they remembered the food but forgot about their tears under the hand of the hard taskmaster Pharaoh. So God left them there to die in the wilderness according to their own word. Then again, when escaping the destruction of Sodom, Lot's wife disobeyed and longingly looked back at the city life filled with corruption. She turned immediately into a pillar of salt. God was not happy about it then, any more than He is now. Drawing or looking back, as Hebrews tells us, directly opposes believing God. "Now the just shall live by faith: but if any man draw back, my soul shall have no pleasure in him" (Hebrews 10:38, KJV).

Only one way and one plan works, God's way! When He says to go, stop, stay, or leave, He means now. Learning the lesson of "one way" sooner rather than later will save us time, money, heartache, and headache. Gomer/Israel would take the long, hard road called "my way" to learn. She was deceived and without knowledge. But God, again, in His righteous anger, still had a "plan." Remember this; God has "...plans for welfare and peace to give you hope..." hope! (Jeremiah 29:11)

God is love; His ways are loving-kindness. All this drama has an amazing purpose and serves as an example. Now God declares His plan through Hosea. According to Hosea chapter two, God promised because she returned to the "old" life that He was about to mess with her plans. First, He starts by taking all the blessing and provision away because she did not acknowledge that it came from Him. This ruined the life she built, exposing her vulnerabilities. With nowhere to run or hide, all the familiar places and faces abandoned her. The Lord would cause all her festivities, celebrations, and wild parties to cease. With that, he destroyed her provision. Because she went after other lovers, forgetting God, He actively reduced her life to nothing. Exposed and stranded, with no one going near her, where could she go, and what could she do now? Next, He then "hedged up her way." Using a hedge of "thorns," He encloses her. Wow, dating 101, get their attention. Get rid of the competition, the comparisons, and the choices, and all the options, nice! There, she could not find or see a way out, nor could the old lovers find her. And even if she tried, bam! Ouch! The thorns told her to get back, don't even try to find a way out. That is how to reduce the odds, clear out the field, and close her in! Surely she will decide to go back to her husband, realizing it was a better deal.

God sets his anger aside and, in His mercy, "hedges" or closes her in and exposes her. He causes the so-called "lovers" to run; they do not come for her. He removes all her "life," as she knew it, because she forgot God. Sounds harsh, but God has a plan. She did not recognize and willingly acknowledge God as her lover, her source, her healer, and her provider. Just maybe you find yourself in a place of solitude, closed in with nowhere to go. Could it be that God is setting His anger aside to show mercy? No matter where you turn, it is like hitting a brick wall; you seemingly cannot go anywhere, and you feel stuck. This is what God, in His jealousy, does for His bride. He never gives up. His jealous love provokes Him to action, not just for Gomer but also for you and me. He will not let us go on forever, turning our back and running away from His love and His goodness without a response. He is angry, but He cannot deny Himself relationship; He loves. Therefore, in His great love, He goes to great lengths to save us from our own destruction, so He comes after us and hedges us in for our own good. It may not "feel" like love, but there is purpose in this place and purpose for the hedge.

God is painting a picture for Israel, the church, for you, and for me, as the "Bride of Christ." He, as the scorned lover, will not sit idly by and let someone or something else receive the affection due Him. Whom do we acknowledge as our source of life: job, education, titles, friends, family, lovers, husband, government, doctors, or worse ourselves? Maybe we think life is found in work, parties, entertainment, kids, houses or spouses, fame or sex, traveling, food, drugs, cars or clothes, or even ministry. Who do we say has the power to satisfy, provide, heal, or fulfill? Are you starting to see? We may not think our choices or decisions could provoke God to jealousy. We often do not think of God this way; He has a soul, He feels. Our daily choices declare whom we acknowledge as our life, our lover. Even in our worship, our hearts may be far from him. God was saying that even in the celebrations, they did not glorify Him. Lord forgive us. Look at what God does next after He hedges her in and gets her all alone to Himself: "Therefore, behold, I will allure her, and bring her into the wilderness, and speak comfortably unto her" (Hosea 2:14, KJV).

The Message says it this way, "And now, here's what I'm going to do: I'm going to start all over again. I'm taking her back out into the wilderness where we had our first date, and I'll court her" (Hosea 2:14, MSG). Interestingly, God strips her life down to nothing, removing every familiarity, comfort, and crutch, including provision, places, people, and parties. True love has come to take her, with all her vulnerabilities, on a journey back through the wilderness. He starts over from the beginning, where Israel first began as a nation. He starts over with her alone, "just you and me, baby!" Taking her by the hand, just as she is, He leads her on a new "first" date into the wilderness.

> *So we have stopped evaluating others from a human point of view. At one time we thought of Christ merely from a human point of view. How differently we know him now! This means that anyone who belongs to Christ has become a new person. The old life is gone; a new life has begun!*
>
> 2 Corinthians 5:16-17 (NLT)

With nothing between them, they walk and talk; He finally has her attention. The old is gone; the new has begun. This may not be the ideal image of your first date to fall in love with Mr. Right, but remember, God wrote the original algorithm for love. He is Love! Now, He "allures" and "woos" her, the rebonding begins. Talking, walking, holding hands, one on one, alone, they get to know each other all over again. Wow! How awesome the potential this place of loneliness or "wilderness" has in your life. Is it possible that God, desperate to get you alone, has orchestrated the circumstances in your life so He can talk to you? Could it be that God has brought you into a wilderness place that you, too, may experience His love again and learn to depend upon Him alone? He has removed all the distractions, so hopefully, you will see Him and hear Him alone say, "Thou art all fair, my love; there is no spot in thee" (Song of Solomon 4:7, KJV).

This wilderness, characterized as a land of drought, a wasteland if you will, is uncultivated and uninhabited. This inhospitable place is a date with your Creator, the Lord your husband. Here, in this dry and thirsty land, as He leans into you, turn and look into His face. See the love the Lord has for you. As you do, fears begin to melt away. Fears that He is not enough or that I am not, that lead to questions like "will you leave me, do you really love me, is this the best life, or will I be happy?" vanish. We see Him; we see love and fears subside. Finally, perfect love casts out all the fears; chemistry is sparked. Experiencing a renewed connection, we turn, lovestruck, repenting and relenting, ready to surrender to the lovesick pursuer of our soul. This wilderness is not the destiny; it is the original *ChristianMingle Meetup!* The broken marriage or relationship experiences new life in the wilderness. The healing begins. It's a *Perfectmatch* by the original *Matchmaker* Himself! Maybe it is a *SpeedDate* or not, but the intrigue tells us this relationship is full of possibility and discovery. The heart and hand of love reaches in and releases the fears and fills our deep-seated desires. The wilderness is wooing.

If you sense you are in a "wilderness" place, thank God, this is going to be good! Here is where you can hear your *Perfectmatch* speak tenderly to you. If you listen, you will recognize His voice. He has something wonderfully intimate and deeply personal to say: "I love you, I have always loved you, and will love you forever." "I am here and will never leave you or forsake you." He begins to share with you the hopes and dreams He has for you. As awkward as this *"do-over"* may feel at times, we are drawn into the mystery of romance, the secret of a King with His Queen. He wants you, "the king greatly desires your beauty" (Psalm 45:11a, KJV). His words tenderly allure our hearts, but the words themselves remain uniquely individual. God knows just what you need to hear. He sees you, He hears you, and He knows you. In this wilderness, He safely and patiently extends true love again.

He has come for you, to romance the you no one else knows, just like you are. Listen for His "still small voice." You are beautiful, special, unique, and one of a kind. Here God spoke to Moses, to

David, to John the Baptist, to Jesus, to Gomer, and now, He speaks to you. He came for me so many times, and yet still He whispers. He came when my first engagement ended, and I felt so unloved. He will move you into a whole new environment to get you out of a mess and into His will. He came again when my husband left after I thought I knew so much about how to love. He came in the midst of disappointments within marriage. He just keeps coming to rescue us from ourselves. You see, He has come alone to comfort and heal our confused, hurting, and broken hearts. He alone fills us with purpose and provision through His love. Here, His all-consuming desire restores, rebuilds, and reignites passion in the midst of loneliness, loss, sorrow, and shadows. Take His hand, go with Him, you will be glad you did. Remember, the shadow never hurt anyone; light is on the other side. He has now brought me back to this place again as my husband has gone on to be with the Lord. How comforting to know this marriage is alive forever.

Desiring true intimacy, full attention from the beloved is shared and enjoyed once again, reuniting the long-lost love. Now, with the fire of love rekindled, God reveals the treasure in the wilderness:

> *And I will give her her vineyards from thence, and the Valley of Achor for a door of hope: and she shall sing there, as in the days of her youth, and as in the day when she came up out of the land of Egypt.*

Hosea 2:15 (KJV) (emphasis added)

Vineyards, a valley, and a song—with these, God restores provision, hope, and joy. Out of the wilderness, the desolation, life is waiting with vineyards and the valley. When we see this, we'll sing for joy as at the beginning. God wants to restore the joy of our salvation, our song. So far removed from her old life, surprised by love, she finds that He has been ahead of her, patiently planting, preparing, and pruning a beautiful vineyard. What a gift! He's about to throw down a real party for her! This first gift of a vineyard foreshadows a celebration, a milestone, a new season, as a suddenly! Signaling our new life in Him is ready and waiting to be fully enjoyed and productive. Life bursts forth up out of the wilderness, that dry place, where and when you least expect it. The vineyard yields her fruit, the grape, and then, in time, the wine is produced. He is the vine, the life, and He produces or yields the hope of this "new wine." A "new wine" that flows from the life of His spirit, filling our spirit, the branch, where finally, our thirst is quenched. Here we find the life we have been looking for—in the vine. He wants to turn your wilderness into a lush, delicious valley of celebration. "Oh taste and see that the Lord is good!" (Psalm 34:8a, KJV) He quenches her thirst with the first drink of celebration as a promise of more joy to come.

> *I am the true vine, and my Father is the husbandman. I am the vine, ye are the branches. As the Father hath loved me, so have I loved you: continue ye in my love. These things have I spoken unto you, that my joy might remain in you, and that your joy might be full.*
>
> John 15:1, 5a, 9, 11 (KJV)

With the vine, though, comes the valley of Achor, which means "trouble" and represented death. Why the valley? Joshua dealt with the disobedience of Achan here. Achan's rebellious act of taking and hiding spoils from the last battle at Jericho brought defeat to the Israelites in their battle at Ai. So, once found out, Achan, his family, and his livestock were all stoned to death and burned in this valley. What was God thinking in bringing Gomer to this valley of death? How could this place possibly bring provision, hope, and joy after all that had happened here? Like Gomer, we, too, can learn from Achan's death and receive the lesson of this *Death Valley!* For Israel, in order to win again and take their Promised Land, the fear, the rebellion, and the disobedience had to die. God was taking Israel back to learn their lesson again through Gomer. Metaphorically, God is asking her, like Achan, to go under the tent and get out everything she is hiding. Get it out, throw it out, and, if necessary, burn it up. Yes, He already stripped everything away in the natural. But now He wants her heart that is now the tent. "For where your treasure is, there your heart will be also" (Luke 12:34, NKJV). It's time to clear out and let go of anything not for you or from Him, sort of a "decluttering" of your heart and your life. There is only room for Him, so go ahead, open all the doors, and clean out the rooms. The Valley of Achor represents the end of ourselves, the dying to our ways, starting over. Achan's stolen treasure hid under his tent brought death. He hid it. Not trusting God, he kept it for a backup, a plan "B," or just a little extra. He disobeyed God, who said to take nothing out of Jericho.

Here in this place, we, too, die, not physically but spiritually. We are done with hiding, with living our way, blessing ourselves. No longer depending on ourselves for satisfaction, we willingly die to self, that is to say, our ego, our flesh, and the world. Here, we let go of the backup plan, no plan "B." Achan did not obey his leaders or trust God for provision; as a result, all of Israel fell to defeat. However, here in Hosea, God, in His great mercy and grace, turns this *Death Valley* into a fruitful garden. We can safely open the doors to all the rooms in our hearts and let Him help us clean out the living room, the kitchen, the bedroom, the office, and of course, the hall closet! Look and see, ask and then remove what has to go.

There, at the end of ourselves, we see the "secret door," a "door of hope." Here He offers a "do-over" door that gives renewed hope for the hopelessness. He is saying what I have for you is better, and what's yours is still yours; it's on the other side. The wilderness and the valley are not the destiny; they lead to the door of hope. This date through the wilderness led to the vineyard, the valley, and finally, the door. He has hacked online dating forever; He has been online waiting! Love, forgiveness, exclusivity, and now hope are all initiated. A confident expectation of good days ahead full of promise floods our soul. Drawn to the mystery behind the door, anticipation and excitement give rise to our song. Our Promised Land awaits; what joy, what rejoicing! The key is in the song. No longer looking back in despair but rather letting go of the past and longingly waiting at the door, she sings with enthusiasm. Praise in the valley! Out of the valley of trouble is heard a new song, a song that opens the "door of hope." It's time to sing! Lift up the song in your heart; He is waiting to hear it! The song is the key that opens the door. He's longing to hear your song, so sing! Your song opens the door to the promises ahead. "But as it is written, Eye hath not seen, nor ear heard, neither have entered into the heart of man, the things which God hath prepared for them that love him" (1 Corinthians 2:9, KJV).

When you think you have nowhere to go and feel as though you are at the end of your rope, perfect! This is your new beginning. Listen, He speaks gently, alluring you to Himself. No more being passed around. He wants to bring you to a door of hope. This wilderness is not a break-up; it's a make-up! It is for seeing and hearing, for letting go of the old and receiving a fresh new start. Look again; there is a door! A door He's waited to show you. In the wilderness, God's provision is given, the door of hope is revealed, and joy is restored. Take His hand, sing your song, and watch the door of your promising future open. There is a celebration just ahead. This is the prelude to the procession.

God took Moses through the wilderness and revealed Himself. Later, He led Moses to take the Israelites through the wilderness to reveal the "Door" into the Promised Land. The Spirit led Jesus through the wilderness to defeat the devil and the flesh and from there ushered Him through the "Door" into His earthly ministry. Now Jesus is saying, "I am the Door" (the way, the entrance). Jesus told Thomas, "I am the way, the truth, and the life; no one comes to the Father but through Me" (John 14:6, NASB). "I am the Door; anyone who enters in through Me will be saved (will live). He will come in and he will go out [freely], and will find pasture" (John 10:9, AMPC).

We can only enter life, the place God has for us, through this "Door," the "door of hope," Jesus. No other door is available. All other doors are dead ends and do not even have a consolation prize! No other door offers the abundant life with a hope and a future, as God promises. There is one door, and He is on the other side, knocking, hoping, and waiting for you to open the door and let Him in, Jesus, the King of Glory.

> *Behold, I stand at the door and knock; if anyone hears and listens to and heeds My voice and opens the door, I will come in to him and will eat with him, and he [will eat] with Me.*
>
> Revelation 3:20 (AMPC)

"Lift up your heads, O you gates; and be lifted up, you age-abiding doors, that the King of glory may come in" (Psalm 24:7, AMPC). Hallelujah! In this place, God says we get a "do-over" where we begin anew and sing again, rejoicing in restored hope. He has brought you to the door, the door of hope; open it with your song! If you have found yourself in the wilderness, where you are dry, thirsty, and unsatisfied, let go of the old, drink of the new wine from His vineyard, and rejoice! This is your place of new beginnings. He's not improving the old; He is doing a new thing, giving you a whole new life!

> Remember ye not the former things, neither consider the things of old. Behold, I will do a new thing; now shall it spring forth; shall ye not know it? I will even make a way in the wilderness, and rivers in the desert. The beasts of the field shall honor me, the jackals and the ostriches; because I give waters in the wilderness, and rivers in the desert, to give drink to my people, my chosen, the people which I formed for myself, that they might set forth my praise.
>
> Isaiah 43:18-21 (ASV) (emphasis added)

He's after the sound of praise, a simple thanksgiving. Have you lost the song in your heart? God will give you reason to praise with a new song! In the wilderness, faith is restored, faith that sings and rejoices evermore! Miriam sang this song when the Israelites looked out over the Red Sea and saw their enemy defeated. Look what God had done! They sang about all the victories God had given them in those early days, in their deliverance from four hundred years of Egyptian bondage. God showed them the door and gave them a song of rejoicing and praise for His mighty works, which He had wrought on their behalf. You must have a deliverance to sing about because you are reading this! He has brought you out of something; sing about it!

He has brought you to this place to show you the door. Your journey starts here. Leave everything you have tried before behind you. Let this be the point of no return, the "end" of yourself, your way, and your plans. Let this be the beginning of His way, His

Lordship. Just open the "Door of Hope," the adventure awaits! God showed Gomer the "door," the way out, and now, as she is singing, overwhelmed by her restored relationship and renewed fellowship, her love bubbles up in a joyful declaration, "Ishi!" "And it shall be at that day, saith the LORD, that thou shalt call me *Ishi*; and shalt call me no more Baali" (Hosea 2:16, KJV) (emphasis added).

"Ishi!" She finally calls God what He has been waiting to hear, "Ishi!" "Ishi," the Hebrew word for, you guessed it, "husband," and not "Baali" or master. She recognizes Him now as her soul mate, her lover, and ascribes to Him the title due to His name, "Husband." She only thought she had love; now she sees Him in all His beauty. Imagine, the God and Creator of the universe is looking for you to simply see Him and declare "my Husband?" What an amazing, patient, extravagant lover! He just wants us to see, know and recognize He has been there all the time. He simply wants to be the "one and only" forever. All the walls of thorns are there to help us, like Gomer, see the true lover of our soul, our husband, is God. It has been Him all along; He's our man! "'And it shall be, in that day,' Says the LORD, 'That you will call Me *'My Husband,'* And no longer call Me 'My Master'" (Hosea 2:16, NKJV) (emphasis added).

Gomer finally says, "He is *My Husband, Jehovah Ishi.*" The ultimate picture of love for the faithless ones, this allegory, portrays the restoration of our relationship to the Lord as a "marriage made in heaven." He has come to claim back His bride, and better yet, she sees Him for the lover He is and declares Him as "the Lord, her Husband." God is bringing Gomer, the *wild woman,* out of slavery where she will not call Him "master" as a slave, but rather calls Him "Husband" as a lover, her "one and only," her "man." She identifies Him as "Husband," as "my Man" because she sees

Him now as her lover, not a slave owner. God wants us to know He loves us best; He is the Redeemer. He took us from death to life, out of bondage into freedom, out of brokenness into wholeness, and out of darkness into light to show His loving-kindness, His mercy, His provision, and His peace (wholeness). How great a testimony to the love and power of God! He's come for us again, to reclaim His bride and take her home.

What a moment of revelation when God opened my eyes to see His work in bringing me to this place of declaration. Finally, I rest, alone with my Lord, my Husband. He wants us to see clearly that our relationship is of the highest order. He is my Husband, my lover, not a slave master. The beginning of a family that would produce precious eternal fruit. How I would treat our relationship from this point would change forever. Now, I had to protect this bond. No, you cannot just date or just date for fun if you are single; you are married to the Creator of the universe. He is pursuing you and providing for your every need, and He wants to be acknowledged. He is the Lord, your Husband. Faithfulness now brings the blessing of God's mate for our lives. Moreover, if you are married, He is still the Lord, your Husband. As we declare Him rightfully and justly, who He is, we give Him legal authority to come into the midst of our marriage and manifest Himself. This changed everything in my new marriage almost overnight. God still wanted to hear me declare Him as the Lord, my Husband, in the midst of this new relationship. He had not left or given me up. He just wanted for me to trust Him, to look to Him and release my husband. Only then could He love me through the life of my fleshly husband. What a turnaround, a complete one hundred eighty degrees in our marriage.

"Husband," just the word conjures a variety of emotions. Some that do not have one want one, and others that have one do not want theirs. Such a dichotomy of feelings! And even still, that can change from day to day. Nevertheless, one thing is certain; we were made for love; love never fails. The relationship between a husband and wife implies a personal, intimate, exclusive, abiding love of the highest order, a holy covenant. The loveliest expression is found in the Song of Solomon chapter six verse three, where the bride says, "I am my beloved's, and my beloved is mine."

Unity, covenant, and exclusivity characterize this relationship. When you have this, you have the secret, love. With God, "the two become one" through Jesus' blood and the new covenant. In Ephesians 5:32, Paul calls this a great mystery concerning Christ and the church, pictured as a husband and wife relationship; the two shall become one. God loves you and desires this relationship with His bride, the Church. When we respond with love, Paul says in 1 Corinthians 3:21b, 23 (KJV), "…For all things are yours; And ye are Christ's; and Christ is God's." If you call the Lord yours, then you belong to God. This is the best relationship, and there is no equal. He is waiting to hear us respond with this declaration: "You are the Lord, my Maker, my Husband." God began connecting the dots for me as He took me back to this promise: "For thy *Maker is thine husband*; the LORD of hosts is his name; and thy Redeemer the Holy One of Israel; The God of the whole earth shall he be *called*" (Isaiah 54:5, KJV) (emphasis added).

In both places, here in Isaiah and in Hosea, we see in the text the words "*called*" or "*declare*" in reference to how God would be addressed verbally or vocally. In other words, we are to give voice or vocally speaking, expressing and declaring our relationship with the term of endearment and respect, "Husband" and *Lord, Jehovah*

Ishi. If I call Him that, I would say speaking to Him, "You are the Lord, my Husband." God is waiting to hear what we call Him. He is not some random person upstairs, like the "*man upstairs!*" That is why it is so important to not take the name of the Lord in vain or for no reason. His name reveals our relationship, and in that is everything. He is not just God, He is the Lord of hosts, the Creator, God of the whole earth, and He wants me to call Him "the *Lord my* Husband"; how simple, yet so incredibly profound!

My confession and declaration is an outflow, the fruit of my heart. The sooner I recognize who my lover is, the sooner I will speak justly or correctly of God. God waits longingly, jealously, and patiently to hear our confession of the Lord as our "husband." He has worked tirelessly stripping, pursuing, hedging, alluring, and preparing to receive His own, His bride. We are His reward. How amazing to realize I am the reward of the Lord, His bride. He goes on to say, "For I will take from her mouth the names of the Baals, and they shall be remembered by their name no more" (Hosea 2:17, NKJV).

Hosea further explains that the name "Husband" is so important that God will take all the names of the other gods out of her mouth and remove all remembrance of them as well. He never wants to hear of them, only who He is to her—"Husband." He does not want to hear about her escapades with Baal or anyone else for that matter. Have you ever talked about your "old" life, including boyfriends, only to have it backfire on you? Then you realize it would have been better if I had just kept my mouth shut. God is helping her out here and taking even the remembrance of those things away, implying that it would be a shame to even mention their names. God does not want you to ever bring it up again. Let it go; it's under the blood of Jesus, forgiven and forgotten. He won't mention it, so neither must we. Stop romanticizing or indulging memories of past relationships or gods; it's in the rearview mirror; look ahead to the Promised Land. Think of it; the all-knowing God has no memory of our past loves. "For I will be merciful to their unrighteousness, and their sins and their iniquities will I remember no more" (Hebrews 8:12, KJV).

Covenant

Now, what comes next confirms this restored love; He explains, "And in that day will I make a covenant..." (Hosea 2:18a, KJV)

On the day of Gomer's song and declaration of her Husband as the Lord, Hosea and God come forward to make an eternal covenant, a vow renewal. A permanent, legally binding agreement or vow, He promises with an oath to keep forever. Different from a contract that is designed with "*escape clauses*," contingencies that provide a way out of the agreement, this covenant is permanent, irrevocable, and immutable, or we might say unchangeable. We live in a culture of broken promises and contracts. As a result, the word "covenant" has lost meaning and significance in our society. Oftentimes items purchased on time get repossessed for nonpayment or failure to abide by the terms of the contract. On one of my dates, my husband took me on a repo run, and I had to let the air out of a tire! If you have ever seen these repo shows, you know what I mean; it can be scary. Nobody wants a repo because it creates a bad "credit score," which inhibits future lenders from extending credit. In other words, the name or word to pay back what is borrowed is not worthy or binding. Even Scripture says in Romans 1:31 and 2 Timothy 3:3 (KJV) that this is a sign of the last days, people will be "trucebreakers, covenant-breakers, and implacable." In other words, they will not even want to make a vow. Fear wins, keeping people from commitments of all kinds, especially in relationships. We live in a temporary, "disposable," "throwaway," non-committal generation. But God wants us to understand that through the promise and the covenant, these two, that He is a covenant-keeping God, faithful. He is not a man that He should He lie. He works through covenant to give us our inheritance.

Here we find that He is longing to enter into a covenant with us. So He, from the onset, offers this "vow renewal," a solemn binding agreement between the two parties. It is a vow, an oath, or a promise usually signified by a token of exchange. Robes, rings, scepters, meals, salt, even shoes but especially blood, are all part of elevating an oath or promise to that of a covenant. As Jonathan gave David his robe, as God gave Noah the rainbow, and as Jesus gave us His blood, we see and understand the gravity of this promise. In betrothal, money and rings exchange as tokens of the promise, and then a year of waiting ensues as the groom prepares to bring his bride home.

In this case, God has sealed His covenant with humanity with His own blood, the blood of Jesus Christ. Not with a man whose blood is tainted with sin, but with Himself. He cannot break His own vow. Man will lie and fail, and the blood of bulls and goats will not suffice, but only the perfect, sinless blood of Christ, born the Son of Man and the Son of God, could seal this covenant forever, making the imperfect perfect. "God is not a man that he should lie; neither the son of man that he should repent: hath he said, and shall he not do it? Or hath he spoken, and shall he not make it good?" (Numbers 23:19, KJV)

> *Know therefore that the LORD thy God, he is God, the faithful God, which keepeth covenant and mercy with*

them that love him and keep his commandments to a thousand generations;

Deuteronomy 7:9 (KJV) (emphasis added)

He hath given meat unto them that fear him: he will ever be mindful of his covenant. He sent redemption unto his people: he hath commanded his covenant forever: holy and reverend is his name.

Psalm 111:5, 9 (KJV) (emphasis added)

"The secret of the LORD is with them that fear him; and he will *show* them His *covenant*" (Psalm 25:14, KJV) (emphasis added). God keeps His covenant, but according to Psalm 25:14, He calls it a "secret" that is revealed to the ones who "fear Him." He has secrets to reveal. When we are living for ourselves, we cannot experience or come to "know" the beautiful secrets of His covenant. God is not just out running around showing this to anyone. It is to the one who fears Him by acknowledging Him as their Lord. Now that He hears "husband" again, He takes away the names of the old loves out of her mouth, so they are never spoken, much less whispered again. Now God is ready to reveal His covenant, the "door of hope" opens. He stands at the threshold, ready to carry you into His Promised Land. God begins with His betrothal vows, His "wooing," as it were, and wants to see what is waiting. He intends to win us back; He's been waiting for you!

Betrothal Vows for His Beloved

1. Vow of Eternity

We pick up with Hosea, representing God to His people Israel then, and to His bride the church today, creating the framework from which their restored relationship will fulfill all their mutual desires with His covenantal vows in verses 19-20: "I will betroth thee unto me *forever,*" and in verse 23, He declares we are "His." "Betroth" is a marital term simply meaning "by one's truth." When God repeats Himself three times, with "I will," He is very intentionally calming our fears of insecurity with the security of His commitment or pledge of honor to take us as His bride forever. Hosea here would take the adulteress Gomer back as his wife, forgiving and releasing her from all her past. Declaring this covenant established forever, confidence is assured in that He is not a man that He should lie. Never would there be any separation or divorce, or even talk of such, the marital union is secure. The Word of God is above His name; His name means nothing if He does not keep His Word. God watches over His Word to perform it. His "I will" is undeniable and irreversible. He has written our name in the palm of His hand and in the "Book of Life." We are His for eternity. He has chosen us from before the foundation of time as His very own special treasure, His bride forever.

Thus, here in scripture, we have the heavenly wedding vows, promises from our heavenly Husband. I cannot even imagine the God of the universe has so passionately and thoughtfully prepared vows, much less that He stands waiting for us to receive them. He has been waiting at the altar, waiting patiently to hear you call Him "Husband" so you can hear Him say these wedding vows. Remember, He is a covenant-keeping God, and He alone knows what we need the most! He is ready to fulfill all your hearts' desire, are you ready? If you will take these vows, one by one, in your heart and receive them, and then respond with "I do," you will walk through this "door of hope" into the Promised Land.

Understand first—God underscores these vows with our deepest need, a sense of security, like most wedding vows state, "to have and to hold from this day forward until death do us part." With God, though, even death cannot separate us. "*Forever*" means an eternal, infinite, unending covenant, surpassing time. His love never comes to an end; it is from "everlasting to everlasting." Take comfort in this security as you begin, only with God; to be absent from the body is to be present with the Lord. When He says "forever," He means it! He will never leave you or forsake you, and He has come for you now. Take His hand, look into His face, and receive these words.

> *That whosoever believeth in him should not perish, but have eternal life. For God so loved the world, that he gave his only begotten Son, that whosoever believeth in him should not perish, but have everlasting life.*
>
> John3:15-16 (KJV)

2. Vow of Safety

The *Lord* vows to His bride as Hosea declares his promises to Gomer in Hosea 2:18:

> *And in that day will I make a covenant for them with the beasts of the field, and with the fowls of heaven, and with the creeping things of the ground: and I will break the bow and the sword and the battle out of the earth, and will make them to lie down safely.*
>
> Hosea 2:18 (KJV)

The Message Bible says it great,

> *At the same time I'll make a peace treaty between you and wild animals and birds and reptiles, and get rid of all weapons of war. Think of it! Safe from beasts and bullies!*
>
> Hosea 2:18 (MSG) (emphasis added)

I love that, "safe from *beasts* and *bullies*!" God is so awesome; He makes a peace treaty with the animals! Studies show the number one need for women is security. Look at God; after He declares

His love for eternity, He then calms more fears by promising to keep the bride safe from danger and harm inflicted by animals or enemies. He promises or commits to provide an environment of peace and protection that will allow her to lie down safely at night, no fights, no friction, and no fear. This is no small promise. He would not remember her sins against her, shaming and blaming or "bullying" her with her own failures and shortcomings, but He would protect her wherever and whenever from anyone else who would try to hurt her. He gives not only peace within the home but peace without. What a great promise He offers!

We are a very blessed nation. Most of us take our safety for granted, but for anybody who has been the victim of being mugged, raped, ransacked, burglarized, threatened, or abused in any way, *safety* is a *big* issue. God knows us better than we know ourselves, and I love how He addresses this directly. Oh, we try to be tough and strong, and even safe; maybe even carrying a gun, some mace, or a baseball bat, but that cannot save us. God says, "Be strong in your spirit, take courage; do not be afraid, for I am with you; I will save you" (Isaiah 35:4). He is the best security system, and His cameras are always on and always monitored, better than *ring 911* or *ADT!* With a promise of peace, He has her attention. God is our refuge!

This covenant speaks literally to us. We live in an area of Florida where animals like alligators, snakes, bees, bats, dogs, gophers, spiders, etc., cannot only be a nuisance but have taken lives. When I walk out my back door, I totally trust the Lord my Husband on this promise of safety. By His marvelous protection, we have lived safely on a lake without any danger. Praise the Lord! We have also been broken into where things were stolen, but we have never been hurt or harmed in any way, thank God! What a powerful promise, "safe from beasts and bullies." God promises an environment of peace to encompass His bride; what comfort to know He is watching and protecting: "Safety is of the Lord" (Proverbs 21:31b, KJV). "He is a shield about me, my refuge and strength, a very present help in trouble, He will fight for you!" (Psalm 3:3; Psalm 46:1; Exodus 14:14) I like this vow!

Now He continues with more:

> *I will betroth thee unto me in righteousness, and in judgment, and in loving-kindness, and in mercies. I will even betroth thee unto me in faithfulness: and thou shalt know the Lord.*

Hosea 2:19b, 20 (KJV) (emphasis added)

Let's unpack this by taking each one out individually and see what He is promising:

3. Vow of Righteousness

The righteousness of God validates the covenant, making it legal and binding, true and proper. It is right. He upholds it with His righteous right hand and His Word, in all integrity. He promises He will come to us in full knowledge of who we are and what we have done, raising us up out of our mistakes and missteps to offer His full pardon and right standing. With favor, as the "apple of His eye," He clothes us with the white gown of royalty as we stand tall with our shoulders back in full assurance that our heart is made right when joined to His righteousness. "For what saith the scripture? Abraham *believed* God, and it was counted unto him for *righteousness*" (Romans 4:3, KJV) (emphasis added).

God promises to give the blessing of His forgiveness, not imputing our sin to us when we believe Him! Your faith in Him and His love counts for righteousness. Will you believe Him? He believes in and approves you and wants to give you this blessing of believing that His robe of righteousness covers our shame. He does not see what we were; He sees what we *are* in Jesus and His righteousness. He puts His faith in you in these words, as He is the author of our faith. It is this faith that sets the relationship straight, puts it on level ground, and clears our conscience. Now, it truly is like the first time as we begin anew. God forgives and forgets our past, never remembered against us again! He separates our sin from this relationship as far as the east is from the west; Hallelujah! Condemnation is gone, and forgiveness enters. He restores the freedom to look into the future and dream once again.

This vow of righteousness means God will always think and do what is right and best for us. God assures us He will never make a mistake! He will never make a bad call or a poor decision. His way is right, and He will do what is right! His ways and thoughts are higher than ours. He is never wrong. His way leads us to life and to blessing. We can trust Him and be thankful for this covenantal promise. Thank God, He is right and trustworthy; we can count on Him, always!

4. Vow of Judgement

"Shall not the Judge of all the earth do right?" (Genesis 18:25b, KJV) Sounds harsh, right? Who wants judgment? This is worthy of celebration! God is committing to give Himself to us according to judgment, that which is fit and becoming—God is able to wisely discern and decide what is best for our relationships, our future, and us. In His judgment, He determines the relationship is now made permanent, the righteousness of Christ is sufficient, and provision is made individually for that which is fit and becoming for His bride. In judgment, God vows that no one can see error in the match. Even if there is a hand raised and a mouth moving,

God gives no place or credence to it and says, "From now on, everyone must hold their peace; she is mine!" "Hearken unto me, my people; and give ear unto me, O my nation: for a law shall proceed from me, and I will make my *judgment to rest for a light of the people*" (Isaiah 51:4, KJV) (emphasis added).

This judgment is our light, our happiness, illuminating our day, giving clarity to our life. It is glorious, shining on us, kindling a fire within our hearts. With God's judgment comes all the rights and privileges legally mine as a wife to a husband. He withholds nothing and offers everything; there is no prenuptial agreement with God! We can count on the judgment of God to be fair; He will always execute fair treatment and do what is right. He offers to take complete responsibility for our well-being, whatever the cost, even His own life. He is not lazy or forgetful; He is ahead or on time in every situation, preparing and doing right. But wait, there's more!

5. Vow of Loving-kindness

He betroths Himself in a "steadfast love" or "loving-kindness," the Hebrew word "chesed," meaning grace and favor. Now He is really getting my attention, speaking my language. He promises to love me no matter what! This is one of the highest expressions of God's loyalty and devotion, an irrevocable commitment to compassion; I am always favored. Hosea is the perfect picture of God's faithful love to the unfaithful. His steadfast love endures forever; He abounds with it. He will never run out of it. He chose me once, and He keeps choosing me every minute of every day. He looks for ways to shower the object of His affection with grace and kindness, unmerited favors. His ear is open to my voice, waiting longingly to hear me. No hiding in a *"man cave"* from me and no *silent treatment*. Whether on a bad day, a good day, a bad hair day, after the honeymoon, and after the third, fourth, or fifth child (and whatever extra pounds come along with that!), he zealously pursues me, His beloved. Always, every anniversary His love remains full—all the time; always the same, never changing—He loves me, even when I am not showing Him love, giving me His best, even when I don't deserve it. He promises to love me always, unconditional! You can receive that love, right? Such love, how could we not receive such beautiful loving-kindness? You are loved without limits and highly favored at all times!

6. Vow of Mercies

"Remember, O LORD, thy tender mercies and thy lovingkindnesses; for they have been ever of old" (Psalm 25:6, KJV). God will have compassion or mercy. He understands, knows, and relates to the feelings of our weaknesses.

> *For we do not have a High Priest Who is unable to understand and sympathize and have a shared feeling with our weaknesses and infirmities and liability to the assaults of temptation, but One Who has been tempted in every respect as we are, yet without sinning.*
>
> Hebrews 4:15 (AMPC)

He promises to show pity and have mercy on us. Now that is more than just being there when we are down. That is a commitment to love us and lift us up out of whatever pit we get into! He shows pity when I blow it, make a mistake, or speak unkindly when I am hurting, broken, or sick. His mercies never end because He understands our weaknesses. He created us, and He remembers we are but dust. He shows mercy when we are tired, overworked, or overwhelmed, whether by the chores, the kids, the duties, the appointments, the traffic, the schedules, deadlines, etc. You name it; mercy is yours! God is never passive; He is passionate, with passion. He commits to fervently and favorably incline to you, or we might say, lean into you. He looks for ways to help carry your burdens and give you rest. Can you imagine someone always moved with compassion for you? Just like Hagar, the slave who became pregnant with Abraham's first son Ishmael, running away, and hiding from the harshness of her mistress Sarai, God sees and hears, and here He provided and blessed her child (Genesis 16:10, 13, KJV). The same God that watched over and blessed Hagar, Jehovah Roi, the God who sees, is watching over you too. He not only sees and hears us; He made us this way. Who could understand us better! He is saying, "I want you, I love you, I am coming for you, and I can handle your life." If you are feeling left out, His abundance of understanding, consideration, and appreciation is waiting for you; only believe.

> *But God—so rich is He in His mercy! Because of and in order to satisfy the great and wonderful and intense love with which He loved us, Even when we were dead (slain) by [our own] shortcomings and trespasses, He made us alive together in fellowship and in union with Christ; [He gave us the very life of Christ Himself, the same new life with which He quickened Him, for] it is by grace (His favor and mercy which you did not deserve) that you are saved (delivered from judgment and made partakers of Christ's salvation).*
>
> Ephesians 2:4-5 (AMPC) (emphasis added)

Thank God for His mercies; they are new every morning! He's got you; will you wake up in His mercy today? There is still more as if this were not enough.

7. Vow of Faithfulness

"I will even betroth you to Me in *stability* and in *faithfulness*, and you shall *know* (recognize, be acquainted with, appreciate, give heed to, and cherish) the Lord" (Hosea 2:20, AMPC) (emphasis added).

God reiterates His covenantal term, betrothal, and now offers stability and faithfulness. How good it is to settle down and settle in. I do like stability; most women and children readily admit to this. There is something comforting about constancy, a place to call home. When you approach the throne room, you come home. God, the Lord, your husband, is always there, and better yet, He knows your name. God is not unstable; up one day and down the next. He is constant and immovable in all of His ways. He is the same yesterday, today, and forever. When the storms of life blow, He is there, solid as a rock, upholding His Word and keeping all His commitments. He is a *very present help* in times of trouble; no matter how bleak the situation looks, He will never bail. How many times and how many ways does man fail at being stable, dependable, faithful, or reliable? It seems vogue these days not to be dependable or stable, to be "free as I wish." People float from relationship to relationship, church-to-church, and job-to-job, not really thinking anything of it and not willing to make any commitments. People are really saying, "I want to keep my options open," or "I don't want to be tied down to anything or anyone," or "I can take it or leave it." Here again, man may fail to fulfill signed contracts or audible agreements, but God never fails.

With God, His Word means everything. He is always watching over it to perform it. He does not want to keep His options open. He already left heaven, laid down His whole life, not tied down but nailed down; and, signed this covenant in *His* blood! He says our relationship is His priority; He is not just taking what He can get; He is delighted and satisfied with His choice. You are not a mistake or the luck of the draw; He wants you just like you are! He will never send us back or trade us in on a newer, better model! Oh, to enjoy stability, the security of finding a place of rest and settling down, when you know where you belong. Paul said it best:

> *That Christ may dwell in your hearts by faith; that ye, being rooted and grounded in love, May be able to comprehend with all saints what is the breadth, and length, and depth, and height; And to know the love of Christ, which passeth knowledge, that ye might be filled with all the fullness of God.*

Ephesians 3:17-19 (KJV) (emphasis added)

What a comfort to be rooted, settled, established, and confident in love. How great is the love of God! He is not changing His mind; He is not confused, He has not moved, and He is not fickle. He does not say one thing today and forget and say something very different tomorrow; He is not "two-faced," as the Message Bible says.

> *Every desirable and beneficial gift comes out of heaven. The gifts are rivers of light cascading down from the Father of Light. There is nothing deceitful in God, nothing two-faced, nothing fickle.*

James 1:17 (MSG)

Do you get the picture? His face is set; He is looking at you, and He will not stop! He wants you to look full into His wonderful face. He boldly declares His faithfulness to us, and His record backs Him up. He has never lied or broken His covenant; we have. Now, He vows, when we come to this place of understanding that we will come "to know" Him truly and fully:

8. Vow of Intimacy

"You shall *know* (recognize, be acquainted with, appreciate, give heed to, and cherish) the Lord" (Hosea 2:20b, AMPC).

Now we come to the best part. God reveals and unveils Himself completely. Because of His eternal love, He declares that Gomer—Israel, His bride (the church), you and I—will *fully know* Him; the *Lord*, the Creator, our *Husband!* In every sense of the word, we will *know* God as we are known. This includes knowing Him figuratively and literally, by observation, recognition, instruction, and yes, even chastisement. We will discover by revelation, discern by perception, and understand with wisdom just *who He is*. We will touch Him, smell Him, hear Him, taste, and see that the *Lord is Good*. Jesus said in His high priestly prayer: "And this is life eternal, that they might *know* thee the only true God, and Jesus Christ, whom thou hast sent" (John 17:3, KJV).

Finally, coming to "know" God, we find life, life eternal, our salvation. In revealing Himself through His vows, we now confidently trust that what we have seen and heard is enough to know our Husband is the Lord. What a divinely inspired love He is ready to bestow upon His bride, pure and undefiled, nothing to hide, and everything to give! To that, we will live in faithfulness, exclusively loving the One who first loved us and giving ourselves wholly and completely. This is now the desired state of matrimonial completion, the unveiling of intimacy.

Oh, my dear sister, He has so much invested. He is waiting for your response. Will you call on Him as "*Ishi*," "Husband" now? He wants you to call Him for your own, "*Lord*, You are my Husband." The strength of His love is so powerful that Gomer, you, and I will finally come to the place of believing He does see me, He does hear me, and He does know my heart's desire. He cares about what concerns you. We now believe He reaches out His hand to take ours and lift us up out of the mire of shame, hurt, despair, loneliness, confusion, and lack. His arm is not short that it cannot save. He wraps His arms around you and comforts you. He has been there all along, keeping you and bringing you to this place. He has been the provider all along, not our brains, or beauty, or brawn. Blessing and favor are from the Lord; He is the One who deserves all the credit, the glory, and the praise. In this, we now know Him. Do you see?

9. Vow of Blessing

> *And it shall come to pass in that day, I will hear, saith the LORD, I will hear the heavens, and they shall hear the earth; and the earth shall hear the corn, and the wine, and the oil; and they shall hear Jezreel. And I will sow her unto me in the earth; and I will have mercy upon her that had not obtained mercy; and I will say to them which were not my people, Thou art my people; and they shall say, Thou art my God.*
>
> Hosea 2:21-23 (KJV) (emphasis added)

Now the blessing is released, we receive the open windows of heaven, the favor of God. When the Lord hears His people call Him by name, Ishi, Husband, the bounty and beauty of heaven and earth are released and lavished, yielding an abundance of blessing and provision upon His bride. The heavens that were brass before are open, sending rain; the earth that was iron now yields her crop. Once held back by God's hand, now a beautiful succession of release as one rolls onto the next, creating "*showers* of blessing" (Ezekiel 34:26, KJV). Blessings hidden are now released from God's own hand upon His beloved. God now refers to His bride as "Jezreel," not as one He "scatters," but as one He "sows."

He plants us in His house, bestows His mercy, and claims us as His family, His people, and His bride. All that is left is our response, "Thou are my God!" God gives a complete turnaround! Oh Lord, You are my God, the Lord my Husband, *Jehovah Ishi*! How could we ever hold our love back from such a faithful, patient Lover?

He has brought me to a place that I finally know Him, acknowledge Him as my source of life, and trust His love for me is good and pure. His provision is complete. In receiving His love, God can now respond because He has found faith. He has found an undivided heart, a tender heart of flesh that now believes. He restores the lost "nobody's" to His dear "somebody's." Through His mercy, we are His anew, sown by God as His bride. The betrothal is complete, and upon acceptance, the marriage is consummated, the two become one. We are His forever.

> *Set me as a seal upon thy heart, as a seal upon thine arm: For love is strong as death; Jealousy is cruel as Sheol; The flashes thereof are flashes of fire, A very flame of Jehovah. Many waters cannot quench love, neither can floods drown it: If a man would give all the substance of his house for love, He would utterly be contemned.*

Song of Solomon 8:6-7 (ASV)

> *A new heart also will I give you, and a new spirit will I put within you: and I will take away the stony heart out of your flesh, and I will give you a heart of flesh. And I will put my spirit within you, and cause you to walk in my statutes, and ye shall keep my judgments, and do them. And ye shall dwell in the land that I gave to your fathers; and ye shall be my people, and I will be your God.*

Ezekiel 36:26-28 (KJV) (emphasis added)

Now, as God's beloved people, with a new heart and a new spirit, we receive Him and His Word sown as seed into the soil of our new tender heart. His Word, the vows of His covenant, is the seed, and as I believe, receive, and confess them, God performs them. When I know Him as He is, I believe and therefore respond, calling Him who He is, the *Lord my Husband*. With the seed of God's word, these promises, sewn in my heart, they can now take root and bear fruit. Finally, God is glorified. The fruit of love from our life reveals God is present. What a beautiful complete picture of God responding to the cries of His people. So, too, the earth and the heavens cry, asking, begging, and beseeching the Sovereign God of all creation to gather the clouds, send the rain, bring water upon the dry ground, and finally cause the soil to germinate the seed. This, in turn, brings forth all the fruit and provision for His people. At one end, man, completely and utterly dependent on God, and on the other end, with all the various elements in between, God, responding. God is waiting to respond when now, the time is right, the acknowledgment has come, "Ishi," and with it a song. He hears her sing once again, free and light, rejoicing and praising. He is provoked once again to send the blessing. What a joy! How He longs to bestow the blessings of protection, peace, and provision. Even the earth and skies are relieved! The cycle of seed, time, and harvest begins again; the showers of blessings fall "round about!"

At this point, I began to realize I had not sown the seed of this Word and allowed it to grow; I had dug it up repeatedly. Then, I was depressed, wondering why I never saw any harvest. How crazy! I had to learn my part in sowing the seed, leaving it there in the soil of my heart, and then how to help it grow. God opened my eyes and showed me what I was to share with you in the pages to come. He was and would always be my Husband, whether single, divorced, married, or widowed. If I trusted Him, He would continue to manifest Himself to me as when I was single, only this time He would also work through my earthly husband, the man He put in my life to represent Him. God took me on this journey, reminding me of what I had learned and how to sow this seed for my marriage. The seed finally had a chance to grow, and within less than a year and a half, every wall, bondage, and barrier to fulfillment and intimacy in our marriage came down. Through the study and teaching of a wonderful book—*Rebonding*, by Donald Joy, we, while leading our whole congregation in the same, renewed our vows and shortly thereafter entered the ministry full-time together. That journey of healing and restoration is what follows.

This precious Word and life-giving seed, "The Lord is My Husband," will bless you, too, as you believe, receive, and sow it into your heart as well. Believe in your heart and call on Him now for your own. He is waiting for you to look in His face and call Him "Ishi, my Husband." Soon, as the seed takes root and bears fruit, the passerby shall see the faithfulness of God and say, "this land that was desolate is become like the Garden of Eden." "Then the heathen that are left round about you shall know that I the LORD build the ruined places, and plant that, that was desolate: I the LORD have spoken it, and I will do it" (Ezekiel 36:36, KJV).

Your life or your marriage that you think is dead, lifeless, and hopeless is just what God is looking to restore and revive. Raising up that which looks dead and desolate into a fruitful garden glorifies God. Why is this? What better testimony to the power of His love, His Word, His grace, and His resurrection power? There is a Garden of Eden on this side of heaven. He says He will do it.

Will you let the water of His Word wash away doubts, fears, and unbelief? Will you allow this Word to give you a new, tender, soft heart of flesh that believes? Simply believe and receive. Remember the Word that states, "Unless we come as a child?" Oh, how beautiful is the simple faith of a little child!

The cycle of "seed, time, and harvest" is part of the Noahic covenant; God said it would never end: "While the earth remaineth, seedtime and harvest, and cold and heat, and summer and winter, and day and night shall not cease" (Genesis 8:22, KJV). The harvest will come if we will take the seed of His word, sow it into the soil of our new heart, and embrace the process of "time." Learning how to see as a farmer or gardener sees is the journey. We look out at the field and see dirt; they look out and say, "That's corn!" Developing the faith of a farmer to trust in the midst of trial and engage in the process required to take us to our physical harvest is now our goal.

What He has declared for Gomer, He is still declaring, down through time, "You're mine, and I want you, I love you. I know the thoughts and plans I have for you," says the *Lord*. God continues to faithfully, steadfastly pursue His bride. He has come for you today. He has told me to tell you, "He is the Lord God your Husband." He loves you forever. He will go to great lengths for you to settle, stand still, and see the salvation of the Lord. God says, "Be still and know that I am God." Do you have an opportunity to "be still?" Would you stop everything, stop your back door exit, your plans, your crying and manipulating, controlling or running? Just stop! Sit still and listen to that still small voice of God whispering, "I love you." Just as God commanded Hosea to go and buy Gomer back from the slave market to be his wife again: "So I bought her to me for fifteen pieces of silver, and for a homer of barley, and a half homer of barley" (Hosea 3:2, KJV).

So too, God sent Jesus to come and buy us back with His precious blood. Such a sacrificial price for redemption has the power still today to speak on our behalf. We are His, redeemed and paid for, but not as a slave, but rather as a bride, a beautiful, glorious bride without spot or wrinkle. He makes us stand before Him, perfected in Jesus through His finished work on the cross, the incorruptible seed God sowed. You see, we are His harvest, and He has long patience for the precious fruit of the earth. "Afterward shall the children of Israel return, and seek the LORD their God, and David their king; and shall fear the LORD and his goodness in the latter days" (Hosea 3:5, KJV).

Hosea demonstrates the unconditional love of God by restoring Gomer, thus illustrating God's unlimited love to look beyond our waywardness, see our great need for His love. After God restores and gives us time alone to settle, we so desire the Lord as our one and only that we now seek Him passionately; and then, not only fear Him with reverence but fear His goodness. That means calling what God does "good" and realizing He will never deny Himself the object of His love. In seeking Him, we come to stand in awe and to tremble at the awesome power, holiness, and beauty of His glorious love and goodness. "Sow to yourselves in righteousness, reap in mercy; break up your fallow ground: for it is time to seek the LORD, till he come and rain righteousness upon you" (Hosea 10:12, KJV).

It is time. Now is the best time to return to the Lord, set yourself, seek the Lord, hear, and receive His word. Like Gomer, our way or ideas get us nowhere, much less the counsel of others. Allow the Lord to come now to you and teach you. As you receive

Him, your healing and restoration begin to manifest. Like rain upon your heart, beautiful harvests of love shine on your face as you begin to recognize the romancing of your heavenly Husband. He tells us how in His instruction to Israel:

> *O Israel, come back! Return to your GOD! You're down but you're not out. Prepare your confession and come back to GOD. Pray to him, "Take away our sin, and accept our confession. Receive as restitution our repentant prayers. Assyria won't save us; horses won't get us where we want to go. We'll never again say 'our god' to something we've made or made up. You're our last hope. Is it not true that in you the orphan finds mercy?"*

Hosea 14:1-3 (MSG) (emphasis added)

He actually tells us what to say, literally, "Take with you these words," they call it "lip-loading." I love it; there is no guessing with God. He is helping us know exactly what He wants to hear from our repentant hearts. I would do this with my husband sometimes; we had so much fun with it. I said something like, "If I could hear you say it like this..." And then fill in the blank. It worked every time, and he eventually "learned" me. So too here with God, He wants to hear us repent, confess, and ask for mercy. Renounce all other loves and denounce the lies. Declare that nothing but He can save you. Then we receive healing, love, growth, and beauty. God once again revives, regards, and watches over His people:

> *I will heal their faithlessness; I will love them freely, for My anger is turned away from [Israel]. I will be like the dew and the night mist to Israel; he shall grow and blossom like the lily and cast forth his roots like [the sturdy evergreens of] Lebanon. His suckers and shoots shall spread, and his beauty shall be like the olive tree and his fragrance like [the cedars and aromatic shrubs of] Lebanon.*

They that dwell under his shade shall return; they shall revive like the grain and blossom like the vine; the scent of it shall be like the wine of Lebanon. Ephraim shall say, what have I to do any more with idols? I have answered [him] and will regard and watch over him; I am like a green fir or cypress tree; with Me is the fruit found [which is to nourish you].

Hosea 14:4-8 (AMPC) (emphasis added)

God promises to heal, to love, to cause us to grow and blossom beautifully, to bless others when we return to God, and bring words of repentance. His promise is to give you a fresh start and shower you so much with His love and grace that you grow and bloom into all you were made to be. It is like a "do-over." God is a God of second chances, third chances, and so on. When we put the idols away for good, idols of self-pity where we give up and go back to the old ways, He promises that we will finally blossom into all we were created for.

For the lovers of God may suffer adversity and stumble seven times, but they will continue to rise over and over again. But the unrighteous are brought down by just one calamity and will never be able to rise again.

Proverbs24:16 (TPT)

He promises to answer, regard, and watch over the ones who give up their idols and rise up one more time. With God, we are then truly satisfied; we finally find the fruit that satisfies. Now is the time to acknowledge Him as Lord and provider, returning thanks to God alone. Nothing and no one else can receive the glory due to Him alone. The wise woman will recognize, this is the right way, the only way that satisfies, the way to live your life. Enter into this beautiful covenant with the Lord as your Husband

and begin a new life, hand in hand with the One who loves you most and is committed to you forever

> *Who is wise, that he may understand these things? Prudent, that he may know them? For the ways of the Lord are right and the [uncompromisingly] just shall walk in them, but transgressors shall stumble and fall in them.*
>
> Hosea 14:9 (AMPC)

May God give you wisdom to understand the power in this word. May you know and understand the Lord is there with you, intimately, never leaving you. He is your Husband. Your story can begin again here at the altar, as did mine. Once I realized He was there all along, hearing, seeing, and desiring to respond, if I would just see Him for who He was, my forever Husband, I could start again. Now I extend the same invitation to you, come to the altar, the bridegroom is calling, "Will you marry me?" Begin again with the author of love, the One who has come for you. He is waiting to hear you say, "*Ishi*, my Husband." Experience the joy of young love and let Him carry you over the threshold and through the door into your Promised Land. Take with you, if you will, these words:

Prayer ~

Dear Lord, hear my plea; I confess my fears and failures in trusting you. I have left off listening to You and followed my own ways. I have not acknowledged Your provision and goodness; please forgive me. Have mercy upon me. I confess you as my Savior, my Lord, and my Husband. I acknowledge You alone are my safety, my shelter, my protection, and my provision. Nothing I have done or could do can save me now, but You, Lord. Forgive me for trying to save myself, for trying to replace your love with people or things. Your great loving kindness and tender mercies are new every morning; thank you. I now receive the seed of this Word into the soil of my heart brought to life by the redeeming power of Your love through the sacrifice of Your life on the cross.

Forgive me for at any time denying and forgetting Your love and Your goodness. I confess and declare You are good; that every good and perfect gift comes down from You. Thank you that as we share this love, you work all these things together for my good according to your perfect purposes and timing. I lift up to You now the sacrifice of praise declaring my thankfulness to Your great love wherein You loved me first. Thank You for coming for me; I give you all I am and ever hope to be. I decree and declare, "You are the Lord, my Husband." I am never alone; Your love is perfect, complete, and truly amazing; it is more than enough. Thank You for healing my heart, for a fresh start, and for causing my life to grow and blossom. Thank you for giving me roots grounded in Your love and for making me a blessing to others. I receive Your strength and beauty. Thank You for reviving my spirit and for leading me to this Door of Hope; I rejoice in You. Thank You for forgiveness. I receive it now and give You the song of my heart, "You are Great and do miracles so great, there is no one else like You, there is no one else like You." I give You my hand and receive the life in Your Word. Help me to never let go of You again. In Jesus' name, amen.

Congratulations, now let Him carry you across the threshold, through the open door, and prepare for His soon coming.

> *Then I heard what seemed to be the thunderous voice of a great multitude, like the sound of a massive waterfall and mighty peals of thunder, crying out: "Hallelujah! For the Lord our God, the Almighty, reigns! Let us rejoice and exalt him and give him glory, because the wedding celebration of the Lamb has come. And his bride has made herself*

ready. Fine linen, shining bright and clear, has been given to her to wear, and the fine linen represents the righteous deeds of his holy believers." Then the angel said to me, "Write these words: Wonderfully blessed are those who are invited to feast at the wedding celebration of the Lamb!" And then he said to me, "These are the true words of God."

Revelation 19:6-9 (TPT)

CHAPTER 3.
MEMORIAL STONES

"And God saith again unto Moses, `Thus dost thou say unto the sons of Israel, Jehovah, God of your fathers, God of Abraham, God of Isaac, and God of Jacob, hath sent me unto you; this is My name—to the age, and this My memorial, to generation—generation."

Exodus 3:15 (YLT)

"The bride has made herself ready, wonderfully blessed, are you!" Welcome, sister, to the journey of your life as we enjoy and prepare for our Groom, *Jehovah Ishi,* the Lord our Husband, to take us home with Him for eternity. As you go through the "Door of Hope," be prepared to write your own story. Pick up a journal and leave a legacy. God's love story with you is a memorial worth sharing and giving to your children, family, or friends. Just as the woman at the well in John four told her story of Christ's love and influenced the entire city of Samaria, so, too, you will want to share what Jesus does for you. Begin in faith, and as David did throughout the Psalms, hold nothing back—your ups and downs, your tears and your laughter—let your life be an open book, poured out as a drink offering, as you drink of the living water. Jesus said to the Samaritan woman at the well,

> *But whoever takes a drink of the water that I will give him shall never, no never, be thirsty any more. But the water that I will give him shall become a spring of water*

welling up (flowing, bubbling) [continually] within him unto (into, for) eternal life.

John 4:14 (AMPC)

The story of Hosea foreshadowed the picture of this well of eternal life. His name means "salvation," but what is beautiful is his father's name, "Beeri," which means "The well of Jehovah." God again gives us a picture; out of the well, Beeri, comes his son, Hosea, "salvation," a spring of living water for eternal life. God wants us to drink and drink the best until we are full and overflowing with His life. Jesus is that life. God is the well of living water from which we draw salvation in Jesus Christ alone. When we drink of the living water, we ready ourselves to give the only drink that truly satisfies others. Keep thirsty, my beloved, for the true satisfaction, and be quenched with the living water flowing down from the throne of God into the wells of salvation in our hearts. Drawing water from this well satisfies our desires to the springing up of eternal life. Hosea, demonstrating the Lord as our Lover, our Husband, becomes known as our "salvation." We will be like this Samaritan woman, who interestingly, like Gomer, as an adulteress, learned to drink of the water that truly satisfies. The woman at the well drank the living water for herself; she tasted and saw that it was good when she received the word of Jesus. Now is the time to drink in the life of love. Jesus loves you! The Lord is not deterred by our past but rather deliberate in offering us something better. Of course, she wanted immediately to share this new water of eternal life and love with the whole town!

Behold, God is my salvation; I will trust, and not be afraid: for the LORD JEHOVAH is my strength and my song; he also is become my salvation. Therefore with joy shall ye draw water out of the wells of salvation. And in that day *shall ye say, Praise the L*ORD*, call upon his name, declare his doings among the people, make mention that his name is exalted!*

Isaiah 12:2-4 (KJV) (emphasis added)

Praise the Lord; His name is above all else! God said when we draw this living water out of the wells of salvation, we would "say, declare, and make mention" of His great name and great deeds. Fill me up, Lord, until I, too, run over, declaring Your goodness for the glory of God. What God is about to do will change your world, so drink up and praise the Lord.

My dear sisters, we are journeying together to know the King. You will want to share the journey's milestones and memories, the challenges and the triumphs. To help us remember the way of this journey, I offer you *eight memorial stones*. These stones are markers representing your passage from the wilderness to the Promised Land, from the land of not enough or just enough to more than enough, from the kingdom of the world to the Kingdom of God, from the *valley* to the *victory*. Yes, upon accepting Jesus as our Savior, God translates us from darkness to light. The challenge from here is to daily receive, remember and identify with the Lord, my Maker, as my Husband. Loving and serving Him with pleasure, not as though He were a slave master but as my dearest treasure, faithfully at all times, I keep saying "yes." As I do, I continuously acknowledge His faithfulness in keeping His vows. That, my sister, is our mission. May these stones be for stepping and not stumbling, for remembering, not forgetting. Let us remember God, His love, His activity, His presence, actively calling to mind who He is and what He has done. With that, we can walk with Him into the glorious plan He has for our lives.

The use of stones is notable yet varies throughout history. We use them today as headstones or tombstones marking a burial plot, identifying the person by name, date, and sometimes, a few tender, memorable words. In state and national parks, they serve to remind us of momentous occasions such as victories won, or again, of famous people. Think of the permanence of stones like those at "Stonehedge" in England, a monument that has stood for likely over five thousand years. Stones, however, are not only used as memorials but as cornerstones for buildings, altars for sacrifice, columns, pavers, even tablets like the ones on which God wrote the original Ten Commandments. But also, what about as weapons, stones were used in the fateful stoning of Stephen, or by David killing the Philistine, Goliath. One stone, slung powerfully, accurately, and confidently, defeated the enemy. How we use these stones determines whether we step in accord with God in victory or whether we stumble. We can use them for evil, throwing them at ourselves or others, or use them for good, remembering God, He is our Rock! We set them up as an altar to God for worship as we memorialize the journey to deeper intimacy with Him, our sure foundation.

The very nature of a stone is symbolic. We have spoken of the permanence and endurance and also of its strength or hardness. Stones can be cut, shaped, polished, or left in their natural state. Altars were built with unhewn or uncut stones, natural if you will, unshaped and untouched by hand or blade. Because of the hardness of the matter in the stone, they demonstrated a certain firmness, strength, and commitment of the participant or worshipper. Jacob, using a stone as a pillow, slept (ouch!) and, after having a dream of the Lord standing above a ladder and speaking a blessing to him, awoke, acknowledging that God was in that place. He then took the simple, easily accessible stone he used as a pillow and set it up as a pillar or memorial. In so doing, He marked that place, declaring it "the Gate of heaven," or Bethel. He began a custom still practiced today, pouring oil on a stone to dedicate or consecrate it for use in worship as an altar to God. Oil is a symbol of prosperity, happiness, and joy. The custom of anointing a thing or person destined for a sacred purpose is of ancient origins. Such unction was, in ancient times, and continues to be in many modern countries and contemporary religions, a symbol of the setting apart of the thing or person so anointed and consecrated to a holy purpose.

> *And Jacob rose up early in the morning, and took the stone that he had put for his pillows, and set it up for a pillar, and poured oil upon the top of it. And he called the name of that place Bethel… And this stone, which I have set for a pillar, shall be God's house…*
>
> Genesis 28:18-19a, 22a (KJV) (emphasis added)

And then, yet again, when God blessed him and called him Israel:

> *And God went up from him in the place where he talked with him. And Jacob set up a pillar in the place where he talked with him, even a pillar of stone: and he poured a drink offering thereon, and he poured oil thereon. And Jacob called the name of the place where God spake with him, Bethel.*
>
> Genesis 35:13-15 (KJV) (emphasis added)

Notice, the stone represented the place *where God spoke with him*, a very special place of God's communion and intervention in his life, a place and/or moment of truth. So named Bethel, meaning the "House of God," the place where He met with God and where he would return. These stones set up as pillars or altars would serve to commemorate the significant meeting places, turning points, and great events in the lives of God's people. God is still speaking today, and my prayer is that here we will find our Bethel. At each chapter, may we set up our marker, a memorial stone first as an altar before the Lord and secondly, as a story, a truth to remind ourselves and to tell others of the goodness of God. As we do, I pray that we each receive a fresh anointing of the oil of the Holy Spirit, setting us apart for Him.

Likely, the story of Jacob's stone altar passed down as hope to each successive generation, reaching the ears of his great-grandson Joshua. So that when it came time, and God asked him to do the same, he thought it not strange and went right to work:

> And Joshua said unto them, Pass over before the ark of the LORD your God into the midst of Jordan, and take ye up every man of you a stone upon his shoulder, according unto the number of the tribes of the children of Israel: That this may be a sign among you, that when your children ask their fathers in time to come, saying, What mean ye by these stones? Then ye shall answer them, that the waters of Jordan were cut off before the ark of the covenant of the LORD; when it passed over Jordan, the waters of Jordan were cut off: and these stones shall be for a memorial unto the children of Israel forever.

Joshua 4:5-7 (KJV) (emphasis added)

Likely encouraged by the stories of his ancestors, he delighted in carrying on the tradition of stirring up the faith of future generations. So when God commanded Joshua, after crossing the Jordan to take up twelve stones out of the river "where the priests' feet stood firm," he was quick to give the instructions. These twelve stones, one for each tribe, were to be a sign, a marker, a witness, which, when seen, would elicit a question of their meaning for generations to come. These questions, in turn, would require a response declaring God's miracle-working power, not only in deliverance but also in defeating their enemies and ushering them into their own land. The testimony of God's love and power would pass from generation to generation, keeping His praise alive and their faith active continually. The memorial stones would serve as a witness of God's goodness to the children forever.

In the New Testament, stones are significant of Jesus and the Church. The stone that the "builders rejected," Jesus, has become the "chief cornerstone" of the church of God. Now God makes us each a "living stone" built up together a *spiritual house*" and brought to life by the Spirit (pneuma, the breath of God). He anoints, consecrates, and sets us apart by the anointing of His Holy Spirit for the work of the ministry. Oil is used also as a traditional way of sealing stone. So too, symbolically, we are sealed by the Spirit of God, represented throughout scripture by oil, marked as belonging to God. We are anointed, sealed, and set apart as holy, living stones brought together by the hands of the master builder.

> *In whom ye also trusted, after that ye heard the word of truth, the gospel of your salvation: in whom also after that ye believed, ye were sealed with that Holy Spirit of promise,*

> Ephesians 1:13 (KJV) (emphasis added)

The smearing/anointing of oil significantly enhances the beauty of a stone. The anointing of God beautifies the believer. Psalm 96:6b (KJV) says, "Strength and beauty are in his sanctuary." God desires that we be "fitly framed together and grow into a holy temple in the Lord for a habitation of God through the Spirit." We are "living stones" according to 1 Peter 2:5, built upon the foundation of the apostles and prophets, with Jesus as our cornerstone. Those who reject Jesus stumble over Him, but to the believer, He is a precious stone.

I give you these stones to remember your God, the miracles, and the stops along the way as an opportunity to worship. To set up a place of worship in your heart, remember the message of each stone: the truth of who I am in Christ—His bride, blessed, anointed, sealed, beautified, and set apart for the Lord. These stones are the rock to stand on, to remember the rock of the Word of God, living words. The Words of life that God watches over to perform "do not return to Him powerless (void or of no effect) but accomplish that for which He sends it" (Isaiah 55:11). As God performed and fulfilled the promises He made to Jacob those many years ago, He continues to fulfill His vows to His betrothed today, who will take Him at His Word. If that is you and you say yes, "I will," then these stones will be places you to revisit and share, your Bethel, the place shared with God. There you, remembering the words He speaks to your heart, will have a reason to worship. These stones will become part of who you are; they have me. Like drawing a line in the sand, I use these to establish my journey going forward, never to go back to any other life than this life with God. "Then said the Lord to me, You have seen well, for I am alert and active, watching over My word to perform it" (Jeremiah 1:12, AMPC). Let us now commit to taking them one stone at a time and ask God to help us "set" them up firmly, establishing them in our life.

Prayer ~

Lord, I entrust the keeping and developing of Your truths in my heart and life. As I progress, may they be established and immovable forever, set as stones for a testimony and memorial of Your great love and faithfulness for generations to come. Would you remove all lies, errors, and deceptions that blind me and keep me from seeing you as my Husband. Anoint me now anew with your Holy Spirit, set apart as a true worshipper. Set Your truth within me, strengthen me for the journey, hold my hand, and open my eyes to see You. Thank You, my Lord, my Husband.

"O Jehovah, Thy name is to the age, O Jehovah, Thy memorial to all generations" (Psalm 135:13, YLT).

CHAPTER 4.
MEMORIAL STONE 1
WAIT

The first stone is perhaps the most challenging of the stones to set up. For most of us, waiting is something we do because we have to or because somebody's in our way or because they have not called our name or number yet, but certainly not because we want to! What does this have to do with our journey? Besides, you might say, "I've been waiting! I'm tired of waiting!" However, the Bible says in:

> *Be still and rest in the Lord; wait for Him and patiently lean yourself upon Him; fret not yourself because of him who prospers in his way, because of the man who brings wicked devices to pass. For evildoers shall be cut off, but those who wait and hope and look for the Lord [in the end] shall inherit the earth.*
>
> Psalm 37:7, 9 (AMPC)

Waiters receive their inheritance. This stone you will not only remember, but you will learn to appreciate. "Wait" is a verb meaning to whirl, shake, fear, dance, writhe, and grieve. Not exactly what I thought. Nevertheless, God showed me something wonderful about this stone. This word has many different meanings, most of which derive from two basic ideas: to writhe in pain and to whirl in motion.

Before you jump in and identify with this stone, calling yourself a "waiter," let us get a better picture of what it takes to set this stone up. Let us get a good visual image, a picture of the waiting room. You know what I mean; you see people's personality in a waiting room. There are all kinds, fidgety ones, readers, watchers, players, talkers, and yes, the impatient, loud, boisterous, and yes, obnoxious ones. Yet, some days may be better than others. The question is how God sees us in His waiting room. We all have to go through the waiting room at some point to move on; how well we wait determines how long we stay. Some, like the Israelites, never left the waiting room, the wilderness, because they did not wait well. They have left us a wonderful example of how not to wait:

> *And all the children of Israel murmured against Moses and against Aaron: and the whole congregation said unto them, Would God that we had died in the land of Egypt! Or would God we had died in this wilderness! How long shall I bear with this evil congregation, which murmur against me? I have heard the murmurings of the children of Israel, which they murmur against me. Say unto them, as truly as I live, saith the LORD, as ye have spoken in mine ears, so will I do to you: Your carcasses shall fall in this wilderness; and all that were numbered of you, according to your whole number, from twenty years old and upward, which have murmured against me, Doubtless ye shall not come into the land, concerning which I swear to make you dwell therein, save Caleb the son of Jephunneh, and Joshua the son of Nun.*

Numbers 14:2, 27-30 (KJV) (emphasis added)

Murmurers lost out. When they murmured against their leaders Moses and Aaron, God said they were murmuring against Him ten times. After all the miracles, God was not pleased with their unbelief; they got what they complained about, dying in the wilderness. "Now all these things happened unto them for *examples*: and they are written for our admonition, upon whom the ends of the world are come" (1 Corinthians 10:11, KJV) (emphasis added). "Do all things without murmurings and disputings" (Philippians 2:14, KJV).

Murmuring in the waiting room was the death of a whole generation of Israelites. We do well to take to heart their example and learn how to wait well. To help us with this stone, go with me to the story of one familiar with the pain of this struggle; her name is Hannah, meaning "grace" and "favor." Found in the book of 1 Samuel, chapter one, we are introduced to a priest named Elkanah and his two wives, yes, two, Hannah and Peninnah. "And he had two wives; the name of the one was Hannah, and the name of the other Peninnah: and Peninnah had children, but Hannah had no children" (1 Samuel 1:2, KJV).

Can we stop here for just a moment? I don't know about you, but are women so different today from back then? Just the idea of sharing my husband with another woman would bring enough questions and pains alone to overcome, not to mention adding anything else on top of that. Although this practice was prevalent and related to us does not endorse it as the standard of God. Scripture reveals the many troubled homes as a result of multiple partners, and this one was no different. Nevertheless, what made it so grievous for Hannah was that although Elkanah loved her and she loved him, he chose another wife to bear him children because she was not able.

The childbearing wife is Peninnah. Now Peninnah knows Elkanah loves Hannah more, so she uses her "mother" status to provoke and belittle Hannah to jealousy. Let's go deeper and find the underlying issues. You see, the story goes on to tell how once a year, Elkanah took his two wives and all his children up to Shiloh, the home of Israel's tabernacle. There they would offer sacrifices and worship. Shiloh represented a place of peace, tranquility, and security, but not so for Hannah. He gave each of them portions to offer, but unto Hannah, he gave a double portion, for he loved her. Although this was generous, it only served to embarrass and grieve her even more, for the Lord had shut up her womb.

> *And her adversary also provoked her sore, for to make her fret, because the LORD had shut up her womb. And as he did so year by year, when she went up to the house of the LORD, so she provoked her; therefore she wept, and did not eat.*

> 1 Samuel 1:6-7 (KJV)

Have you ever been so upset you could not eat? Maybe you were endeavoring to worship God, but all you could do was cry? However, what is worse, her husband's double-portion of favor and blessing was no comfort and most likely incited Peninnah to jealousy and more provoking. Even if he had given her a triple or quadruple portion, it would not have helped, for she wanted a child. No amount of money could replace the feeling of empty arms. Her fulfillment could not be bought. God was in control.

Is it not bad enough to carry the weight of the burden, but then seeing and hearing your adversary mock and ridicule you? Can you just hear this woman, Peninnah? She knows Elkanah loves Hannah, but because she has given him his posterity, his namesake, she gloats. To a Jewish woman of that time, not bearing children was a blot, a social stigma. They believed the "fruit of the womb was the reward of God," but more than that, they were looking for the Messiah. By taking Peninnah to birth his posterity, Elkanah implied Hannah "wasn't enough." As if she did not hurt enough already, now she had to deal with feelings of insufficiency and inadequacy. Because she was barren, she was not "enough," and so he went and got another woman. Then Elkanah's payoff, as if giving her more offering was supposed to make her feel better. This just intensified the misunderstandings of her unfulfilled purpose and desires.

How many times the enemy has tried to make us feel like we are not enough—not pretty enough, not smart enough, not capable, talented, or gifted—and from those who love us? Is there any real comfort in a double-portion? How ridiculous! She loved him and wanted to meet his needs and fulfill the dreams and hopes they shared together. How devastating to think some other woman had now done this for him! If she could not give the one she loved and have for herself this precious gift—a child—why was she here? What was her purpose? I am all too sure she struggled with these and other questions. The temptation to murmur was plentiful, but we never hear of any spoken, or even whispered, grumbling. She exemplified the meaning of "wait," though, to writhe in pain. She hurt. She cried and wept sore but never murmured against either of these two, her husband or the mother of his children.

Then, to make matters even worse, her husband, instead of comforting her with understanding, asked her, "Why are you crying? Why are you not eating? Why are you so grieved? Am I not better to thee than ten sons?" (Verse 8) Isn't it just like a man to make it all about him? (I mean that in the nicest way possible, it is in there.) Here she is, barren, unfruitful, and dealing with another woman sleeping with her husband and giving him all these children. Where are the compassion and mercy? Elkanah knew what he was doing, and now he is reaping the fallout of his decision and trying to act like it is no big deal. How difficult it would be to make it right, he would have to put them all out, just as Abraham did with Hagar and Ishmael.

I can just see the joy on his face as he holds his children, watching them, playing with them, teaching them, showing them off. What immense pain as she daily watches and listens. Is she really to just settle and be glad for her man who thinks he is all that and a bucket of chicken? Certainly, he was one of the few devout men who took his family faithfully each year, as a testimony to his neighbors, to the tabernacle for the annual sacrifices and feasts. This he did even when the priest's sons were using their positions hypocritically, as we will see later.

Yes, he did give her a double portion, and for this, she could be grateful. However, how could a double-portion possibly make up for a child? This cold, heartless response only left her feeling more desolate and forsaken, wondering if he, her own husband, does not understand who will. So Hannah did the only thing left to do. She left where they were eating and drew near to the tabernacle, her soul hurting, weeping greatly; she prayed to the Lord, pouring out her soul. What a great response! Instead of getting mad at God for getting her into this relationship and for closing up her womb, she drew near to God. Instead of harboring anger and bitterness toward Elkanah and Peninnah and trying to get God to change them, she went to God with her greatest desire, her heart's cry.

Where do you go? When you are in the midst of immense pain, suffering, and anguish, what comforts you, another relationship, temper tantrums, texting, tweeting or posting on social media, wine, drugs, TV, friends, shopping, running away, hiding, eating, or maybe even a cleaning spree? What is it? After all that, to only find out, nothing brings lasting comfort. Do you try everything else, or is your first inclination to go to God? "Do you go to the phone or to the throne?" as Joyce Meyer says.

Hannah came boldly before the throne of God. She lays out her request before the Lord and asks for a child, specifically for a "man child." However, she adds a vow to her request, possibly for the first time. How many times have we done that, "If only You will God, then I will____?" Fill in the blank. We make some promises to God with great intentions, but all too easily, we forget and think God does too.

> *When thou vowest a vow unto God, defer not to pay it;*
> *for he hath no pleasure in fools: pay that which thou hast*
> *vowed. Better is it that thou shouldest not vow, than that*
> *thou shouldest vow and not pay.*
>
> Ecclesiastes 5:4-5 (KJV)

Wisdom would say be very careful before making a "deal" with God; He will hold you to it. Better not to make one if you do not plan to remember, and keep it. Nevertheless, Hannah does. She promises to give the child back to the Lord all the days of his life and not allow his hair to be cut. What a vow! After all these years, I believe she gives God what He has been waiting for, her strongest desire, the baby. Until now, she had not made this offering, but what an offering; to give him completely up to the Lord. She literally is willing to sow her "first fruit," her firstborn child, to the Lord. A beautiful foreshadowing of what God would do in giving his only son for all humanity.

While she is praying, Eli, the priest, notices her mouth moving and sees her weeping, but he did not hear what she was saying. He immediately assumed she was drunk! As if it wasn't bad enough with the other wife laughing at her, society looking down on her, and her husband being insensitive (clueless or weak, one or the other); now here is the priest, the man of God, who thinks she is drunk! Here she is pouring out her soul, hurting and crying, and now she has to explain herself and her pain to the priest to prove she is not drunk. (Sometimes it is just easier to let people think whatever they want, as just explaining can be too painful.) Listen to how Hannah handles the situation:

> *And Hannah answered and said, No, my lord, I am a woman of a sorrowful spirit: I have drunk neither wine nor strong drink, but have poured out my soul before the LORD. Count not thine handmaid for a daughter of Belial: for out of the abundance of my complaint and grief have I spoken hitherto.*
>
> 1 Samuel 1:15-16 (KJV)

She simply denies the charges and declares her condition and her action. She was "sorrowful" and "talking to the *Lord*." Interestingly, she did not give any details or some long, drawn-out story. She was a woman of few words, focused and intent on her business at the tabernacle. How many times do you go over and over the story, only embellishing it more with each telling? You rehearse and repeat the pain. Oh, how we need to pay close attention to her example and stop hitting the replay button! When nobody understood or felt her pain, through cruel mocking, ridicule, and even accusation of wrongdoing, in her broken, grieving, sorrowful state, she maintains a meek and humble position before the Lord and his priest. She offers few words, no offense—what a great example! Could she have easily become more hurt, maybe even walking away from the tabernacle? Sure! Sometimes the best thing to say is nothing at all.

Maybe you or somebody you know has gotten mad at the pastor, or a deacon, or elder, or maybe just another member and walked out of church only to completely miss what God had for them. Not Hannah; she wanted her blessing too badly to take up any offenses. Oh, Lord, help us to stay that focused in our prayers. She was not drawn into a pity party, saying, "Nobody loves me; I'm all alone in this; nobody understands me; I'm the victim." She simply stated her condition, her action, and her Lord. She took the burden and the pain to God and handed it over.

The issue was never about Peninnah, Elkanah, and the children, or now, even the priest; it was always, and only, the desire of her heart to bear a child, specifically a "man child." How many times and how many ways do we get distracted from our true desire? Where is your focus? Hannah went to the Lord and waited on Him. She fought internally and externally to wait on the Lord. As she did, so must we—stay, wait, and plead with God. "Call unto me, and I will answer thee, and shew thee great and mighty things, which thou knowest not" (Jeremiah 33:3, KJV).

> Confess to one another therefore your faults (your slips, your false steps, your offenses, your sins) and pray [also] for one another, that you may be healed and restored [to a spiritual tone of mind and heart]. The earnest (heartfelt, continued) prayer of a righteous man makes tremendous power available [dynamic in its working].
>
> James 5:16 (AMPC)

Then Eli, the priest, agreed with her and answered, "*Go in peace*, and the God of Israel *grant thee* thy petition that thou hast asked of him" (1 Samuel 1:17b, KJV) (emphasis added). "Again I say unto you, That if *two* of you shall *agree* on earth as touching anything that they shall *ask*, it shall be *done* for them of my Father which is in heaven" (Matthew 18:19, KJV) (emphasis added).

The Power of Agreement

Maybe you have been hurting and even praying but have not yet had someone to agree with you concerning your request. Get your hopes up and believe for the best; go to your pastor, and ask him to "agree" with you. Stop repeating the problem; go to God, bring it before Him, lay it down, leave I, receive your word and call it done! I believe Eli saw and heard her passion. He knew this fervent, effective prayer brings the power of God into the midst of a situation. Hannah knew exactly what she wanted. Her prayer was heartfelt and specific and certainly fulfilled God's command to "multiply." Eli could thus agree with her prayer and blessed her with peace.

She received not only her request but also *peace*—"Shalom," everything in its place, order, well, favored, happy, and in good health. In peace, she could go walking in the wholeness of God, nothing missing or lacking in her life. She was now enough, complete! Hannah, favored, finally found Shiloh to be the place of true peace. Now the child would belong to God. Her dream released, given away, and laid at the altar brought in return so great a gift, peace. In letting go, the supply of heaven flows. The power of fulfillment, in her vulnerability and weakness, she finally found agreement. Oh, how we need others of "like precious faith." Her request—heard and granted, her hope—restored; God's peace was now hers.

> *Do not fret or have any anxiety about anything, but in every circumstance and in everything, by prayer and petition (definite requests), with thanksgiving, continue to make your wants known to God. And God's peace [shall be yours, that tranquil state of a soul assured of its salvation through Christ, and so fearing nothing from God and being content with its earthly lot of whatever sort*

that is, that peace] which transcends all understanding shall garrison and mount guard over your hearts and minds in Christ Jesus.

Philippians 4:6-7 (AMPC) (emphasis added)

Now, the most beautiful response: "And she said, Let thine handmaid find grace in thy sight. So the woman went her way, and did eat, and her countenance was *no more sad*" (1 Samuel 1:18, KJV) (emphasis added). No fear and no more sadness; she is content! What just happened? Was she holding a baby? Was she even pregnant? No. However, do you remember the definition of our word "wait"? It is not just to "writhe in pain," but to "whirl in motion!" Now Hannah still has to wait, but the "writhing" has turned to "whirling"! She is no longer sad; now she can eat! The circumstance is the same, but her heart has changed. She is not the victim anymore but rather the victor! God is in control; He is on the scene; He's got this! With the Priest in agreement with her, he blesses her, and at that moment, she believed and received. He gave her a prophetic blessing, and now her mourning turned to joy. The rejoicing comes after the victory. But wait, where and when was the victory? On her knees, waiting and praying before the Lord. This is the victory, even our *faith*, faith, believing God, that waits in prayer.

This book of 1 Samuel opens with the cry of a godly woman. While the people are crying for a king, Hannah is crying for a child. God builds the throne on a woman's cry. When a woman takes her exalted place of prayer, God builds her a throne. I can just see her whirling her way out of the tabernacle, people looking on, wondering what has happened to Hannah. She believed, but there is more; believing alone would not deliver her destiny; what else? "Therefore I say unto you, What things soever ye desire, when ye pray, believe that ye receive them, and ye shall have them" (Mark 11:24, KJV).

According to this passage, what do you receive? What you believed you received when you prayed. You receive it when you pray, believing. Just like ordering something on TV or the internet, you call/click, order the item, pay for it, and then you wait for it! Is it yours? Yes! You paid for it, so what do you say now? It is mine; it is processing and on its way. In seven to ten days, it will be here unless you have Amazon Prime, but is it in your hand now? No. Is it yours? Yes! Do you see this? Hannah was "no longer sad." Why? She believed she received when she prayed. She knew she would see her baby boy, look into his eyes, and hold him. Maybe not today or tomorrow; there was work to do, but then one day, her answer would manifest. Believing is seeing. We get it backwards so often; we think seeing is believing. No, seeing is seeing! Once you see it, you do not need to believe in it; you can look at it, touch it, and hold it. No, believing comes first; then seeing, "For we walk by faith, not by sight" (2 Corinthians 5:7, KJV).

> *For we are saved by hope: but hope that is seen is not hope: for what a man seeth, why doth he yet hope for? But if we hope for that we see not, then do we with patience wait for it.*

Romans 8:24-25 (KJV) (emphasis added)

Patient waiting rejoices now for the joy to come. We know Hannah believed she received when she prayed because she left freed from sadness and filled with peace. Hannah left the tabernacle that day spiritually impregnated with a Word from God, a "seed." She believed and therefore received. Did you realize God speaks to us through our "shepherds?" Hannah had respect for the word of her priest and received it as a Word from God. When

Eli said, "God grant thee thy petition," Hannah received! How many times has God tried to speak to us through our pastors, shepherds, or rabbi, and we would not listen, receive, or maybe, were not even available, still in bed on Sunday mornings! Or, we might have heard God speak, but we did not care, or even take it to heart what God said through them? I am speaking to myself here. This is how I went down the wrong road. Oh, dear sister, have respect for the gifts God places in the church. Bring yourself under your pastor and hear from God. How many blessings do we miss because we are not listening and receiving our Word from God through His chosen vessels? God has set these people in the body as it has pleased Him. He gives the gifts. If we are too lazy, apathetic, or proud, we can miss our "seed" by not heeding the gift of prophecy in the church.

Eli's family would lose the priesthood because Eli, her priest, was not bringing his sons into obedience. Even when there is sin in the priest, God works through order and uses authority in our life to protect, provide, correct, and bless us. Honor all those who are in authority. God sets these offices, or gifts, in the church to help us grow up in Christ to do the work of the ministry as one body. Without them, we will never grow up or rise up into all God has for us. The blessing of Eli rested upon Hannah, and she left that day with her answer. Nobody or nothing else could give her this peace but God. Through patient endurance, she got her answer. God understood, He heard, and He answered. What a great High Priest we have today, Christ Jesus! He sees you, hears your cries, and better still, He understands.

> *Inasmuch then as we have a great High Priest Who has [already] ascended and passed through the heavens, Jesus the Son of God; let us hold fast our confession [of faith in*

*Him]. For we do not have a High Priest who is unable
to understand and sympathize and have a shared feeling
with our weaknesses and infirmities and liability to the
assaults of temptation, but One Who has been tempted in
every respect as we are, yet without sinning. Let us then
fearlessly and confidently and boldly draw near to the
throne of grace (the throne of God's unmerited favor to us
sinners), that we may receive mercy [for our failures] and
find grace to help in good time for every need [appropriate
help and well-timed help, coming just when we need it].*

Hebrews 4:14-16 (AMPC) (emphasis added)

How do I get this kind of faith that believes I receive when I
pray? Then, when do I know I have it? Good question; glad you
asked! "So then faith cometh by hearing, and hearing by the word
of God" (Romans 10:17, KJV).

What you "hear" or give attention to determines what you put
your faith in. If you listen to doubt, fear, and unbelief, then you
have more faith in hopelessness, failure, and loss. If it is, on the
other hand, the Word of God, you are receiving the incorruptible
seed that produces faith in God and His promises. As you give
yourself to hearing and meditating on the Word of God, whether
through godly teaching, preaching, reading, studying, or singing,
you build your faith. Your spirit is coming up or rising up in the
glory of God. Truth dispels lies, restores hope, and builds faith in
God. The Word says we go from "faith to faith" as we learn "line
upon line and precept upon precept."

We come into a more intimate knowing of who God really is
and then begin to experience Him. We recognize Him. We see His
hand at work now, when before we did not recognize, much less
acknowledge, Him. When we have greater personal knowledge,
we trust Him more. We believe Him. You know you have this

faith when you walk out of your prayer closet, that secret place, rejoicing, praising, and giving God thanks, worshipping Him now with your life as a "living sacrifice." You know you have this kind of praying faith when this love of God now results in loving others. You see, faith works by love.

> *For [if we are] in Christ Jesus, neither circumcision nor uncircumcision counts for anything, but only faith activated and energized and expressed and working through love.*
>
> Galatians 5:6 (AMPC) (emphasis added)

Love activates faith. What counts, what God is looking for is faith expressing itself in loving others. Jesus so trusted and believed God would raise him from the dead that He was able to lay His life down for sinners, unconditional love. The cross of Calvary represents the greatest act of love for humanity while revealing the greatest depth of faith in God by our Savior, Jesus. He is the author of our faith; He wrote the book on it! We love because He first loved us. If Hannah had not made the choice to love Peninnah and her children, her faith would not have worked. If she had not chosen to love and give herself to Elkanah, she would have never given birth to Samuel. Faith in God works by love. Who has hurt you that you can love? Ask God how you can show them His love. Find someone to love, especially an enemy.

It is also important to note that we know Hannah forgave all those that hurt her—Peninnah, Elkanah, Eli the Priest—and any others because God would not have forgiven her, nor heard and answered her cry if she had not.

> *And when ye stand praying, forgive, if ye have ought against any: that your Father also which is in heaven may forgive you your trespasses. But if ye do not*

forgive, neither will your Father which is in heaven forgive your trespasses.

Mark 11:25-26 (KJV) (emphasis added)

"But your iniquities have separated between you and your God, and your sins have hid his face from you, that he will *not* hear" (Isaiah 59:2, KJV) (emphasis added). "If I regard iniquity in my heart, the Lord will *not* hear me" (Psalm 66:18, AMPC) (emphasis added). The Lord heard Hannah's prayer; nothing separated her from her God. Her heart and her conscience were clear before the Lord. She did not hold onto any offense or unforgiveness against those who did not understand her struggle nor those who capitalized on her pain. She forgave. God could look, hear, and answer. Forgiveness gets God's attention; He says, "That's my girl!" If we love Him, we obey His command, "Love your neighbor." Love forgives. That is the gospel. If Hannah had not forgiven them, she would have shown God that she thought she was more important than He was. Her hurts would then be an idol in her life. Nevertheless, not Hannah; she forgave and took no offense. Think of it; she had to not only forgive Peninnah for mocking her; her husband, Elkanah, for not understanding and praying with her; but also the Priest Eli, for accusing her of drunkenness when she was seeking the Lord! Likely, she had to forgive herself as well for thoughts of guilt and condemnation, thinking she was no good to anyone as if God didn't know what He was doing. Yes, forgive myself; accept Jesus' forgiveness.

The beauty of God is He understands our weakness. He grants us the mercy to forgive, the grace to love, and the power to heal. We cannot hold on to hurts, taking offense, and expect that the Lord will hear and answer our prayers. His law has always been and always will be "love."

"Teacher, which is the great commandment in the law?" Jesus said to him, "'You shall love the LORD your God with all your heart, with all your soul, and with all your mind.' This is the first and great commandment. And the second is like it: 'You shall love your neighbor as yourself.' On these two commandments hang all the Law and the Prophets."

Matthew 22:36-40 (NKJV) (emphasis added)

The greatest commandments are number one, to love God, and number two, to love others; simple, love! By loving God and loving others, Hannah did not allow the hurt the Scripture speaks of in 1 Samuel 1:5 that says, "...although the Lord had closed her womb," to make her bitter. She may not have understood, but she would pursue Him through, and in, her pain. As badly as she wanted a child, God still wanted her to want Him more. This trial was sacrificial love. She came to the point of giving up her dream, her child, to the Lord. She made a vow offering her dream, her unborn son, to the Lord if He would grant her one. This vow she would keep. Her firstborn son was the first prophet of Israel after Moses, and the last judge, marking the end of the judges. Samuel, meaning "asked of the Lord" or "son of God," belonged to God now. By dedicating Samuel to the Lord, she opened the door for God to give her more children.

She vowed, saying, O Lord of hosts, if You will indeed look on the affliction of Your handmaid and [earnestly] remember, and not forget Your handmaid but will give me a son, I will give him to the Lord all his life; no razor shall touch his head.

1 Samuel 1:11 (AMPC)

She refused to allow her desire to become an idol; she vowed to give him back to God. Holding on too tight to your dream will ensure its demise. The dream is your seed, and in order to germinate and grow, first, we must sow it. Let it die and let God resurrect it. If you want it more than you want God, you will lose it. God is a jealous God. What you compromise, you lose. Laying it down and giving it to God allows God to pick it up and give it back. Pleasing God with sacrificial faith is the faith He rewards. When we delight in Him, He gives us the desire of our hearts. Our desires line up with His will for our lives. Make Him your first love, with all your heart, soul, and mind, and watch Him move in the affairs of your life. When she committed the desire of heart, her baby boy, her seed to God, God gave it to her and opened her womb.

God helps us to do likewise; release hurts that have caused an offense, forgive, pray blessing, and give our heart's desire to God. Let God hear you; He will come and heal you and bind up your broken heart. Show Him your love by forgiving and praying for those who have used you or hurt you.

> But I say unto you which hear, Love your enemies, do good to them which hate you, Bless them that curse you, and pray for them which despitefully use you. But love ye your enemies, and do good, and lend, hoping for nothing again; and your reward shall be great, and ye shall be the children of the Highest: for he is kind unto the unthankful and to the evil.

Luke 6:27-28, 35 (KJV)

Hannah's reward was great, she gave birth to Israel's greatest judge, and then God blessed her with five more children! No telling what extending forgiveness, love, goodness, and blessings will release in your life! Love my enemies? Yes! Do good to people that hate me? Yes! Bless those that curse me? Yes! What a love standard! The moment you chose to forgive, love, do well and pray, you please God; this is the faith God rewards. Faith in God's love gives love to others. Without loving, we do not exercise faith; without faith, there is no reward. As long as we love, God is working. Love always wins. "Love never fails" (1 Corinthians 13:8a, NKJV). When you love, you win! How is your love walk? Is there someone you do not love, God, your husband, maybe his ex-wife, maybe his children from another mother, a friend, neighbor, co-worker, the in-laws, or even your pastor? Who has God given you to love? Repent, ask for forgiveness, and pray for them. Ask God to give you His heart of love for them and show you how to bless and do them good. Watch God start working things together for your good. It is awesome to see! Showing love reveals your life is in God's hands, that you totally trust Him to lay your life down and take up your cross.

> For this is the message that ye heard from the beginning, that we should love one another. We know that we have passed from death unto life, because we love the brethren. He that loveth not his brother abideth in death. Hereby perceive we the love of God, because he laid down his life for us: and we ought to lay down our lives for the brethren. And whatsoever we ask, we receive of him, because we keep his commandments, and do those things that are pleasing in his sight.
>
> 1 John 3:11, 14, 16, 22 (KJV) (emphasis added)

Faith pleases God. Faith works by love. Love pleases God! That is our faith working! When our faith is working through love, we can ask of the Father and receive. Love puts us, or positions us, to come boldly before the throne of God's grace and give our petitions. No love, no answer from God, simple. Start today, right where you are, showing love. Ask God to love through you and show you what love will look like for each person.

Hannah, by placing her trust in God, went from grieving to believing, from hurting to surrendering, and from sadness to gladness. So can you! By faith working through love, God heard and answered her prayer. She would now go expectantly, praising God and holding fast to her promise, having received her petition by faith. She was pregnant with promise! Now, she is waiting well. There would be more to do and a vow to keep. For now, though, she had her "word," the priest agreed and released the blessing over her. Remember, with God, all His promises are "yes and amen in Christ Jesus." "All things are possible with God." This "word" now brings hope, the anchor of our soul. One word is enough to bring hope and stability in the midst of a storm. Nothing could move her now. "Which hope we have as an anchor of the soul, both sure and steadfast, and which entereth into that within the veil" (Hebrews 6:19, KJV).

Jesus, the Word, our hope, entered the Holy place, and now, as our hope, He comforts and secures our soul just as an anchor holds its vessel steady. Hope is powerful. Have you ever noticed how some naysayers say, "Don't get your *hopes* up?" Why not? That is my Jesus; He came not only to get our hopes up but also to be our hope! He is the "door of hope." Get your hopes up! Be the most hopeful person you know. Without hope, our faith is ungrounded. God gives faith for today and hope for tomorrow, a joyful and confident expectation in God's Word and His goodness.

Hope in God's Word brings stability and rest to our soul; that is, our mind, will, and emotions. With this hope, we can be at peace in the midst of a storm. Hannah could wait well now;

with her soul anchored to this word, she could go home with hope in her heart and continue on this journey. She dropped her anchor, and now the issue is settled. Drop your anchor! Settle the question like Hannah. Yes, she has other stones to set up, but the hope brought her into "whirling," a state of joyous anticipation, much like a secret. A deliberate, decisive turning towards hope that changes everything. An expectant hope that starts preparations, buying the clothes, getting the room ready, etc. Our mind needs hope to rest, our emotions need hope to be stable, and our will needs hope to make good choices or decisions for our "future" and not our "feelings!" Our mind is now free to think on things above, our will submitted to choose life, and our emotions filled with eager anticipation. Imagine such fulfillment and joyous expectation. God created us for this hope and expectation, a hope that brings rest, peace to your whole body! You feel better; you may even experience physical healing, as you hope in the Lord. "Therefore my heart is glad, and my glory rejoiceth: my flesh also shall rest in hope" (Psalm 16:9, KJV).

Now we likely, for the first time, experience the true peace that only comes from God. With this hope, we can now believe God and live by faith, trusting Him no matter what things look like in the natural, and no matter how long they may take to change, God will keep His word. With this word, you can wait patiently, with composure, or, even excitedly with great anticipation, whirling like a little child, hopeful. "Wait for the Lord; be strong, and let your heart take courage; yes, wait for the Lord" (Psalm 27:14, NASB).

You literally take courage (strength, energy) into your heart when you take God at His Word. With God's instruction to wait comes the grace, the power to do it patiently, until we see it. Give Him time to work, have the faith of a child. Your heavenly Father knows what you have need of before you ask Him. Oh, the joy you experience as you allow God to do it for you. "Strengthened with *all* might, according to his glorious power, unto *all* patience and longsuffering with *joyfulness*" (Colossians 1:11, KJV) (emphasis added).

God can so strengthen us with might by His power that we wait joyfully; this is what waiting well looks like. Such beautiful waiting is a testimony to others in the waiting room of life. This is now someone with whom you would want to share the waiting room. Did you realize that is what the strength of God accomplishes? Maybe you missed it, "strengthened with all might according to the power of God" to *wait*! Maybe you have not waited well. What you need now is the strength of God. Nehemiah 8:10b (KJV) says, "…the joy of the LORD is *your strength*" (emphasis added). With joy in waiting, we receive God's strength; now, we can wait for the manifestation of our promise, just like Hannah. Her faith was "it," what she hoped for, a child, the confirmation of him. By faith, she received him. With faith in God as her proof, the truth now supersedes and overrides the immediate reality of barrenness. Faith contradicts facts because faith is unseen. The supernatural supply takes control over the natural when we let go. Let go, and the supply will flow!

> *Now faith is the assurance (the confirmation, the title deed) of the things [we] hope for, being the proof of things [we] do not see and the conviction of their reality [faith perceiving as real fact what is not revealed to the senses].*
>
> Hebrews 11:1 (AMPC) (emphasis added)

Her faith is the reality, the proof of ownership, like her confirmation number, of her hope. More real to her than her sense of sight, sound, touch, smell or taste, is the sixth sense, faith! She is now an expectant mother even before she is with Elkanah. One word from God changes everything! This word, the answer to her prayer, becomes her seed that eventually produces a quiver full of children, a full house! Giving God her firstborn opened the door for God to fill her to the full with children. That was all He was waiting for, the commitment of her child to God. She would make good on her promise to give Samuel, her firstborn, to the Lord. He became one of the most significant prophets of the Lord, anointing the first King of Israel, Saul, and later, David.

Hannah believed God would reward her, and He was pleased with that. Do you understand that? When we delight to do God's will, to pursue Him at all costs, earnestly and diligently seeking Him and nothing else, He delights in giving us the desires of our heart. He wants to do it! How futile it is to be mad at God; He is the rewarder!

> But without faith it is impossible to please and be satis-factory to Him. For whoever would come near to God must [necessarily] believe that God exists and that He is the rewarder of those who earnestly and diligently seek Him [out].
>
> Hebrews 11:6 (AMPC) (emphasis added)

We begin in faith with God and continue in it every day of our life. Are you believing, or are you hurt by the perceived activity or inactivity of God? Seek Him! Take your hurts and desires to God, wait on Him, and seek Him earnestly and diligently until you find Him. When you find Him, you will understand His love for you; and receive strength and encouragement to wait. Let nothing stand in your way in your pursuit of God; keep on keeping on, lean into God. "Keep on asking and it will be given you; keep on seeking and you will find; keep on knocking [reverently] and [the door] will be opened to you" (Matthew 7:7, AMPC).

Get alone in a quiet place and invite the Lord to speak to you. Maybe like Hannah, you can go to your house of worship and bow before the Lord at the altar. Get alone and get with God. Wait on Him, and while there, ask, seek, knock until you receive, find, and see the open door. Take this word and put it into the soil of your heart. Receive it. The Lord, your Maker, is your husband. He loves you and wants to manifest Himself to you. He is your source, your provider, your protection. If you believe, you will see. Now take this word to Him and ask Him to make it real to you. Then wait. Just wait on Him. The seed of God's Word is a treasure, a pearl of great price. Properly tended to, this seed will take root and grow into a fruitful harvest or tree:

> *And he said, so is the kingdom of God, as if a man should cast seed into the ground; and should sleep, and rise night and day, and the seed should spring and grow up, he knoweth not how. For the earth bringeth forth fruit of herself; first the blade, then the ear, after that the full corn in the ear.*
>
> Mark 4:26-28 (KJV)

> *And he said, whereunto shall we liken the kingdom of God? Or with what comparison shall we compare it? It is like a grain of mustard seed, which, when it is sown in the earth, is less than all the seeds that be in the earth: But when it is sown, it groweth up, and becometh greater than all herbs, and shooteth out great branches; so that the fowls of the air may lodge under the shadow of it.*
>
> Mark 4:30-32 (KJV)

Trees start with a seed; they need soil, water, air, sun, and time to grow. You are God's seed; He has long patience for you, and, He desires that your life bears fruit, and is productive, producing fruit, thriving, and prospering. As we continue on our journey of setting up our stones, we will see and know just how precious this seed is and how to tend to it that we may glorify God in bearing much fruit. A process of progress *is* prospering. "And he shall be like a tree planted by the rivers of water, that bringeth forth his fruit in his season; his leaf also shall not wither; and whatsoever he doeth shall prosper" (Psalm 1:3, KJV).

Now you have been given a seed, "The Lord is your Husband." Receive it, believe it, sow it, and hope expectantly, patiently waiting to see "first the blade, then the ear, after that the full corn in the ear." Just like Hannah, you are expecting. You can say that over to yourself, "I'm expecting!" We are expecting God to bring forth fruit from the seed of His Word He has planted in our hearts. Faith in His word is your vision. This is helpful:

> And the LORD answered me, and said, Write the vision, and make it plain upon tables, that he may run that readeth it. For the vision is yet for an appointed time, but at the end it shall speak, and not lie: though it tarry, wait for it; because it will surely come, it will not tarry.
>
> Habakkuk 2:2-3 (KJV) (emphasis added)

Wait for it! The vision is happening; it is yet for an appointed time. Though it seems to take time, give the time to God, trust Him with the "when." Believe Him when He says, "It will not tarry." Time is in His hands. He knows when the "appointed time" is, we do not, and He is under no obligation to tell us. That is why He requires faith. When you do not know everything, He does; stop thinking, start trusting. Then, keep on trusting.

Cast not away therefore your confidence, which hath great recompense of reward. For ye have need of patience, that, after ye have done the will of God, ye might receive the promise. For yet a little while, and he that shall come will come, and will not tarry. Now the just shall live by faith: but if any man drawback, my soul shall have no pleasure in him.

Hebrews 10:35-38 (KJV) (emphasis added)

God will come. The time prolongs because we have "need of patience." Why? So that after we do the will of God, we might receive the promise. We do His will first. His will is to "live by faith, not by sight." We do not "try" faith; we "live" by it. If we say we tried faith and it did not work, we gave up. Rather, faith tried us, and we failed faith; however, faith that remains in God receives the rewards. God is watching and waiting to see how we do. He will pass over a thousand people to respond to a heart and life of faith. God never fails, nor does His Word! What then is the will of God?

"In everything give thanks: for this is the will of God in Christ Jesus concerning you" (1 Thessalonians 5:18, KJV). Thanksgiving, this is the beginning of God's will; thankful to God for yesterday, today, and tomorrow; for life's precious moments. This is how faith sounds, thankful, grateful, and hopeful. Faith sings, rejoices, and is "no longer sad!" What do you sing, "gloom, despair, and agony on end?" Are you like Eeyore from Winnie the Pooh, buying into "Murphy's Law: anything that can go wrong will go wrong?" It is time to turn that around and give thanks.

Start now giving voice to your thanks. This is God's will, ministering to the Lord through our thanksgiving. Good waiters are good ministers. He wants to hear us give Him thanks. Think about it, if you are not thankful for what you have, how will you be thankful for more? Remember, you have what you believed you received when you prayed. So now, you know you received it if you are giving thanks. God wants to hear thanksgiving from a thankful heart. How about it, can you give God a thanksgiving? You can start with this word, "Thank You, God, for this Word, the truth of Your Word, and the power in it. Thank You, Lord, for watching over this Word to perform it." After we do the will of God, we receive the promise. Got it? Just do it!

We are thankful. Just practice saying, "Thank you." Say "thank you" for everything, no matter how big or how small. Even the things you do not understand. Thank God. Now, my dear sister, you are ready to wait. "But they that *wait* upon the LORD shall *renew* their strength; they shall *mount* up with wings as eagles; they shall *run*, and not be weary; and they shall *walk*, and not faint" (Isaiah 40:31, KJV) (emphasis added).

Expect, look for, and welcome the Lord. When you wait like this, your strength is renewed; you mount up on His healing wings, refreshed by the water of His Word and encouraged by His continuous presence. You will be able to run and walk without getting weary or faint, with no discouragement or depression. Oh, how marvelous; oh, how wonderful is the amazing grace of God! His grace is the empowering of His Spirit to strengthen us in order that we may wait well. Waiting well gives Him glory.

Hannah's waiting turned around that day from writhing in pain to whirling in motion. The power of one word from God can turn your writhing into whirling. Wait on the Lord, listen until you hear a note of victory or confirmation, then wait well! Be found in praise and glory to His great grace. Now go ahead, feel free, and whirl while you wait; it's our dance! I am whirling with you!

Not long after they returned home, Hannah conceived. Just to note here, that means she had to "get busy" and put some action to her faith, but that is another stone. She finally gave birth to her first child, a son, Samuel. "Wherefore it came to pass, when the time was come about after Hannah had conceived, that she bare a son, and called his name Samuel, saying, because I have asked him of the LORD" (1 Samuel 1:20, KJV). What joy in the house! Now, with her hope fulfilled and her faith seen, she kisses the face of her promised child. Yet, the time would go by quickly; she had a vow to keep. The only thing that could be worse than an empty womb was an empty vow. Elkanah agreed, take the child when you are ready and think best. Therefore, she fulfilled her vow and gave Samuel to Eli in Shiloh to remain.

> *And she said, Oh my lord, as thy soul liveth, my lord, I am the woman that stood by thee here, praying unto the LORD. For this child I prayed; and the LORD hath given me my petition which I asked of him: Therefore also I have lent him to the LORD; as long as he liveth he shall be lent to the LORD. And he worshipped the LORD there.*
>
> 1 Samuel 1:26-28 (KJV)

Hannah sang and worshipped the Lord, and God blessed her seed sown with a beautiful harvest:

> *And Eli would bless Elkanah and his wife and say, May the Lord give you children by this woman for the gift she asked for and gave to the Lord. Then they would go to their own home. And the Lord visited Hannah, so that she bore three sons and two daughters. And the child Samuel grew before the Lord.*
>
> 1 Samuel 2:20-21 (AMPC)

"How long must we wait," you may ask. "Until" is the only correct answer, until your faith, "it," is sight. Settle this question once and for all. If someone asks you, just say "until," and forget about the timing; leave that to God. God's will is for you and me to whirl while we wait. Do you know the saying, "time flies when you're having a good time?" Well, you have it; have a good time with God! Enjoy whirling with Him while He is working for you. You wait well, and He works. This is our first stone; *wait*. You will go back to this stone many times, remembering the times you waited on God and heard from Him. Be sure you mark it well. Write it in your journal; it will be worth remembering. I am *waiting and whirling* with you!

Prayer ~

Thank you, Lord, for this beautiful woman of faith, Hannah, and her great example of waiting well. Forgive me where I have failed in the waiting room, whether impatient through murmuring, grumbling, unforgiveness, apathy, bitterness, hatred, or contempt. I am sorry, Lord, and repent. Help me to forgive, love, and bless others while I seek your will, waiting expectantly on You. I cast my cares, burdens, and desires upon you, trusting that your will is done in my life. Help me to wait well, whirling with a grateful heart, like Hannah. Thank you for this waiting room and this seed; the Lord is my Husband. I trust you for the harvest, in Jesus' name, amen.

CHAPTER 5.
MEMORIAL STONE 2
WORSHIP

"But the hour cometh and now is, when the true worshippers shall worship the Father in spirit and in truth: for the Father seeketh such to worship him".

(John 4:23, KJV)

Sometimes a journey is planned, and sometimes it is spontaneous. My husband loved to surprise me by going places. Either way, it starts, whether suddenly or expected, it started with an idea, or a word, let's go_____, fill in the blank. The idea, the word, came from a place of desire. A desire to see, experience, travel, go, leave, or just the surprise of adventure. Maybe you saw someone's vacation pictures or an advertisement, and then suddenly the seed was sown, and now it's on your "bucket list." The word, the seed, the waiting leads to anticipation, the hope of fulfilling the dream. Do you remember a time you waited with expectation, anticipating the day you would leave? You may have to do all sorts of things to get ready like buying new shoes, new clothes, sorting, condensing, planning, booking, researching, etc. What you are doing is giving attention, value to this dream with your time and money. You have joined forces with the vision to create the reality or fulfillment, the actualization of it. The vision leads to participation. The seed of God's word does the same when it is sown into our hearts. We participate with the seed by valuing and tending to it. How is this done, you might wonder. We participate with the word through worship. The waiting that brought the seed leads us to worshipping. When we worship, we agree with the vision, the dream, the seed, and we begin to move toward the dream with our thoughts, our time, energy, and finances. This participation becomes our second memorial stone to set up on our journey, "Worship."

The old English word for this is "worth-ship." What we give ourselves inordinately to in time or money, exceeding reasonable limits, placing in value above all else, we give "worth-ship," rather, as we would say, our worship. Ultimately, what we give the best of ourselves to, and the first of our money to continuously, declares who or what we deem is of worth or value. That, in essence, is what we serve. This is the basic principle for all worship, and King David said it this way, in 2 Samuel 24:24 (AMPC),

> ...No, but I will buy it of you for a price. I will not offer burnt offerings to the Lord my God of that which costs me nothing. So David bought the threshing floor and the oxen for fifty shekels of silver.
>
> 2 Samuel 24:24 (AMPC)

Our offering of that which is of value, the highest, and best, to the object of our affection then becomes our god. We are always serving or worshipping something or someone, in attitude and activity, even if we do not realize it. We are made to worship and to worship God. The question is not whether we worship; it is what or who we worship, one of these two:

> No one can serve two masters; for either he will hate the one and love the other, or he will stand by and be devoted to the one and despise and be against the other. You cannot serve God and mammon (deceitful riches, money, possessions, or whatever is trusted in).

Matthew 6:24 (AMPC)

Worship reveals value through adoration, reverence, honor, and obedience to the god or God served. What we value, we willingly spend the best of our time, money, honor, and reverence on, either the provision or the provider, but not both. Maybe you have heard it said, "price determines value," or could it be value determines price. The worth or value of something in large part is affected by how well we know someone or something.

In determining the value of something, The Antiques Roadshow brings in experts or specialists on the items appraised. They quote an estimated price of something's worth, but it is not until someone is willing to pay for it that value is determined. I have been in many antique stores where the proprietors just laugh when people quote the prices from this show telling the owners, "good luck with that." Even real estate establishes a true value when a willing seller receives payment in exchange for his property from a willing buyer.

Determining accurate value requires the employment of many principles. However, in the end, value is established through an actual monetary exchange. "Value expresses an economic concept. As such, it is never a fact, but always an opinion of the worth of a property at a given time in accordance with a specific opinion of value" (uspap.org, page 201). Just watch the stock market for a week, or look at how cars, furniture, or jewelry change value over time. When you pay for something, you are making an exchange of "legal tender." You give something of yours for something else. You are saying this thing is "worth" to me what I am giving for it. In addition, by the way, as my Dad always told me, nothing of value is ever free; in the end, it will usually cost you something. Money is the international unit of exchange; currency we call it, whether it is dollars, euros, pounds, or pesos, or cyber money like "*Bitcoin*." This most often represents one's time, part of you. You may have heard it said, "time is money," meaning your time, which represents you, is valuable and is worth money.

Time is valuable, and your money represents your time. What you give your time and money to represents what you think is valuable. What do you think is valuable? What is worth your time and money: your job, your family, your home, your church? Think about it. Go look at your bank statements. Where does your money go? On what do you spend it? Look at your schedule; what do you do from the time you get up to the time you lie down? You are declaring the value or worth of the things and people in your life by what you give the first and best of yourself to; and, this speaks of what you think of yourself. What value would you place on your life?

Nothing and nobody has known you and understands your worth more than God understands; He created you. God created us for relationship with Himself, thereby declaring our value. Then enters the competition, a jealous former worshipper, Satan, who also desires to declare our value. He held the highest position as a worship leader in heaven, but He chose the wrong thing to worship, himself. Since he subsequently lost that position forever, he endeavors to prevent anyone from worshipping God in his place. Therefore, when God's first man and woman, Adam and Eve, entered the picture, he went to work. Satan tempted Eve to question, disbelieve, and distrust God by looking at and finally tasting the forbidden fruit. She then, in turn, shared it with her husband (not husbands). With the fall of Adam and Eve to this temptation came the promised severing of relationship with God; sin and death then entered because of the curse. The curse of death

God spoke would come if anyone ate of this forbidden fruit. Our hearts now darkened and separated from God; Satan thought he won. Although man did not esteem the relationship with God as valuable, God did.

He showed His love by making a way to bridge the divide, restore life, and eventually, the relationship. By giving His treasure, His only Son, Christ Jesus, He delivered us from death and paid the price, life for life, blood for blood. The Principle of Substitution now declares our value, an equally desirable substitute was required, and only God's Son qualified. Life is in the blood; the penalty was death; someone had to die, and blood had to be shed, "without the shedding of blood, there is no remission of sin." That is the power of Passover, the cup that we drink represents the blood of Jesus, and God said, "When I see the blood, I will 'Passover' you." Why? Because the blood on the doorpost of every Israelite home in Egypt said, death had already come to their house. And so it is with you and me when we accept the blood of Jesus as our atonement, or payment, He passes over our sin. When the Son of God, Jesus, took our place on the cross, shed His blood, and gave His body to be broken for ours, He redeemed us from the curse. He bought us back from death, hell, and the grave. We now have better promises established on a better covenant because the blessings of Abraham are now ours. (See Deuteronomy 28.)

God said you are worth it all, paying the ultimate price, His life. He participated with mankind in leaving the throne and becoming a man. He had the vision and sowed the seed of His Son that He might bring many sons to glory. In turn, we worship Him when we participate with Him, the Word, the seed of His truth and spirit He sows in us through salvation. Some things money cannot buy. God has given us an example of how to participate, how to give value, and show worth. He gave the best He had for us and paid a debt He did not owe and one we could not pay. Jesus said to the Father, "I will leave heaven," thereby willingly giving His life. He stripped off His regal robes of glory and humbled Himself by putting on human form. He became not only a man but also a servant, yet without sin, the perfect, spotless, sacrificial Lamb of God to take away our sins, breaking the curse of death, hell, and the grave. "Just as the Son of Man came not to be waited on but to serve, and to give His life as a ransom for many [the price paid to set them free]" (Matthew 20:28, AMPC). "For God so loved the world that he *gave* his only begotten Son, that whosoever believeth in him should not perish, but have everlasting life" (John 3:16, KJV) (emphasis added).

> *Forasmuch as ye know that ye were not redeemed (purchased) with corruptible things, as silver and gold, from your vain conversation received by tradition from your fathers; But with the precious blood of Christ, as of a lamb without blemish and without spot:*

> 1 Peter 1:18-19 (KJV)

> *Christ purchased our freedom [redeeming us] from the curse (doom) of the Law [and its condemnation] by [Himself] becoming a curse for us, for it is written [in the Scriptures], Cursed is everyone who hangs on a tree (is crucified);*

> Galatians 3:13 (AMPC)

When God raised Jesus from the dead, He accepted the payment of His blood. Now that blood forever speaks for us on the mercy seat of heaven with Jesus ever interceding on our behalf. He has given His all for you in full participation with mankind. Why? He wants a relationship with you. You are worth the very life of God. He has established and declared you are worth the life of His Son. He came to save, deliver and set us free from the power of sin's hold on our life. Now we are free to experience and enjoy love and life again with God, love and life we can share with others. Look at Hannah's prayer of worship after she gave Samuel, God's answer, her firstborn, to the Priest:

> *Hannah prayed, and said, My heart exults and triumphs in the Lord; my horn (my strength) is lifted up in the Lord. My mouth is no longer silent, for it is opened wide over my enemies, because I rejoice in Your salvation. There is none holy like the Lord, there is none besides You; there is no Rock like our God.*
>
> 1 Samuel 2:1-2 (AMPC) (emphasis added)

She is no longer silent. Do you remember how careful she was in not murmuring? She had held her peace, but now, she "opened wide" her mouth to exalt, magnify, and rejoice in her God over her enemies! This unashamed, abandoned worship in response to God glorifies Him. Imagine, the child she longed for, wept for, waited for, and now weaned, is given over to the priest. Imagine how difficult that would be; as some scholars say, Samuel might only have been three years old at the time. Here is Hannah, giving up and back to God, her long-awaited son, with her best praise. A people that respond and represent Him by showing His love and goodness to a dying world glorify God. When we glorify God, accurately reflecting Him and who He is to the world, we show forth His worth. Our lives magnify Him and make Him great and renown on the earth. This is "worth-ship." "For ye are bought with a price: therefore glorify God in your body, and in your spirit, which are God's" (1 Corinthians 6:20, KJV).

She worshipped God with the sacrifice and gift of her son. Worship is an individual, as well as a corporate response of reverence, submission, and exaltation in spirit, soul, and body to the love of the Almighty, Holy, and Creator God. God is looking for the heartfelt response to His love where the believer, the beloved, ascribes value to God with their life. This sacrifice, simply our participation with God, is worship.

In recognizing God is our all in all, giving Him our first and best, we lift Him above all else in our life. We acknowledge Him, His goodness, His life, and love by enjoying Him. Like a lover, we desire their time, attention, their caresses, and kisses. We enjoy each other through participation in all our days. Like texting, calling, talking, meeting, joining our loves, we do so with our Lord, our Lover, our Husband. We hang on His every Word, we read and reread His love letters, we express our love, appreciation, and admiration. Somehow we find a way to get close to Him, to get His attention, to be where He is. That is our only acceptable worship, worshipping Him in every area of our life. God once spoke to me as I was on my way to the Lord's house to sing, to start now, and "worship Him in my driving." Honoring His presence in my car. God is so intimate He watches everything and can be glorified in every aspect of our life, even our driving; that means obeying the rules of the road—speed limits, no texting, full stops, etc. He wants us to acknowledge Him for who He is: our God and Lord, our Master, our source, our provider, our Savior, our Husband, our Deliverer, our Shield and Buckler, our Strong Tower, our Refuge, our Shepherd and Helper, our Comforter and Counselor. When we see and know God, we will value God for who He is, and then we can worship Him in the beauty of holiness.

This may be one of the hardest stones to set up, and yet we think it is so simple. A few songs, a prayer, giving a little tip every now and then to the church or charity, and we think God, the Creator of heaven and earth who formed us, should be satisfied. We most likely need to adjust our focus and our thinking. We conclude then that what we give ourselves to inordinately, in time and money, we worship. God is a God of order. Jehovah Shalom means the "*Lord* is Peace," He is the *Lord* our Peace. Peace is "nothing missing, nothing lacking, and everything in its place." You see, there is a place for things, and yet those things have to be put in their place. Order is peace. No order, no peace. When things are "out of order," they do not work properly.

Take children, for example; God gives children as a "heritage," a "reward," and calls them a "blessing" that we might raise up godly seed. Children require time and money. The question is not whether we take care of them and provide for their physical, spiritual, and emotional needs; God already said that "a man who doesn't provide for his own is worse than an infidel." The question is how much time and how much money; how much is too much? When does providing for them become idolizing them? Children, just like a host of many other things, can be over-indulged, thus taking the place or time God would have us give to Him. Why would we do that? Maybe out of guilt, or maybe out of trying to satisfy our own childhood shortfalls, or maybe even pride, we set our children up as a god-like entity only to be sadly disappointed.

Remember Hannah; she could have easily made the child Samuel her world. With an insensitive husband and a mean "baby momma" Peninnah, she could have easily lost herself living for her first baby. This is not peace. This is a home and a relationship out of order because God would not have been on the throne;

the baby would have been. The same goes for husband or wife. Anyone, or anything, that attempts to take the place, the throne of my life, the habitation, and the throne for the God of this universe alone are out of order. Nothing else is big enough to take the seat created for the infinite God. Fortunately, Hannah refused to make an idol of the child by keeping her vow and giving Samuel to the priest. God thereby kept His rightful place in her heart, received her worship, and blessed her with five more children.

When He is in His proper place, on the throne, and I am on the stone, fallen and broken, then everything else will begin to take its proper place; peace. When I am on the throne, being in charge, setting the agenda, God said that the same stone that the builders rejected would fall on me and take me. Without peace with God, I find everything in my life is "out of order."

> *Jesus saith unto them, Did ye never read in the scriptures, The stone which the builders rejected, the same is become the head of the corner: this is the Lord's doing, and it is marvelous in our eyes? And whosoever shall fall on this stone shall be broken: but on whomsoever it shall fall, it will grind him to powder.*
>
> Matthew 21:42, 44 (KJV) (emphasis added)

Our choice is either to fall and be broken or be ground to powder. One is a vessel God can use, or one is trampled on; that is the choice. You are either on the throne or fallen on the stone of Christ; one becomes the heart filled with God or, one becomes powder. The choice is clear, the throne or the stone, which will it be. God dwells in the broken and contrite heart. Fall on the stone and be broken lest it fall on you, and "grind you to powder." Acknowledging my need, I fall into the arms of Jesus, find true rest and peace for my soul. He is the stone the "builders rejected," but not for the believer; we must trust in His Word. Falling on the stone of Jesus and allowing myself to be broken creates a place for the Most High God to dwell.

> *The high and lofty one who lives in eternity, the Holy One, says this: "I live in the high and holy place and with those whose spirits are contrite and humble. I restore the crushed spirit of the humble and revive the courage of those with repentant hearts.*
>
> Isaiah 57:15 (NLT) (emphasis added)

The contrite ones are the broken ones who have fallen on the cornerstone, Jesus Christ. He is our example. He gave up His throne and became the Chief Cornerstone. He took on humanity, broken and bleeding for us, becoming the perfect, acceptable sacrifice. In giving up His glory, He took on Himself the pain and suffering of our sin, paying our debt, death. When we receive Him as our life, we experience revival and restoration. Revived, brought to life in Jesus, we are restored to right relationship, seated with Him in heavenly places.

> *But He was wounded for our transgressions, He was bruised for our guilt and iniquities; the chastisement [needful to obtain] peace and well-being for us was upon Him, and with the stripes [that wounded] Him we are healed and made whole.*
>
> Isaiah 53:5 (AMPC) (emphasis added)

We have all these ideas of healing or wholeness for ourselves, yet Jesus asked for our life. He comes to live in the heart of the broken, the one which has fallen on the stone of Jesus Christ. This is the beginning of our worship, experiencing life in Him and with Him. Come on and join the dance, maybe for the first time, or maybe for a long time; your partner holds out His hand. "Or else, let them *take hold of My strength and make complete surrender to My protection, that they may make peace with Me*! Yes, let them make peace with Me!" (Isaiah 27:5, AMP) (emphasis added)

Recognizing God as the Almighty, I take hold of His hand, His strength, surrender to His protection, and in so doing, I live in peace with God. You see, worship begins with releasing what I cling to so tightly and taking hold of the strength or power of God. Like a wallflower, He says, "Leave the wall, take my hand, and dance with me." When I am holding on to Him for life, my focus is on Him. Surrender declares He is my life. I am then one with Him; everything is now in order. *True* peace occurs now as the soul revolves around its center, Almighty God, craving for nothing but what God continually supplies, its passions subdued to itself, itself lovingly loyal to God, in harmony with God and His laws. Anything less than this, our created purpose, will leave us dissatisfied and searching to fill the emptiness; and whether the cravings are high and lofty or as possibly base, neither supply is large enough to bring peace to our soul. All else are false gods, always promising but never delivering. Worship begins when our soul finally finds its rest in and makes peace with the infinite God. From here, the door opens to a life of fulfillment, meaning, and purpose.

To remember and help us set up this stone of "worship," let us look at one of the most beautiful examples recorded in the book of Luke. Jesus gives us a memorable illustration of the giving and receiving of worship. In this story, Jesus, with the help of a woman of ill repute, gives a subtle, then powerful rebuke and an equally subtle, yet passionately charged plea to a Pharisee. The challenge is to examine our own hearts as to our understanding of true abandoned worship that brings peace. Jesus engages His contemporaries, rising to the occasion:

> *And one of the Pharisees desired him that he would eat with him. And he went into the Pharisee's house, and sat down to meat. And, behold, a woman in the city, which was a sinner, when she knew that Jesus sat at meat in the Pharisee's house, brought an alabaster box of ointment, And stood at his feet behind him weeping, and began to wash his feet with tears, and did wipe them with the hairs of her head, and kissed his feet, and anointed them with the ointment. Now when the Pharisee which had bidden him saw it, he spake within himself, saying, This man, if he were a prophet, would have known who and what manner of woman this is that toucheth him: for she is a sinner.*

Luke 7:36-39 (KJV)

Simon, the Pharisee, invites Jesus to his house for dinner. Jesus accepts. As He sits to eat, a woman in the city, known popularly as a sinner, comes in and stands behind Him, "weeping." How could she do this? Think about this for a moment. Was she invited? As the story unfolds, we sense she was not necessarily on the invitation list. How this would change! Word had spread; Jesus was coming to Simon's house. The time was nearby for the fulfillment of prophecy. An air of excitement surrounded Jesus; could He be the Messiah? As was custom in that day, however, when a person of wealth entertained a notable guest, family and friends received an invitation to stand in the surrounding courtyard to witness the moment of celebrity. Bravely and courageously, she put aside her fears of public harassment and shame and enters the place where her Savior would dine.

The Messiah who looked at her with love, not lust, who gave her a new life and wiped away her past, the One who is healing the sick and raising the dead, He is in town tonight! How could she not set aside her fears and bring Him a gift and, at least, hear Him one more time? Taking a place near his feet as He reclined at the table, she listens; the guests could be seen and not heard. However, she could not have known how her reaction to the power of His forgiveness and love would set the course for the dinner conversation. She, moved to tears, is visibly weeping. Her tears have found their way onto Jesus' feet. What a scene! Imagine how everyone must be looking and wondering, "How is He going to handle this? How is He going to respond?" She then breaks custom by letting her hair loose to dry his feet. Oh my! What does she think she is doing?

Now to make matters worse, she has brought in with her an alabaster box of very precious ointment, a gift, most likely an expensive perfume or oil. An ointment like this was worth a whole year's wages. Such extravagance was fraught with danger, but she, compelled, would now open this box, and as the aroma filled the air, poured out the perfume, anointing Jesus' feet and then kissing them. This is the perfect picture of true worship, literally, "to kiss the feet of." She has surrendered all that she has and is at the feet of Jesus, bowed in humble adoration. I can hear the gasps, the whispers. *Does He know who this is?* Simon wonders, thinking to himself. Jesus, wisely discerning their thoughts, tells a story. We will pick up here:

> *And Jesus answering said unto him, "Simon, I have something to say to thee;" and he saith, "Teacher, say on." "Two debtors were to a certain creditor; the one was owing five hundred denaries, and the other fifty; and they not having wherewith to give back, he forgave both; which then of*

them, say thou, will love him more?" And Simon answer-
ing said, "I suppose that to whom he forgave the more;"
and he said to him, "Rightly thou didst judge."

Luke 7:40-43 (YLT)

This is an obvious answer to a poignant question. The one forgiven the most loves the most. Simon has now answered himself, opening the door for Jesus to make the comparisons. Simon first, for whatever reason He even invited Jesus, had not shown Him even the customary courtesies. Guests, commonly being offered water, washed their feet since sandals and dirt roads were the norm. Simon had not done this. The woman, on the other hand, had washed Jesus' feet with her own tears but also wiped them with her own hair. Simon did not give the usual greeting of a kiss, and yet she had not ceased to kiss his feet. What humble worship, bowing down at His feet, washing them with her tears! That's a lot of tears! Simon did not anoint Him with oil, but this woman had anointed His feet with the most expensive of oils, perfume. Imagine how silence gives way to Simon's rebuke while the aroma of this precious ointment fills the air. What a contrast! Let's continue,

"Therefore I say to thee, her many sins have been forgiven,
because she did love much; but to whom little is forgiven,
little he doth love." And he said to her, "Thy sins have been
forgiven;" and those reclining with him (at meat) began to
say within themselves, "Who is this, who also doth forgive
sins?" and he said unto the woman, "Thy faith have saved
thee, be going on to peace."

Luke 7:47-50 (YLT) (emphasis added)

She demonstrated her thanksgiving and love for Jesus with abandoned sacrificial worship. Through an outpouring of extravagant love, she expressed publicly in humble sacrifice the gift of her whole heart. Jesus' final response to this love and adoration was, "Thy faith hath saved thee, go in peace." Wow, Jesus not only receives her worship but in His acceptance, He responds so powerfully to justify her with His added blessing of peace. In so doing, He allows judgment to pass on to the others. Her act of complete abandonment lives on, memorializing her forever. Her faith rewarded; He saved and made her whole. Jesus gave her peace, a life now revived and restored. In the presence of all who would judge and esteem her least, Jesus shows her to be just as forgiven, just as clean, and now, just as free to live in wholeness, His peace.

Peace came through worship; abandoned, unashamed—giving of all I am with the best I have at the feet of Jesus. Simon missed the heart of the matter, the heart. While he withheld his love, she poured out it out with her whole heart, and that, willingly not grudgingly. This living sacrifice is the path of peace. Our soul is at rest. We are filled with His presence, His peace. What if this woman, many believe Mary, had been too busy, too afraid, too ashamed, too anxious, or too worried to go into Simon's house? Because she knew what God already thought of her, she chose not to hide, not to miss the only thing or person that mattered. In order to give Jesus her best, her worship, she refused to give into fears or worries of what people might think. She knew who she was, but she chose to think about who He was—her Lord, her Christ, her deliverer, and Redeemer.

How would hiding have benefitted her? Why do we think hiding will benefit us? Think for a moment with me what that does. Number one, hiding is prison; it is not freedom. Number two, it is bondage, not peace. And finally, number three, hiding is darkness, not light. Prison, bondage, and darkness, all a result of "overthinking" or "worried" what other people think! Jesus is offering this peace or wholeness, a rest from our activity. When we come out to the open and step into the light, concerned only with giving Him His due reverence and worship, we enjoy the strength and peace He gives. And in return, He also honored her in the sight of all the guests. A child-like faith responds to His mercy from a true heart of loving thanksgiving to fear His name alone. Trust His love and goodness and lift up to Him the highest and best praise!

When we hide, we are really saying, "I don't believe You, God. You can't handle my mess; I don't trust You." That is why Jesus said to this woman, "Thy faith has saved thee." What unbelievably bold and courageous faith to walk into that house and put herself all out. Hiding from God has never been an option or way to peace. Jesus knew what everybody was thinking in the room. There is nothing hidden from Him, so go on, give Him your all, your best! Be deliberate; look for the best things you have to give. That is why God asked for the "first fruits," the best. We give Him our best, and He takes the rest and makes more out of it. You can never "out-give" God!

I am reminded of just such an opportunity when I was "single again" and had recently ended a relationship of which God had instructed me severely, "to flee." Left with some beautiful gold and diamond jewelry I loved wearing, I had a choice. Sadly they represented a dead relationship. Well, it was soon to be Easter Sunday that year, and I needed to be prepared to give my best offering. What could I give? That is right; you guessed it, the jewelry. You say the jewelry, really? Yes, really. I put them back in their beautiful black velvet bag. That Sunday, as I was sitting in the choir and the offering bucket came by, I gently laid the best gift I had in the bottom. What a relief and what a joy! I had released the most valuable "thing" I had, and at the same time, released any remaining emotional ties to the giver. I felt so free. How God has blessed that simple act. I could never have dreamed the beautiful gifts God would give me to replace that which had no meaning with that which does. Blessed be God who keeps His Word; He gives seed to the sower that reaped a beautiful harvest. This may sound simple or strange, but either way, obedience honors God. You may have something like that; ask God, He will let you know.

Sometimes we give God any old thing we have and think God should be happy. How sad He must feel. Can we, like her, take some time out of each day to fall at His feet and kiss Him, to give Him our tears or joys of love? What a wonderful challenge, just to know and respond daily to how much He loves me with my whole heart and all my worship. What a deeper romantic relationship we enter when we recognize and acknowledge the great price He paid for our lives, our salvation, our destiny, and our healing! Worship ascribes worth and thanksgiving to the thing or person adored; it declares "you are worthy of all my time, all my money, all my adoration," not just some, all!

Lay down our life, take up our cross, leave houses, and mothers, and fathers...the call is great, help us, Lord, to leave and cleave! If you hear Him coming, stop what you are doing and go to Him, take your best gift, and worship Him. Then you, too, can "go in peace." What liberation! What freedom we experience as we are forgiven of sin, freed from bondage, and filled with His love!

> *I appeal to you therefore, brethren, and beg of you in view of [all] the mercies of God, to make a decisive dedication of your bodies [presenting all your members and faculties] as a living sacrifice, holy (devoted, consecrated)*

and well pleasing to God, which is your reasonable (rational, intelligent) service and spiritual worship.

Romans 12:1 (AMPC) (emphasis added)

Our reasonable act of worship is to give God what He bought, our life, as a living sacrifice. In other words, you bring yourself to God, giving Him your life and all that includes—your talents, abilities, gifts, passions, desires, hopes and dreams, everything—and lay it before Him. This is our "reasonable" duty. That means we make a rational thinking decision in light of the mercies of God, to say "yes" to God and "no" to ourselves. We reason in light of the mercy of God and decide conclusively; there is no other reasonable alternative; this is what I will do. Then, through a simultaneous action of leaving the world and following Jesus and His Word, we now prove or show forth God and His ways to the world around us. We fulfill the will of God, not the will of man or myself. This sacrifice of ourselves, through the cleansing blood of Jesus, the power of the Holy Spirit, and a renewed mind is the action of a "true worshipper," or rather a worshipper who worships "in truth."

This is the place for our very own Bethel; like Jacob, we wholly take God as our God, the place where we set up our stone by laying our life on the altar. Here we lay anything and everything on the altar that appeals to our will, and we take up His will. We then find that everything in our life becomes an avenue or opportunity to worship the Lord. When He has the throne, we then offer Him and His word true worship, the glory due Him, our highest loyalty, devotion, and respect in every area of our life: relationships, finances, work, recreation, etc. Our life models the motto, "Father knows best." We seek to reveal God, to show Him our lift Him up in all of our life.

I mentioned driving earlier; you can worship God with your driving. Have you ever noticed someone with a Christian bumper sticker driving like a crazy person? Not a very good testimony. Or maybe you have had someone cut you off racing into the church parking lot to get the best spot. Think about it, does that worship God? Some things are so automatic we may not even realize how we keep God out of our daily decisions and routines. Open it all up to God's scrutiny, invite Him to change it, and order it up how He wants it. Acting on a heart of faith with thanksgiving is worship that proves I believe, revealing whether my worship is in "truth." My worship is daily, hourly, minute by minute, 24/7, not just for an hour or two on Sunday morning.

All of my life, in everything, I have a reason to worship. To lift Him up and for Him to be seen is my purpose because He forgives, loves, saves, and delivers me, and one day soon is coming to take me home to be with Him forever. It's time to doubt your doubts! If you have held back in any area of your life, looking for advice or a "word" from someone else, stop, trust God right there. Give Him first place, and first "say," and then give Him your best praise.

When we have waited on God and received our word, that precious incorruptible seed, then we must release it. The word the "Lord is my Husband" is a seed given me that I offer you to offer back in worship. Let go of all the hopes and dreams and release them into the hand of God. Come out of hiding in what you think is safe but is only a tomb. Trust Him! By releasing the seed, we are actually sowing it into the supernatural ground of love. This is our faith. We believe God with the Word He has given us, trusting Him to bring it to harvest. The seed is given to sow in order to grow. Release it. Right now, give Him a "living sacrifice," putting all, including your hopes and dreams, on the altar. I remember the moment I repented for not keeping it in the ground and declared it once and for all, "The Lord *is* my Husband!" Everything changed that day in my heart. When faith was released, peace returned, hope was restored, and joy revived.

Just like Abraham when he prepared to worship, offering his promised child Isaac to the Lord, we, too, can believe that God can even raise our promised seed from the dead. Only to see, there in the thicket, was the provision, the ram, just at the right time. God's prepared provision was found in a ram that went up the other side of the mountain, all alone, possibly at the same time, matching every step as Abraham climbed higher to this place of sacrificial worship. Abraham declared of God there; He is Jehovah Jireh, the "*Lord* who's provision is seen." God gives the seed, the offering; when we sacrifice it, we sow it. Our worship, our sacrificial sowing, brings the performance of the promise. He receives honor when we worship Him with our highest and best. Abraham would go on to be the grandfather of Jacob, who fathered the nation of Israel as we know it today, and, as believers today, we are the seed of Abraham. What an incredible harvest he reaped and is still reaping!

When we honor Him with our faith, He honors us. We worship Him with the word of revelation He has given us of Himself; He is the Lord, our Husband! Our help is in the name of the Lord. Trust Him to bring this to pass. Jesus tells us, "Verily, verily, I say unto you, except a corn of wheat fall into the ground and *die*, it abideth alone: but if it *die*, it bringeth forth *much fruit*" (John 12:24, KJV) (emphasis added). "Thou fool, that which thou sowest is not quickened, except it die" (1 Corinthians 15:36, KJV).

Who knows what "much fruit" will look like in your life! When God, the giver of the seed, and the harvest says "much fruit," you can get your baskets ready. God will raise up, "quicken," or give life to the seed! Moreover, it will look exactly how He makes it; He is the Creator. Put it in the ground, let it die, and leave it! God will give it life! He will quicken that which is dead. Do not go digging it up to see if it is growing as I did. Pray over it. Thank God for it. He will raise it incorruptible, in glory and power. Our praise is our perfume. God is always listening, and so is the devil. What you say and do determines which one you are giving the right to operate in your life, God or the devil. You can tell where your faith is and where you are going by what you are saying. Listen to yourself sometimes; what are you saying? If it is "true worship," it will bring glory to God and grace to the hearers by magnifying His word over your circumstance. "For by your words you will be justified and acquitted, and by your words you will be condemned and sentenced" (Matthew 12:37, AMPC). "Death and life are in the power of the tongue: and they that love it shall eat the fruit thereof" (Proverbs 18:21, KJV).

My words carry power for good or evil, to justify or condemn, for death or life, and what I say, I will eat. God declared it first, "you will eat your words," so make them something good. This word, the "Lord is my Husband," offered with a voice of thanksgiving, is my worship, anytime, anywhere.

> Let your character or moral disposition be free from love of money [including greed, avarice, lust, and craving for earthly possessions] and be satisfied with your present [circumstances and with what you have]; for He [God] Himself has said, I will not in any way fail you nor give you up nor leave you without support. [I will] not, [I will] not, [I will] not in any degree leave you helpless nor forsake nor let [you] down (relax My hold on you)! [Assuredly not!]
>
> Hebrews 13:5 (AMPC) (emphasis added)

Through Him, therefore, let us constantly and at all times offer up to God a sacrifice of praise, which is the fruit of lips that thankfully acknowledge and confess and glorify His name.

Hebrews 13:15 (AMPC) (emphasis added)

What name? Start with Ishi! The sacrifice of praise I offer is thanksgiving that He *is* the *Lord, my* Husband! He will never fail me, nor give me up, nor leave me without support; He will not leave me helpless, not forsake me, nor ever loosen His hold on me, hallelujah, praise His name!

As you begin to praise God, giving thanks that He is the Lord your Husband, something wonderful begins to happen; this seed germinates and begins to take root in my heart and life. As I worship, the rain of the Holy Spirit falls and brings with Him the necessary power of God to nourish the seed. Soon, and in due time, the "blade" begins to come up out of the ground, and before you know it, the seed is manifesting in my life. The process is sure. God watches over the seed, His word, to perform it. You may not even recognize your marriage when God gets through, giving it a makeover! People may look on and call it an "Extreme Makeover!" Let God do His work; you become a true worshipper. You wait and receive, and worship and believe.

In releasing our hold, we take hold of Him, partaking of His strength, His glory, His great grace. In this, He receives worship. He is ascribed the power due to His name. Release the most precious thing you have to Him and hold on to Him. Honor Him with it by giving it to Him, let it die, and trust Him to bring it to life and to give it a body. He will put things in order. Ascribe to Him the Glory and honor due to Him, the Almighty, everlasting King of Kings and Lord of Lords.

And that which thou sowest, thou sowest not that body that shall be, but bare grain, it may chance of wheat, or of some other grain: But God giveth it a body as it hath pleased him, and to every seed his own body.

1 Corinthians 15:37-38 (KJV)

God will give your seed, your marriage, your husband, a body as it pleases Him. Give Him the opportunity with your worship, a life, and words of thanksgiving, to create something beautiful, something pleasing.

So many beautiful women of worship in scripture who, when confronted with the power of the love of God, respond overwhelmingly with praise and worship, even in the face of uncertainty and possible persecution. Miriam, Moses' sister, as the Red Sea envelops the enemy of the Egyptian army, leads Israel in worship; in the wilderness, with no visible means of food and water and no Promised Land in sight, they worshipped. The Samaritan woman at the well worships by influencing the whole city to "come and see Jesus." Mary, the mother of Jesus, sings her song of worship we call the "Magnificat," after her cousin, Elisabeth, confirmed the word of the Lord that she will give birth to the long-awaited Messiah. Imagine preparing to give birth to the King of Glory, Immanuel, and offering her worship without fear of what the future would now hold for her.

We have already mentioned the worship of Hannah as she returns her first child to the priest Eli in order to keep her vow. These women of worship have shown us, as we remember them, how to remember our God in worship. Take strength and encouragement now to your soul as we set up our own memorial stone of love to worship with them, without hindrance, the same God. As He honored them, He will honor you. As you offer your worship, honoring Him and giving Him the highest place in your life, He, pleased, can now respond on behalf of a "true worshipper," just as He has done time and time again. He is no respecter of persons, just "true worshippers." He is seeking such, will you be one now, for good? A "true" worshipper fears God only, not man. Lord, help us please you. "The LORD taketh pleasure in them that fear him, in those that hope in his mercy" (Psalm 147:11, KJV).

> He will fulfil the desire of them that fear him: he also will hear their cry, and will save them. My mouth shall speak the praise of the LORD: and let all flesh bless his holy name forever and ever.
>
> Psalm 145:19, 21 (KJV)

Whom you fear you worship; whom you fear has power over of you. Fear ascribes value. When I fear God and His word over other's opinions or life's circumstances, I worship God in holiness, showing He is above all in my life. This reverential worship pleases Him so much that He promises to fulfill the desire of such a one. If I fear man, I give him power to control me, but when I fear God with all my worship, I give Him the right to move in my life. Just as the woman with the alabaster box feared Jesus and not the crowd, He exalted and blessed her. Determine what matters most, the thoughts, opinions, and ways of God or man. Then out of a heart of holy fear, awe, and reverence, offer your worship, releasing and inviting God to move on your behalf. Now we can add to our patience, or waiting, hearts and mouths of joyful thanksgiving, true unashamed, abandoned, fearless worshippers now ascribing worth to the object of our affection, God!

I worshipped God when I first received this word. Matter of fact, I wrote my praises with liner on my mirror, so every time I looked into it, I offered up my praise with thanksgivings. I thanked God He was my Husband, I thanked Him He was gathering my mate for me, that He had good plans for me, for a hope and a future. At some point, after I was married, I lost my praise. Disillusionment set in, and I began to question God until I was encouraged by my friend Debbie to remember the Lord was still my Husband. Then, from my mentor Vicki, who said when the Lord gives you a word, that is your answer. I repented there and began again to praise God; He was still the Lord my Husband, *in* my marriage. It is all about the praise, recognizing, and giving God thanks continuously. Praise brings the "performance" of the promise. Start now to give God the praise; soon, you will see the power of God manifested in your midst.

Now, I find myself, single again, widowed. I felt to update this book as I journey through this new season. This word means as much to me now as ever. I know I am never alone, and He will never leave me or forsake me. He has been, and always will be, faithfully, the Lord, my Husband. What God did in one season, He can do in another. He's the same yesterday, today, and forever!

Put your trust in God, please Him with "true" worship. Worship Him only. Remove and take down every idol; the thoughts, places, people, activities, and things that have taken your time and attention. Offer yourself as a "living sacrifice, holy, acceptable unto God, which is your reasonable, rational, intelligent service"; in other words, it is the only good choice. Commit now to turn your worry into worship. Bring Him your cares, lay them down, and worship Him with all your heart, soul, and mind as a "true" worshipper in spirit and in truth, for He cares for you. When you release a life of sacrificial sowing into the heart of God and His kingdom, you position yourself to receive His best. Look out!

Prayer ~

Oh, gracious heavenly Father, I praise You and bless You. Thank You for Your loving kindness and patience in waiting for me. With all that is within me, I now give myself wholly to You, spirit, soul, and body. May my life be a sweet aroma, a living sacrifice before You. Thank You that You love me and call me as your bride. Having given Yourself as the Lord, my Husband, to me, I now give myself to You. Thank You that You keep that which I have committed to You and that You watch over this covenant. May I keep it with the same fervency that You do! Thank You for redeeming, forgiving, choosing, loving, and calling me according to Your plans and purposes.

I love You, Lord, and give You all my worship. I bow before You and relinquish my hold on all other gods. Would You show me any idols I have worshipped and help me to remove them and take them down! I desire to worship You only, in spirit and in truth. All I am and all I have is Yours. You are my God and King, my deliverer, my Savior and Redeemer; I live to glorify and praise Your name forever... Forgive me for any unwillingness and stubbornness; today, I surrender and say, "Yes, Lord," to Your will and to Your way. May my life be a praise to Your glory and great grace. I sow the seed, that word You have given me by releasing it, letting it die, and bringing it to You as my worship. You are the Lord, my Husband; I receive, believe, and confess You with my praise.

Thank You for receiving me. You are the Lord of the Harvest, so I trust You to manifest Yourself, in your time, giving this seed a body. You alone are my all in all. All my life is in You, Lord. Glorify Your name in me, forever. Praise your holy name, in Jesus' name, amen!

"...For those who honor Me I will honor, and those who despise Me shall be lightly esteemed" (1 Samuel 2:30, AMP).

CHAPTER 6.
MEMORIAL STONE 3
WATCH

Welcome to the bridal party! Keep on praising while we continue on this journey. Now that we are "waiting," having received the revelation word, the seed, into our heart, and "worshipping" offering the seed back to God with thanksgiving, we are ready to stand our "watch." Our third memorial stone to set up is "watch." "*Watch* ye, stand fast in the faith, quit you like men, be strong" (1 Corinthians 16:13, KJV) (emphasis added).

Paul's admonition is to be watchful, wake up, and keep watching. Be alert, be on your guard, keep your eyes open, like a ninja, looking for a spiritual opportunity or danger; be very courageous. God is at work, look and see where He is working. Jesus said:

> *Watch therefore: for ye know not what hour, your Lord doth come. But know this that if the goodman of the house had known in what watch the thief would come, he would have watched, and would not have suffered his house to be broken up.*
>
> Matthew 24:42-43 (KJV) (emphasis added)

We watch for the Lord and keep watch for the enemy. The Amplified Bible explains "watch" as "give strict attention to, be cautious and active." This is proactive. Your seed is valuable; you must watch over it, guard it, and be alert to opportunities God sends your way to nourish it. Think of something important to watch. How about our little children, especially when we are in a public place? We must keep watch that they do not hurt themselves or each other, but also that some stranger does not hurt them or take them. We are always on the alert. What else do we watch? TV, our favorite shows, the latest "tweet" or status update, our gardens, our pets, or people. People-watching can be quite a pastime; you can learn a lot from observations. Watch to see what people might need, how they are getting along, how they act in certain situations. Did you know God is a people watcher? He is watching you and me to see how we will respond if we will notice what He does. Have you ever set up a surprise and then hid, just for the fun of seeing how someone would respond to the surprise? What fun that can be!

Well, God desires that we are on the lookout for Him, and certainly, He hopes we will recognize His set-ups for us and acknowledge Him for them. He likes to surprise us too. Developing sensitivity to the working of God only comes as we quiet our spirits, prepare to say "yes," and discern the happenings that come in front of us. On the other hand, if you are waiting, worshipping, and wondering, you will be certain to miss God's activity. I have missed His activity only later to greatly regret it. There is no place here for wondering, only watching. When you and I wait, hear from God, and worship Him with all our hearts giving Him the sacrifice of praise, like the imprisoned Paul and Silas in Acts 16, we don't wonder; we know God inhabits our praise, and one way or another, God will show up!

You may know of the story of Peter in jail when the church gathered together to earnestly pray for his deliverance from King Herod's clutches. An angel came to his rescue, and Peter didn't even recognize that the rescue was real. Then, after it finally dawned on him, he went to the house where they gathered to pray for him. Rhoda responded to his knock and heard his voice but didn't open the door. When she told the others, they didn't believe that Peter was at the door, they thought she was crazy, or that it was an angel! How quickly and easily we forget what we are praying and believing. How many times do we have to release a matter to God in prayer and then go and take it right back before we realize God wants to answer us! He wants us to see that He is working.

So, how do I watch for Him? Start to notice what happens next; stay alert. When we are watching for God, the enemy will not confuse us; we will know God is making a way in the desert. He is coming down to open the prison doors; we just may not believe it like Peter.

Now, consider with me this situation and see if you, too, would recognize God at work. To help us further with this stone "Watch," let us look at another "woman of ill-repute," this one named Rahab. In Joshua 2, the story unfolds. The new leader of Israel, Joshua, sends two men to spy secretly and view the land of Jericho. While there, they found the "red-light district," as it were, and hid in the house of a "woman for hire" named Rahab and lodged there. Now meanwhile, the King of Jericho finds out and tells Rahab to "bring the men out." Instead, she hides them; and tells the King that they have already left the city and, if they hurry, they will overtake them. Therefore, the king's men left and went after them. Rahab then speaks to the spies.

> *And she said unto the men, I know that the LORD hath given you the land, and that your terror is fallen upon us, and that all the inhabitants of the land faint because of you. For we have heard how the LORD dried up the water of the Red sea for you, when ye came out of Egypt; and what ye did unto the two kings of the Amorites, that were*

on the other side of Jordan, Sihon and Og, whom ye ut-
terly destroyed. And as soon as we had heard these things,
our hearts did melt, neither did there remain any more
courage in any man, because of you: for the LORD your
God, he is God in heaven above, and in earth beneath.

Joshua 2:9-11 (KJV) (emphasis added)

Rahab said, "I *know* that the Lord hath given you the land..." Hearing the wonders and miracles of their God, she firmly believed. Therefore, when they came and asked for help because a holy fear of their God had entered her heart, she recognized the opportunity for an advantage and seized the moment. With faith in the word she heard, she was convinced their God was God. Any courage to stand or fight against them "melted" away. The fame of God had gone ahead and prepared her to help the winning side. Paul tells us in Romans 10:17 (NKJV) that "Faith comes by hearing, and hearing by the word of God." Because she had a confident assurance, she also had an expectation of deliverance by their God. She then appeals to their kindness for her salvation:

Now therefore, I pray you, swear unto me by the LORD,
since I have shewed you kindness, that ye will also shew
kindness unto my father's house, and give me a true token:
And that ye will save alive my father, and my mother, and
my brethren, and my sisters, and all that they have, and
deliver our lives from death.

Joshua 2:12-13 (KJV)

Convinced of their certain victory, she asks that her kindness returns to not only her but to her family to deliver them. They agree, "Our life for yours, if ye utter not this our business..." She must bind a line of scarlet thread in her window as a sign; this is the house to save. Even here, God paints a picture of the blood of

Jesus as our salvation through this scarlet thread; all those inside will be saved. The spies left and hid for three days before they returned to Joshua. Before you know it, she looks out her window and sees an army. Here come the men of war marching before seven priests with trumpets, followed by the Ark of the Covenant with all the Israelites after that, encompassing the city. After six days of continued marching without a sound, the seventh day comes. Only this time, they march around seven times, at which time she hears a loud shout. Suddenly, the walls of the city fall flat, and the men go rushing in.

However, at her door, there is a knock. What would be your thought? Would they keep their agreement? Were they there to save her and her family? Sure enough, she opens the door to receive a safe escort for her and all her family outside the camp. She did not have to shout; she had to make a cord, put it in the window, and wait. Lo and behold, her faith finds her mentioned in the lineage of Christ Jesus the Messiah in Matthew 1:5, where she is the mother of Boaz, the great grandfather of King David.

> *And Joshua saved Rahab the harlot alive, and her father's household, and all that she had; and she dwelleth in Israel even unto this day; because she hid the messengers, which Joshua sent to spy out Jericho.*
>
> Joshua 6:25 (KJV)

God rewarded her faith. She heard the stories, believed, and feared their God. Because of her faith, her whole family receives salvation. Powerful, one woman who dared to trust God gives salvation to her whole house. When presented with an opportunity, she recognized it as God, received her word, seized it, and watched for her deliverance. This was an intelligent, reasonable, rational decision. Go with God! Her actions proved what was in her heart, faith in God and a holy fear of God. She proved the will of God was to save her and her family. This holy fear resulted in ultimate love for her family and love for God. She was willing to take a risk—a step of faith. Believing, she acted on the words she heard and then waited and watched. We do not read of anyone else in the city of Jericho who made it out alive, only Rahab and her family. She is named as one of the few women mentioned in the Hall of Fame of Faith: "By faith the harlot Rahab perished not with them that believed not, when she had received the spies with peace" (Hebrews 11:31, KJV).

Faith watches. Imagine, every day preparing for your home to be destroyed, hoping for the word of these men to bring salvation to you and your family. Resting on the hope that a scarlet thread hanging from the window will save them, they agree to prepare. They must have had the most beautiful bright red cord, long and thick, easily seen, hanging out their window. Patiently, she waited and watched for her time. Calling all the family together, they watch, ready at a moment's notice to escape. So many "what if's," but because she acted consistent with her agreement, patiently waited, and watched, they were ready when the rescue came. Are you ready? Have you prepared what God has required of you? Are you watching for God? Maybe you have given in to hopelessness, to fear, an unholy dread or worry. Listen to what you are saying. If you are rehearsing the "what if's," then you are re-hear-sing, hearing over and over again anything other than the Word God gave and giving voice to fears. Stop! Change your tune; sing a different song, a song of deliverance. Testify to yourself the word God gives you. Start repeating, "Thank You God for Your Word, I believe You, not what I see!" Thank God, He has sent you His Word and begin to declare He is God.

Then they cry unto the Lord *in their trouble, and he saveth them out of their distresses. He sent his word, and healed them, and delivered them from their destructions. Oh that men would praise the* Lord *for his goodness, and for his wonderful works to the children of men! And let them sacrifice the sacrifices of thanksgiving, and declare his works with rejoicing.*

Psalm 107:19-22 (KJV)

You may have started noticing a pattern. On this journey, with every stone, we are beginning the habit of praise. In our watching, we continue waiting and worshipping, offering God the sacrifices of rejoicing in whom He is, giving thanks to His name. With our eyes focused intently, looking for God, we are not as prone to yield to the enemy's distractions. One step, and one day at a time, we yield to the leading of the Lord through His Holy Spirit. We have an "unction," a knowing from the Holy One that keeps us steady as we look out over the landscape of our life. As in lining up the target through the sharpness of a scope, we are single-minded, focused on the activity of the Lord.

Rahab had a secret; now, too, her family has one. Imagine the temptation of distraction just even to tell a near friend, but no. The surprise would remain a safe-kept secret. Nevertheless, how many times did they repeat the wonders of God to keep themselves encouraged? From the time they had heard the miracles, their hearts melted; they were convinced the God of Israel was God. They no doubt rehearsed the many stories of the Israelites repeatedly, declaring God's work with rejoicing. They believed that the two spies would keep their promise, and undoubtedly, salvation was eminent. Some time transpired, though, before Joshua and the Israelites would arrive on the scene. Patiently though, they kept their watch until finally, there they were, in sight and the day of deliverance, at hand.

Watching requires that not only your eyes are "peeled," but all your senses as well are engaged. Even a slight whisper is noticed when you are on "high alert." Although temptations loom to draw our gaze away, let that be only for a moment, a glance, and quickly reset your gaze above.

> *Looking away [from all that will distract] to Jesus, Who is the Leader and the Source of our faith [giving the first incentive for our belief] and is also its Finisher [bringing it to maturity and perfection]. He, for the joy [of obtaining the prize] that was set before Him, endured the cross, despising and ignoring the shame, and is now seated at the right hand of the throne of God.*
>
> Hebrews 12:2 (AMPC)

Jesus set the example; He never lost sight of the cross. "Look away" like Jesus, from distractions to Jesus. Set your sights; He is the Lord, your Husband; stay focused on Him. Focused like a laser beam locked on to its target, where nothing can move you, neither internal nor external factors. Storms may come from without and disturbances from within, but staying "locked on" to Jesus, you are not moved. Distractions will begin to be so obvious that they may even become laughable. Look away and look up. Keep returning to your setting; the Lord is my Husband, focusing intently on Him. This look is far more than a casual glance. It is an attentive, steady, absorbing gaze to look with pleasure and anticipation, to look for your life. If the Lord is your Husband, He will show up, manifesting His faithful loving-kindness to you. Watch for Him and keep the faith. Keep your lamp trimmed with oil. Like the bridesmaids waiting on the bridegroom, when you hear something, you can quickly turn on the lights and see! See God! If you keep looking back, you will stay in fear and discouragement, doubt and unbelief; if you look around, you will get over into confusion, bitterness, and unforgiveness; but, if you look up above all else, you will see Jesus.

> *A Song of Ascents. I will lift up my eyes to the hills [around Jerusalem, to sacred Mount Zion and Mount Moriah]— From whence shall my help come? My help comes from the Lord, Who made heaven and earth.*
>
> Psalm 121:1-2 (AMPC) (emphasis added)

Do you think Rahab gave looking back one thought at all? No, of course not; she had a holy fear of God. She was ready, watching for an escape route, her "door of hope." Do you look to Him as the *only* help? If God be for us, who can be against us? Our help is in the name of the Lord! God gave us the rainbow, not only for us to look at and remember His promise but also for Him to look at and remember. He told Abraham to "look" at the "stars of the sky" and the "sand of the sea" to get a vision that he would have more descendants than these in numbers. Those Israelites bitten by the fiery snakes were told when they "looked attentively" at the brass snake Moses had made and placed on a pole, they would be healed (Numbers 21:9).

Maybe you struggle, and like Lot's wife, look back longingly at a life of worldliness and sin, from which God has delivered you out. She gives us a lesson of "what not to do." God sent His angel to deliver Lot's family from the wicked cities of Sodom and Gomorrah, and as He was burning them up, she looked back, lingering. I am sure it was tempting, but God was pouring out His wrath and indignation on the evil He hated. She must not have understood clearly how God abhorred the sin, and in an instant of looking in the wrong direction at the wrong thing, her turned gaze is memorialized forever as a "pillar of salt" (Genesis 19:26). Salt acting as a preservative to remind the onlooker that even on our way to freedom and deliverance, we must hate what God hates, keeping our eyes fixed on the His way, the highway of holiness. We can choose every moment to look forward to God's grace or look back at past sins. In order to go forward, we must keep looking forward toward where God is leading, away from death toward life. God is calling.

What about Rahab, she had a past and a shameful reputation, but when she heard of the God that delivered with power, unlike Lot's wife, she feared and believed. When the opportunity presented itself, she recognized it and willingly participated. Acting on her understanding, she proved her faith in God. Think about it; it had been forty years since the Israelites crossed over the Red Sea. She had been waiting and watching in anticipation of their arrival for a long time. She could, but she chose not to judge the future God had for her by looking at her past. Not only could she not afford to do that, but also neither could her family nor can you. In so doing, her actions demonstrated her faith and belief in their God. Stop holding your future captive to your past. Let God capture your gaze with His love; watch Him, look to Him. Let go of shame, guilt, or condemnation and grab hold of His hand. Let us say with the psalmist: "In the morning You hear my voice, O Lord; in the morning I prepare [a prayer, a sacrifice] for You and watch and wait [for You to speak to my heart]" (Psalm 5:3, AMPC).

> *O my Strength, I will watch and give heed to You and sing praises; for God is my Defense (my Protector and High Tower). My God in His mercy and steadfast love will meet me; God will let me look [triumphantly] on my enemies (those who lie in wait for me).*

Psalm 59:9-10 (AMPC)

May we say with Micah looking with confidence to the Lord: "But as for me, I will *look* to the Lord and confident in Him I will *keep_watch*; I will wait with hope and expectancy for the God of my salvation; my God will hear me" (Micah 7:7, AMPC) (emphasis added). May we receive the exhortation from Jesus in:

> *Keep awake then and watch at all times [be discreet, attentive, and ready], praying that you may have the full strength and ability and be accounted worthy to escape all these things [taken together] that will take place, and to stand in the presence of the Son of Man.*
>
> Luke 21:36 (AMPC) (emphasis added)

Watch, not just occasionally, at all times, attentively, with energy and purpose, sober and alert, on duty, looking for the activity of God. Like the first time you saw your favorite movie. By now, you have probably become a student of that movie, able to recite even the lines. God is moving, will we recognize it? How many times do we miss what He has for us distracted by fears or other voices, living off-duty? Paul urges us to keep alert and watch with strong purpose:

> *Pray at all times (on every occasion, in every season) in the Spirit, with all [manner of] prayer and entreaty. To that end keep alert and watch with strong purpose and perseverance, interceding on behalf of all the saints (God's consecrated people).*
>
> Ephesians 6:18 (AMPC) (emphasis added)

In other words, put blinders on if necessary. Let the purposes of God's will and His plans keep you focused on Him. The world, or the devil, will try to distract you and get you to look at other things that might seem better now, but persevere, be of good courage, and keep watch for God. John warns us to keep awake and watch in:

> *So call to mind the lessons you received and heard; continually lay them to heart and obey them, and repent. In case you will not rouse yourselves and keep awake and watch, I will come upon you like a thief, and you will not know or suspect at what hour I will come.*
>
> Revelation 3:3 (AMPC) (emphasis added)

Here is one last thought on this stone "watch":

> *Exercise foresight and be on the watch to look [after one another], to see that no one falls back from and fails to secure God's grace (His unmerited favor and spiritual blessing), in order that no root of resentment (rancor, bitterness, or hatred) shoots forth and causes trouble and bitter torment, and the many become contaminated and defiled by it—*
>
> Hebrews 12:15 (AMPC) (emphasis added)

We are to be on the "watch," looking after our brothers and sisters in the Lord. Whoa! You might think, "Who wants that?" Or much less, "Who wants to do that?" As once a pastor's wife, I know this is tough. People want you to solve their emergency but then do not want you in their business. Then, when things start going downhill, they want to know why you did not get in their business. Crazy! When you do, and things turn around, sometimes they get uncomfortable and leave. It is so easy in big churches to slip in and out unnoticed. People like it that way, more of a spectator mentality. However, it was not always that way. Clearly, we see here, that is not how God intends the body to function. He is saying, "Look after one another to see that no one falls back."

We are encouraged to "go to the one," and in another place, "to go after the lost sheep," in a spirit of meekness endeavoring to restore such a one. This is what God did for us in Christ, and He has now given us this ministry of reconciliation:

> *It was God [personally present] in Christ, reconciling and restoring the world to favor with Himself, not counting up and holding against [men] their trespasses [but cancelling them], and committing to us the message of reconciliation (of the restoration to favor).*
>
> 2 Corinthians 5:19 (AMPC)

We are to share the message of reconciliation, restoring others to the right relationship, favor with the Father. Ask, and then watch for the opportunity and/or need to do this. God will use you, look around, you will see the need is great, people need the Lord. We are looking to love, simply let them know they are loved, and just as Christ forgives us our sins, we are to forgive the sins of others. "Behold, I come as a thief. *Blessed is he that watcheth,* and keepeth his garments, lest he walk naked, and they see his shame" (Revelation 16:15, KJV) (emphasis added).

Determine to keep your watch well. Which way are you looking, backwards, down, or up? Now is the time; set yourself to watch; He is coming, and coming for you, be on the *lookout!* Practice perspective, look past the natural to the supernatural. Remember, like Rahab, what God has done, see Him and seek Him, nothing is impossible with God. He loves you and has a good plan; trust Him now. Like Rahab, prepare your house, throw out your cord of faith, recite the goodness of God and sing your praises. Watch attentively, watch for the suddenly, the strange, the unexpected; He is coming! Look for Him, especially in the little things. He has been working behind the scenes; get ready; He may just surprise you!

Prayer ~

My heavenly Father, my Lord, forgive me for where I have looked longingly at that which has not glorified You. Help me to hate what you hate. Help me to fix my eyes, my gaze on You, keeping watch for You alone. You are Lord over all the days of my life from this day forward; I look to You, waiting, worshipping, and watching with hope and expectation, believing You will come with power and might, shining light in the darkest places. Help me to recognize your activity and to keep alert, with my eyes "locked on" You. I commit to look for you, open my eyes to see You. You alone are God and worthy of all my praise. Thank you, Lord, for your word that you watch over to perform, that you are not a man that you should lie, but that you keep the covenant. Thank you that you keep watching over me. Praise You, Lord, and thank You.

I am watching with you and for you, my sister. God bless you!

> *"I ask—ask the God of our Master, Jesus Christ, the God of glory—to make you intelligent and discerning in knowing him personally, your eyes focused and clear, so that you can see exactly what it is he is calling you to do, grasp the immensity of this glorious way of life he has for his followers, oh, the utter extravagance of his work in us who trust him—endless energy, boundless strength!"*

Ephesians 1:15-19 (MSG)

CHAPTER 7.

MEMORIAL STONE 4

WALK

"But they that wait upon the LORD shall renew their strength; they shall mount up with wings as eagles; they shall run, and not be weary; and they shall walk, and not faint."

Isaiah 40:31 (KJV)

Praise God; you are continuing on this journey with me; together, we will see the harvest. God is no respecter of persons, but He is a respecter of faith. Now that you have waited on God and received the seed, "The Lord is my Husband"; continuing in worship with thanksgiving for your seed, and keeping your watch, then you are now prepared for the next stone—"*walk.*" Setting up our fourth memorial stone on this journey, "*walk,*" may seem easy. You may even say, "Oh, I've got this, I'm already doing this one," at least I thought so. Not so quick, however, sure, most everyone can walk, but scripture paints a very unusual picture of this stone, and as we look at this, may we examine ourselves in its reflection.

Yes, we must get up and get moving. Walking implies action, forward movement, a steady pace. While hopefully not in a circle like the Israelites in the wilderness for forty years, or backwards like we have seen, we come to the place of employing our energies to act on our seed. Walking is the way we conduct our life now or live as believers. We never walk alone when we take daily, habitual steps with the Lord, our Husband. Instructions like "walking by faith" and "walking in the spirit" call us to set up this stone in a dynamic way. Trusting God, not for what we see, but rather, full of His spirit by faith, we take each step holding tightly to our Father's hand into the unseen or unknown. When God told the Israelites to "walk in His ways," He added this blessing:

> In that I command thee this day to love the LORD thy God, to walk in his ways, and to keep his commandments and his statutes and his judgments, that thou may live and multiply: and the LORD thy God shall bless thee in the land whither thou goest to possess it.
>
> Deuteronomy 30:16 (KJV)

Coming into His presence, raising our hearts and hands in worship, giving voice to our praise, keeping our eyes "locked" on Him produces an inner strength to safely follow the leading of the Holy Spirit. With our hearts attuned, we can hear His directions, trusting God's GPS. His guidance system is dependable, sure, and safe. Through His Word and the Holy Spirit, He leads us to our desired destination. Even if you have gone "off-road" a few times like me, the GPS, *"God's Positioning System,"* reroutes us, getting us back on track. No matter how far off we get, He will still get us to our destination!

How and where we walk is of vital importance; just like our eyes and our mouth, it can mean life or death. Because God inhabits our praise, He brings with Him all that He is, including His peace. With His peace, we can now, as Ephesians 6:15 (KJV) says, "And your feet shod with the preparation of the gospel of peace;" shod, or rather, put the shoes of the gospel message to our faith. His peace is rest, but it is not inactivity. It is Spirit-directed activity reconciling man with God. Without His peace, our message falls short of the Gospel. Let us learn to go walking with the Lord, in His way, and in His spirit by looking at the "walk" of another inspirational woman of faith, Ruth. Definitions vary slightly, but according to the Merriam-Webster dictionary, Ruth means "friend, companion, or refresher; compassion for the misery of another; satisfier." In this story, we will see how love finds a way.

This love story opens up with an Israelite family, Elimelech and his wife, Naomi, and their two sons, Mahon and Chilion, who had fled their homeland of Bethlehem, meaning "house of bread," because of a famine. Oddly enough, this was likely the result of the disobedience of God's people worshipping the idols of the heathen nations around them rather than the one true God, Jehovah. Upon settling in the foreign land near Moab, Elimelech dies, leaving Naomi with her two sons. They each take a wife from Moab, a godless people, and enemies of the Israelites, Ruth and Orpah. Together they dwell there with Naomi for ten years. Suddenly, the two sons die, leaving all three of the women widows.

Unfortunately, it is interesting to note here that the very thing they were trying to save, their lives, in fleeing the famine and forsaking the loving discipline of God, they have now lost. Naomi's strength, all her men, are gone. Elimelech and his family followed their own way and, in so doing, came to the seeming end of their family name. Sometimes in an effort to avoid pain, we open ourselves up to more unnecessary pain and suffering. Divorce is often like this; we may think the "grass is greener on the other side," only to find out there is just a different set of baggage. In leaving God's land and His people for the enemy's land and people, Naomi exchanged a famine for three funerals.

Better to be in the will of God and suffer for your good than to go your own way and suffer loss. God did not leave His people hopeless; He is the All-Sufficient One, El Shaddai; His goal is revelation and restoration of who He is and how He provides.

With the famine now over, and her homeland blessed with bread once again in the harvest, Naomi determines to return to Bethlehem-Judah. After encouraging her daughters-in-law to go back to their families, which ultimately included their gods, she kisses them goodbye. But they, weeping and mourning at the thought of the broken relationship, refuse to go at first. Orpah, however, decides to return home, but Ruth cannot. How disappointing that this woman of God would encourage these young girls to return to a godless life after seeing and hearing of her God for ten years. At an all-time low, Naomi may have hoped to somehow save her family name and face in returning to Bethlehem emptied-handed. Possibly, without the girls, no one would ever know her sons had taken wives from the godless Moabite nation.

Why try to cover our past mistakes? It is of no avail. God sees, He knows, forgives, and even more redeems when we confess and surrender to His way. Interesting here, God was working powerfully through the young Moabite girl. She had seen and heard enough of this talk, and Ruth would have nothing of it. With her heart and eyes fixed on Naomi and her God, she determines to go with her, leaving the family, gods, and homeland of Moab. Notice her eyes are not looking back like Orpah; she is looking with anticipation as to what the new land will hold for her; trusting in the God of Naomi, she's ready to take her first step of faith. Although she was going to a place and a people she had never known, she found the true God and a life of peace with Naomi. She chose to walk by faith and not by sight, to walk away from her past into her destiny. By declaring her infamous covenant, she strengthens and seals her resolve even further:

And Ruth said, Intreat me not to leave thee, or to return
from following after thee: for whither thou goest, I will go;
and where thou lodgest, I will lodge: thy people shall be
my people, and thy God my God: Where thou diest, will I
die, and there will I be buried: the LORD do so to me, and
more also, if ought but death part thee and me.

Ruth 1:16-17 (KJV)

That is closely following; what a powerful bond in their relationship. In the ten years of marriage to her son, Ruth must have seen and felt something in Naomi that she was not willing to give up but rather follow. Wherever Naomi walked, that is where Ruth wanted to walk, all the way to the grave. Knowing the hopeless life of going back to the way of her family, Ruth was determined. Relentlessly, she vowed to go or to stop whenever and wherever Naomi did. She started a journey with Naomi and was not about to stop now. After seeing and hearing the determination of Ruth, Naomi accepts the commitment and starts the walk home in silence. The strength of purpose and resolve was irresistible to Naomi. We serve a covenant-keeping God, and He expects us to keep our covenants as well, and as we do, He is there to uphold our commitments and us. While these two women, now in covenant and on the same journey, walk towards provision, one walks in anticipation of good, looking forward, the other, however, in fear of shame.

Maybe you started out your marriage with a resolve similar to Ruth's and have since faltered. Receive this as encouragement to strengthen and renew your commitment as one who does not draw back, but as one who trusts God, willing to walk by faith forward into your destiny. It is one thing to know God; it is entirely different to put your life in His hands and trust Him for all your needs. The secret is you are *not alone*; He is with you, in the morning and the evening, and your coming and going, He is *for you!* He walks with you, my beloved.

Upon their arrival in Bethlehem, word spreads throughout the city. Naomi's friends greet her with surprise and shock, wondering, "Can this really be Naomi?" Naomi, whose name means "pleasantness and delight," defied her name; she even says to her questioning friends, go ahead, and call her "Mara," meaning "bitter." She was identifying herself as one with whom the Lord had dealt very bitterly. She said, "The Lord has brought me home again empty," meaning no husband, no children, no grandchildren, and broke. Not only did she arrive with an empty home, but empty hands and an empty heart as well. She is bitter but not broken. She did not even recognize or acknowledge the gifts she still had: life, opportunity, God, friends, and this faithful daughter-in-law, Ruth. Poor Ruth, what was she, "chop liver?" Imagine having committed yourself to someone your whole life, and he or she just declares to everyone that she has nothing!

Naomi is having an emotional meltdown, simply put, a "pity party." Have you ever seen the look on someone's face that is wallowing like this? All I had to do was look in the mirror! I've been right there, not recognizing and acknowledging the gifts of God while feeling sorry for myself; what a slippery slope to fall down! Her friends did not even recognize her; downcast and despondent, she recited her pain. When focused on our losses, it is impossible to be grateful for our blessings. Worse, now though, she is actually identifying with her losses, calling herself, and even naming herself "Mara," "bitter." Even if no one else ever called her that, she saw herself this way. What a dangerous trap we set for ourselves if we intend on responding to God in anger, mad at God for a road we took without Him. God's mercy is staring at her in the eyes of

Ruth. Maybe you are mad at God; look around you, maybe right in front of you shines the mercy of God on your situation.

Acknowledging His abundant showers of blessings is the beginning of softening our hearts to receive His loving-kindness again. The Lord is working to reveal Himself as Husband, not only to these two women but to you and me; if we will open our eyes, we will see His love. Naomi could not possibly consider at this point, in her abasement, how she would come to value the vow of love from her daughter-in-law, Ruth, who would fulfill her name as a "companion and refresher."

Even though Naomi did not consider Ruth at the time a blessing, God was with Ruth. She was not deterred, nor offended, and did not leave. With love for Naomi as her own mother, she sensed in her heart that the plan and purpose for her life was walking this out with Naomi and her God. Somehow, over the last ten years watching and listening to Naomi, she learned to trust and believe that she knew the way of life. To this belief, she committed her life; not even this momentary setback would cause her to doubt. Her love and respect for Naomi and her God kept her focused. Look at a verse her great-grandson would pen: "Though I walk in the midst of trouble, You will revive me; You will stretch forth Your hand against the wrath of my enemies, and Your right hand will save me" (Psalm 138:7, AMPC). Wow! God revives; His right hand saves me! God finishes what He starts and will keep us alive in the thick of things when we do not see the end. Think of what your great-grandchildren will learn and repeat from you! Let's go on:

> *And Naomi had a kinsman of her husband's, a mighty man of wealth, of the family of Elimelech; and his name was Boaz. And Ruth the Moabitess said unto Naomi, Let me now go to the field, and glean ears of corn after him in whose sight I shall find grace. And she said unto her, Go,*

my daughter. And she went, and came, and gleaned in the field after the reapers: and her hap was to light on a part of the field belonging unto Boaz, who was of the kindred of Elimelech.

Ruth 2:1-3 (KJV) (emphasis added)

Amazing, good for her; she got up and got moving. She "walked" out faithfully her commitment to Naomi, who at this point is still wallowing in her pain. Not seeing God in any of this, she withdraws as a victim, isolating herself from the community. I can just hear her weak dejected tone telling Ruth to go, feeling forsaken yet still letting Ruth figure it out. Somewhere within her, she recognized by now, this was no ordinary daughter-in-law; this was a "daughter-in-love," a girl she termed dearly, "daughter." Ruth did put feet to her faith, got up, and went out to gather some food. Walking by faith into the face of certain odds, as an impoverished widow, with no sons, no jobs, and a likely weakened or sickly mother-in-law, Ruth, the foreigner, displayed great courage initiating a survival plan.

With the possibilities of danger, abuse, and/or ridicule, she launched out to find work in a strange land. What is interesting, though, is a small little word we see here, "hap." "Her hap" was to end up in the field of a man, and kindred, named Boaz. "Hap," defined as a "fortuitous chance," means she was walking so closely in submission to the Lord that she was led to this field by the sovereignty of God, even though God is not mentioned. "The steps of a good man are ordered by the LORD: and he delighteth in his way" (Psalm 37:23, KJV).

"And your ears will hear a word behind you, saying, this is the way; walk in it, when you turn to the right hand and when you turn to the left" (Isaiah 30:21, AMPC). Ruth began walking out her covenant, expecting that she would find "grace" or "favor" in the eyes of someone. She had hope, that is, a positive expectation of something good. And with that hope, she walked on her way forward, God ordering her steps to find a field of provision. Maybe you are waiting on God, but He may be waiting on you. You cannot steer an idle ship; start moving by following the "unction" or leading of the Lord. Scripture tells us, as believers, we have this "unction" or "anointing": "But ye have an unction from the Holy One, and ye know all things" (1 John 2:20, KJV).

Ruth knew they would need food to survive, so she took the initiative, and with Naomi's blessing, she went on her way to find some. Word got out and probably spread quickly in the little town of Bethlehem. This is Naomi's daughter-in-law, who has abandoned her homeland and committed her life to Naomi, her God, and her people. Amazingly, she boldly walks right up and, as scripture will reveal, tells her story to the overseer of a field, who then allows her to start reaping immediately. Boaz, the owner, arrives, and upon seeing her, asks her story from the supervisor; and, after hearing of her resolve and reputation, he addresses her directly. As a close relative to Naomi, she did not know he extends special favor to Ruth, which would prove to be highly significant.

> Then Boaz said to Ruth, "You will listen, my daughter, will you not? Do not go to glean in another field, nor go from here, but stay close by my young women. Let your eyes be on the field which they reap, and go after them. Have I not commanded the young men not to touch you? And when you are thirsty, go to the vessels and drink from what the young men have drawn." So she fell on her face, bowed down to the ground, and said to him, "Why have I found favor in your eyes, that you should take notice of me, since I am a foreigner?" And Boaz answered and said to her, "It has been fully reported to

*me, all that you have done for your mother-in-law since
the death of your husband, and how you have left your
father and your mother and the land of your birth, and
have come to a people whom you did not know before.
The L*ORD* repay your work, and a full reward be given
you by the L*ORD* God of Israel, under whose wings you
have come for refuge." Then she said, "Let me find favor
in your sight, my lord; for you have comforted me, and
have spoken kindly to your maidservant, though I am
not like one of your maidservants."*

Ruth 2:8-13 (NKJV) (emphasis added)

Beautiful, Boaz offers her a place, protection, and provision, even asking the reapers to drop extra for her. He guarantees her a place in his field, promises to keep her from harm and to feed her. Trusting in the Lord, God has sovereignly led her to this field of peace and comfort. How glorious is the favor of God! Boaz offered her continual work reaping in his fields, protection from harm, and a continual supply of food and drink. As a foreigner with no husband, locals could easily mock and ridicule her, but also, much worse, as Boaz knew, the young men could have raped her. He commanded them not to touch her but rather to give her drink and even leave extra grain for her. Thankfully, Ruth gleaned almost three quarters of a bushel that day, unheard of for the poor.

Upon arriving home, Naomi, seeing the abundance, asks surprisingly, "Where did you glean today?" Ruth told her, "In the field of Boaz." How exciting, now Naomi's spirit comes alive, she has the vision. She was watching! She praises the Lord and invokes God's blessing on the man. Now she connects the dots. (Lord, help us with this because sometimes we are not watching closely enough to see God is always moving and working.) God has revealed Himself as Husband in extending the grace of first, comfort and kindness in His words to Ruth, but then, protection from harm, as well as provision.

> *And Naomi said unto her daughter in law, blessed be he*
> *of the LORD, who hath not left off his kindness to the living*
> *and to the dead. And Naomi said unto her, the man is near*
> *of kin unto us, one of our next kinsmen.*

Ruth 2:20 (KJV)

Naomi sees the light! Finally, her perspective is lifted from the pit of despair to the passion of hope. God has opened a door of hope, and she, now encouraged, agrees, Ruth should stay in his field until the end of the harvest. Knowing this, that Boaz, as a kinsmen-*redeemer*, or rather, one of the close relatives of Elimelech, her deceased husband, could be charged with the responsibility of *buying* Naomi's land back from "foreclosure" and raising up seed to her through Ruth. Naomi enthusiastically instructs Ruth, "Do as he has said." With her courage restored, her desire is "to seek rest for Ruth; that it may be well with her." Wow! What a change. She has gone from walking away from God to walking with God, from wallowing to worshipping, from wanting to send Ruth away to now seeking her best, a home. She threw open the door, the door of hope, and is now ready to walk through into the light and see what God will do. Thank God for the tenacity of her daughter-in-law, who believed God enough to stay and seek God's plan. She watched God enough before recognizing, this must be God!

Naomi is reaping a harvest of love and faith. Somewhere in their time together, she has clearly sown into this Moabite girl, an association so important that it was vital to her existence and future. Naomi must have walked out on a day-to-day basis, a living, vibrant real faith in her God, so much so that Ruth would not even consider Naomi's depressed condition as a deterrent or distraction. Ruth walked out her faith in the middle of the mystery, right into the field of providence.

Think about who you are with on this journey of life right now. I have heard it said, if you look at your friends, you could see your future. Look around and ask yourself, who are you following—walking behind, with—walking beside, and leading—walking in front of? You may need some new friends, friends of faith. Whether or not we share our faith, the stories of God's goodness, with the next generation or those around us can make a difference whether we are encouraged in our time of need. Oftentimes, as we encourage others, we, too, are encouraged. What we sow, we reap. Naomi sowed faith, and now in her hour of need, she is reaping through the faith of her "daughter." She was refreshed by the "refresher," Ruth. "…whoever refreshes others will be refreshed" (Proverbs 11:25b, NIV). "Two are better than one, because they have a good reward for their labour" (Ecclesiastes 4:9, KJV).

I believe as Ruth saw the life come back into Naomi, she got excited as well. God gave these two to each other, and as one encourages the other, the other encourages her right back. As they were, so are we, better together! We are not made to walk alone. So now Naomi has a great idea and gives Ruth a plan:

> *Wash thyself therefore, and anoint thee, and put thy raiment upon thee, and get thee down to the floor: but make not thyself known unto the man, until he shall have done eating and drinking. And it shall be, when he lieth down, that thou shalt mark the place where he shall lie, and thou shalt go in, uncover his feet, and lay thee down; and he will tell thee what thou shalt do. And she said unto her, all that thou sayest unto me I will do.*
>
> Ruth 3:3-5 (KJV)

Ruth sensed his favor, and Naomi had a "knowing," Boaz was already showing himself as a husband, a kinsmen redeemer, through the wooing and allurement of his speech and blessing. Remember the picture in Hosea, God spoke "comfortably" to Gomer in the wilderness, speaking to her heart words of love and care and then showing her the door of hope. Boaz, with his words of comfort and respect, has inspired not just one woman but also now two. He is not just any boss man but one of their kinsmen redeemers. Although not the nearest, he is still a relative with the position, responsibility, and means to redeem them both from their impoverished life and even fulfill their dreams of an heir, as he was also single.

Now, Naomi has seen the door of hope! She is on it. With a future in sight and her hope back, she plans to strike while the iron is hot! They choose to walk out their faith and put it all on the line. The time has come for Ruth to step out, but first, she must prepare for a special meeting. Naomi instructs her to clean up, put her perfume on, change her clothes, go, and present herself to this man. However, do not get too excited. Wait until he has had plenty to eat and drink, then watch where he lies down, go quietly, and lay down at his feet. This will let him know you are available for marriage. Then, wait to hear what he tells you to do. Notice here how God gives His direction through a woman, Naomi, as Ruth walked in submission to her.

Much symbolism here no doubt inspired authors of the New Testament, like Paul, Luke, and James, to charge the believer with washing, cleansing, and purging oneself in preparation to approach the Lord, our Husband. This is a beautiful picture of Romans 12:1 (YLT), "You present yourself, a living sacrifice, holy and acceptable unto God..." We are changed and become new through the washing of the blood of Jesus and the water of the Word. We are clothed with new robes, a sweet aroma, white robes of righteousness and new shoes, "peace pumps," the preparation of the gospel of peace (Ephesians 6:15). Now we can come boldly to the throne of grace.

How many changes of clothes she must have gone through, imagining what he would like, what his favorite color was. In complete obedience to Naomi, Ruth prepares and pampers herself. Excitedly, and yet likely with some apprehension, she musters all the boldness necessary and continues her walk of faith. Even if she was afraid, she did it. What encouragement!

> *"and if in the light we may walk, as He is in the light—*
> *we have fellowship one with another, and the blood of*
> *Jesus Christ His Son doth cleanse us from every sin;"*
>
> 1 John 1:7 (YLT)

On her walk, Ruth prepares emotionally and mentally to present herself for marriage in a most humble yet risky and vulnerable position. Imagine how she felt as she took this walk, perhaps wondering if anyone sees her. She is bravely walking in the light of the truth Naomi gave her, but will others think ill of her; what will happen? What if he rejects me? Even if she had these concerns come through her head, she kept walking, one step at a time. God's word is a lamp to each step she takes and a light to her path. Familiar with the mystery, though, she walks on trusting Naomi's word, knowing she is not alone. God made a way before; He will do it again! Finally, she arrives at the "threshing floor," likely an open, airy hard spot where they could beat out and winnow the grain, with possibly a temporary covering, where the men would work and guard the harvest from possible thieves. They would eat, drink, and then find a place to rest.

She did exactly as Naomi had instructed. Ruth had learned to trust Naomi taking her as her covering, her "rabbi," a spiritual mother. As a great example of the power of submission, especially, and most importantly, in the face of uncertainty, Ruth waits and watches, encouraging herself no doubt with the goodness and faithfulness of God to even bring her to this place.

If you do not have a spiritual "mother" or "rabbi" by now, this should encourage and inspire you as to the value of having one. Could God be asking you to be a spiritual mother? God said it is the responsibility of the "older women to teach the younger women." Has someone fondly attached herself to you? Watch for God at work, and do not be too quick to brush them aside; it may be your pathway of blessing like it was here for Naomi. Walking by faith and not by sight, Ruth now fully trusted Naomi; how beautiful! Naomi's influence on Ruth would save both of their lives, but it was through the determination of Ruth's commitment to God and Naomi. Naomi knew about God, she knew His name, but now she has learned to trust God. He truly is El Shaddai, the All-Sufficient One, the Lord, her Husband.

Ruth walks out the instructions and waits until Boaz lies down. She has waited patiently, and now, the moment of truth. One fact is sure: ignoring and neglecting Boaz was not the way to win his affection. If there were any hope of marrying him, Ruth would have to approach him, make herself available to him, and express her desire for him to take her as his wife. Hopefully, he will not be mad or get angry at the possible infringement on his upright reputation. Walking gently, maybe even tiptoeing over to where Boaz lies, she quietly uncovers his feet and lies down. Let's pick up here:

And it came to pass at midnight, that the man was afraid, and turned himself: and, behold, a woman lay at his feet. And he said, Who art thou? And she answered, I am Ruth thine handmaid: spread therefore thy skirt over thine handmaid; for thou art a near relative. And he said, Blessed be thou of the LORD, my daughter: for thou hast shewed more kindness in the latter end than at the beginning, inasmuch as thou followed not young men, whether poor or rich. And now, my daughter, fear not, I will do to thee all that thou requires: for all the city of my people doth know that thou art a virtuous woman.

Ruth 3:8-11 (KJV)

I wonder how Ruth felt lying there, waiting for Boaz to wake up. How would he respond to her presence? Would he be intimidated, angry, embarrassed, violent, or even interpreting it as perhaps an opportunity for a sexual encounter? On the other hand, would he understand and accept his responsibility as near of kin? How uneasy she might have felt, but she lay there just as Naomi instructed. Then, in the middle of the night, he wakes up. Interesting, the Scriptures say Boaz was afraid, not Ruth. Imagine that! He has a woman lying at his feet; what could she do to him? He asked who it was as though he could not see or did not recognize her. It must have been dark, or she really cleaned and fixed herself up!

When he discovers it is Ruth lying at his feet, a symbol of service, and that she has asked him to "cover her with his skirt," symbolizing a request for marriage, he blesses her for her interest and recognition of him as a "kinsmen-redeemer," a close relative with the right to marry her and redeem their land. He applauded her request in noting that he is not a young man and that she could have any of the young men she wanted; she was a real catch. She was very courageous in coming to him, and he agrees to do all she requires! What a moment of relief and exhilaration! Because her reputation is that of a virtuous woman, in keeping her covenant with Naomi to stay and take care of her, he blesses her and accepts her proposal. However, he tells her of a nearer relative he must offer her to first before he can take her as a wife.

Boaz sends her home in the early morning with her veil full of barley; lest someone would by chance notice her, this would make her appear as though she was most likely in the field gleaning early. Upon receiving the generous gift, Naomi is convinced; Boaz will not rest until he takes care of this business. Now they must wait, sit still, and see the salvation of the Lord. So patiently and expectantly, they wait and watch.

The lessons, once learned, continuously present themselves, and fortunately, this one, they got. They would not run around contriving some plan like so many women would. We might parallel this to dating around while you are waiting on the right man. That is not waiting! Exactly how could that ever be considered waiting when God says He will gather my mate for me? That is feeding the flesh and walking in your own ways. Stop wasting precious time and energy, and sit still while God moves on your behalf. On the other hand, maybe you have a plan B, just in case he does not come back. That is not faith either. Faith does not have a plan "B!" If you are married, give up the private checking account you are hiding (for a back door escape), and get "all in" on God's plan and will for your life. God will not only work but also show Himself strong on behalf of him whose heart is perfect; that is, an undivided, believing heart with one plan, God's!

Boaz goes immediately, gathers ten of the town elders, and then calls for the closer relative to come and take care of some business. Boaz then informs him of his right to buy the land first from Naomi and asks if he wants it. At first, he says yes until Boaz reminds him of his role as kinsmen redeemer; he must also take in the two widowed women, Ruth and Naomi, and raise up seed to their deceased husbands. As the plot thickens, he says no, as this would bring trouble to his house. I imagine he must have already been married. As he passes, this gives Boaz the next right of refusal. Only this time, Boaz gladly, willingly, and quickly claims not only the land but also the women. He declares his intention to raise up seed to this family, and in so doing, the town praises him and pronounces a blessing on him and his seed that he will be famous and fruitful. Here we are, over two thousand years later, telling of him, their prophetical prayers and praises fulfilled.

Not the way we imagine marriages coming together in our Hollywood-crazed culture. Nonetheless, Boaz struck the deal, which was signed and sealed with a shoe—yes, a shoe! That was their signature in those days, a public revoking if you will of his right to walk through the land, and symbolically giving Boaz possession of the land, the right to walk in it! God had told Abraham, Joshua, and Moses to "walk through the land for I have given it to you," and "every place that the sole of your foot shall tread that have I given you." The shoe represented ownership, the right to walk on the land. Boaz now has the shoe, and with it, the right to walk and redeem not only the land but also the women. A powerful word picture in a shoe, walk-in authority, in all the rights and privileges of a possessor, an owner. Boaz could boldly go forth to declare his purchase and rightfully claim his new family.

Off goes Boaz, blessed with praises from the city and carrying a shoe, representing his new land, wife, and family responsibility to the name of Naomi's husband, Elimelech, to raise up seed.

So Boaz took Ruth, and she was his wife: and when he went in unto her, the LORD gave her conception, and she bare a son. And the women said unto Naomi, Blessed be the LORD, which hath not left thee this day without a kinsman, that his name may be famous in Israel. And he shall be unto thee a restorer of thy life, and a nourisher of thine old age: for thy daughter in law, which loveth thee, which is better to thee than seven sons, hath born him. And Naomi took the child, and laid it in her bosom, and became nurse unto it. And the women her neighbors gave it a name, saying, There is a son born to Naomi; and they called his name Obed: he is the father of Jesse, the father of David.

Ruth 4:13-17 (KJV) (emphasis added)

How exciting as Ruth sees Boaz come through the door, he has kept his promise. Through waiting and watching in submission and obedience to Naomi, Ruth started this walk of faith and finished it by receiving her reward. Boaz keeps his word, redeems the property, and takes Ruth as his wife to raise up seed for Elimelech, his kinsman, and Naomi. The women in the town, seeing the reversal of fortune by the salvation of the Lord, bless Naomi and her new grandson. How overwhelmed with joy she must have been. So much so that she takes the child to nurse and invites her neighbors to name her child! Can you imagine? What fellowship of love there must have been for Naomi and Ruth to include in this moment of joy the very women that gave them a hard time, in the beginning, no hard feelings, only rejoicing!

Naomi and Ruth reaped their harvest of faith, and Obed was his name, meaning "serve." Maybe a reminder of how God blessed Ruth because of her service to Naomi. He was the grandfather of King David, from whose lineage would bring the Messiah, Jesus. They gave their hurt and pain to God, trusting Him and walking out their faith, waiting and watching to see what the Lord would do. They "walked by faith and not by sight," submitting themselves to God, to each other, and to their redeemer, and now their faith became sight, believing first, then seeing.

Oh, look and see what the Lord has done; it is marvelous in our eyes! He is worthy; He is faithful; He can be counted on. Will you put your trust in Him today as these women did? Lay aside the hurts and insults, and take the hand of your kinsman-redeemer, Jesus; He has come to save you and restore to you what the enemy has stolen. Walk on in faith; your husband is here; you are not alone. You have not been left to fend for yourself. God has a marvelous plan! "Yea, though I walk through the valley of the shadow of death, I will fear no evil: for thou art with me; thy rod and thy staff they comfort me" (Psalm 23:4, KJV). Walk "*through!*" Do not set up camp in the valley of the shadow of death. If you have, get up and get moving! Walk on in and claim the promise. The *Lord* is your Husband; He has bought you with the blood of Jesus; He is your kinsman-redeemer! Listen to Him; His Word will comfort you as you walk. Worship Him with His Word. Fear no evil. "For we *walk by faith,* not by sight:" (2 Corinthians 5:7, KJV).

Walk through every minute in faith, watching and worshipping, taking each step as He lights your way; listening as He speaks in your ear which way to turn. Like Ruth, take the walk of faith and listen as the Lord instructs you in which way to go. If she had looked around, she might have gone back like Orpah or stayed at home like Naomi, but Ruth dared, took the risk, put herself out there trusting to God, and He led her to the right man. It is easier to steer a moving vehicle than a stationary one. Maybe now is the time for you to get up and start walking with God, with faith that lets Him lead the way. Yes, Jesus, take the wheel while

I get in the back seat where I can rest, like in a limousine. I do not even have to map out the course, just ride. "He leadeth me beside the still waters. He restoreth my soul: he leadeth me in the paths of righteousness for his name's sake" (Psalm 23:2, 3 KJV).

> *Then Jesus said unto them, yet a little while is the light with you. Walk while ye have the light, lest darkness come upon you: for he that walketh in darkness knoweth not whither he goeth.*
>
> John 12:35-36 (KJV)

God expects you and I to walk in the light He gives us, not the light we do not have. This word, the Lord is my Husband, is light to your path, one step at a time, walking with God, trusting Him. "His word is a lamp unto your feet, a light unto your path" (Psalm 119:105, KJV). There is a path on which to walk called the "Highway of Holiness," where the redeemed walk with God. For those He redeems and calls His bride, He made this highway safe and lights it with His Word. I hope I see you there! Walk on, worshipping, watching.

> *And a highway will be there; it will be called the Way of Holiness. The unclean will not journey on it; it will be for those who walk in that Way; wicked fools will not go about on it.*
>
> Isaiah 35:8 (NIV)

There are four more ways in which scripture tells us to walk on this Highway of Holiness:

1. **Walk in the Spirit**

First, walking in the Spirit is to be filled to the full and overflowing with the Holy Spirit so that we follow the voice of the Holy Spirit, sensitive to His leading. He will always lead in line with the Word of God, never contradicting God's revealed will. Walking in the flesh or according to my fleshly desires is the opposing temptation. That is why I need to "die daily," taking up my cross. Know this; you can never trust your flesh, no matter what your record may be. "This I say then, Walk in the Spirit, and ye shall not fulfil the lust of the flesh. If we live in the Spirit; let us also walk in the Spirit" (Galatians 5:16, 25, KJV).

Ruth may have wanted to stay home, not walk up to a stranger and ask to reap, or stay home and not risk going down to the threshing floor where Boaz would find her. Nevertheless, she courageously and bravely overcame her fleshly fears and walked on in the spirit to fulfill the plans and purposes of God by pursuing His will. God met her in the field and made provision for a family in abundance. Sometimes you may feel like you have been walking around in circles, not going anywhere or getting anywhere. The Israelites ended up walking in circles because of the unbelief they demonstrated in their murmuring and complaining. Giving thanks to God, keeping your praise on, and your eyes up will help to keep you walking in the spirit and on the "way of holiness" that leads to the life and blessedness God promises. Be filled with the Spirit of God:

> *...but be filled with the Spirit, Speaking to yourselves in psalms and hymns and spiritual songs, singing and making melody in your heart to the Lord; Giving thanks always for all things unto God and the Father in the name of our Lord Jesus Christ;*
>
> Ephesians 5:18b-20 (KJV)

How do we walk in the Spirit? Speak and sing to myself and to the Lord, giving thanks always for all things to God. Faith sings, faith speaks, and faith gives thanks. Thank you, Lord!

2. Walk Circumspectly

Secondly, Paul encourages us to walk "circumspectly." "See then that ye walk circumspectly, not as fools, but as wise" (Ephesians 5:15, KJV).

Do you know the song "Tiptoe through the tulips"? It is like this, walking very carefully and precisely, like a cat walking through glass, watching and looking while you walk. Very different from "lollygagging" around, or drifting along, rather, purposefully and wisely placing each step. Ruth purposely walked with Naomi to Bethlehem, then to a field, and finally, to the threshing floor. Her walk was careful, deliberate, and precise and yielded a life God rewards. As the signs say, watch your step. Walk, but keep watch where you step. People are watching where you go. The whole town was watching the path Ruth and Naomi took. God honored them with favor by lifting them out of poverty into prosperity. Invite God to lead you carefully by His spirit on the "Highway of Holiness," that as man sees you, they see a wise woman who honors God whether anyone is watching or not. I doubt Ruth even considered that she was the "talk of the town," but she still just kept on walking out her faith, loyally serving God and Naomi. God sees your walk.

3. Walk Worthy

And thirdly, we are to walk worthy:

> *I therefore, the prisoner of the Lord, beseech you that ye walk worthy of the vocation wherewith ye are called, With all lowliness and meekness, with longsuffering, forbearing one another in love; Endeavouring to keep the unity of the Spirit in the bond of peace.*
>
> Ephesians 4:1-3 (KJV) (emphasis added)

God also calls us to "walk worthy" or walk in a manner worthy, fitting, or deserving of identifying with the Lord. As Ruth walked out her values, she was "known" as a virtuous woman. She cared deeply for her mother-in-law, and in doing so, her reputation was one of great character. She endeavored to maintain her relationship with Naomi, even when Naomi did not want her. Ruth kept the bond of peace with Naomi, walking worthy to be in the lineage of Christ. Peace made a place for the promise. God has a call on your life. How do I know? Because you are reading this. Walk worthy of that call; people are watching and affected by how well you love and forbear, making and following peace with all men. People watched Ruth; Boaz watched her and heard others speak of how well she walked, caring for Naomi. He was pleased to give her his name, his possessions, and his posterity. God fulfilled His promise in a woman of faith who walked worthy and circumspectly.

4. Walk in Love

Finally, scripture admonishes us to "walk in love." "And *walk in love,* as Christ also hath loved us, and hath given himself for us an offering and a sacrifice to God for a sweetsmelling savor [aroma]" (Ephesians 5:2, KJV) (emphasis added) (brackets added for clarity).

The Amplified Bible describes this walk of love as "esteeming and delighting in one another." Notice here that this is a way of life, not a feeling. The more you walk in love, the more you love, the greater the aroma of your life abounds toward God. Paul helps us to understand how strong our thinking must be concerning a "walk of love" when he gives us the example of Christ's offering and sacrifice on the cross. He overcame his emotion to continue in His walk of love. Look at his comment to Peter, "Watch and pray, for the spirit is willing, but the flesh is weak."

Our flesh challenges love, so we pray that we might yield to our spirit and continue to love, esteeming, and delighting in another. When Naomi wanted nothing to do with Ruth, Ruth determined by choice of her will to stay with her, commit to her, and go wherever she went. She esteemed Naomi, which means she valued and looked up to her, even through her own personal rejection, and continued to walk in a "covenant" love. We may experience the same challenges of rejection, fear, uncertainties, etc., but as we take hold of our Lord's hand and walk on the highway of holiness, we will begin to enjoy the blessings of intimacy, which is peace with our God. Ruth blessed the life and name of Naomi forever with her winsome love: "And may he be to you a restorer of life and a nourisher and supporter in your old age, for your daughter-in-law who loves you, who is better to you than seven sons, has borne him" (Ruth 4:15, AMP).

Ruth is extolled as a woman who, walking out the will of God daily, trusting in His holy ways, separated herself from a people to a purpose. Ruth lives on in infamy as a glorious example of how when you have seen and know the Lord, you can lay everything down, including yourself, and take up His blessing. With fears aside and faith fulfilled, she stirs our hearts to believe once again; we can hold His hand and walk boldly into the unknown. He is faithful; if we fall, He holds us up. He takes us to our destiny. Will you put His shoes of peace on today and walk with Him; He wants to take you on the journey of your life. Lay aside the fears and embrace the adventure; if you knew everything, it would spoil the surprise.

So what does this have to do with my marriage, you might ask? Living out the truth, I believe and receive the Lord as my Husband, and as I do, God begins to reveal Himself through my husband. I walk out love and respect towards my husband not because he has earned it, but because God has, and he is my physical representation of God. Walking in the spirit means I am full of the spirit in such a way that I bear the fruit of His presence in me: love, joy, peace, goodness, gentleness, kindness, meekness, temperance, and faith. Maybe you have been tempted to turn back and, like Orpah, go back to the familiar, the comfortable. However, notice, we never hear of her again, not so with Ruth. Or, maybe you have been tempted to get back or get even. Take the example of Naomi, who, even in her despair, walked toward God, facing her loss and receiving His provision. As Ruth stayed focused, yielding to none of the distractions along the way, and as a result, found favor, you, too, can take the risk, walk courageously in love and find the blessing in the adventure. Remember, where you look is where you go; look to God, take His hand, and walk with Him. He is with you, before you, behind you, beside you, and within you; you are never alone. As you continue to progress, walking in the way of holiness, in the light, your path gets brighter and brighter. Keep looking to Jesus; keep your eyes off the "seen" and on the "unseen." That is where God is taking you; trust Him, walk by faith, and enjoy the journey!

Prayer ~

Oh Lord, our Lord, the One and true gracious God, lead us in the way everlasting, the way of holiness. Send Your light to guide us and lead us in the path of truth, Jesus' way. We declare You are our way, our truth, and our life. Strengthen us with the might of Your Spirit that we may walk in the light, in the Spirit, and by faith. Forgive us where we have gone off road and show us the way back to You, keep us on the way of holiness. We now give you complete access and authority to our lives to remove anything that is not of faith or holy.

We commit to laying aside the weights and the sins that hold us back and to running with patience the race that is set before us. Help us to walk on the straight path that we may be healed, following peace with all men. Thank You for loving me enough to discipline me when I get off the straight and narrow path. I love You, Lord, and give You my heart. Thank You that I never walk alone, that You never leave me nor forsake me. In Jesus' name, amen.

I pray: "That ye might walk worthy of the Lord unto all pleasing, being fruitful in every good work, and increasing in the knowledge of God" (Colossians 1:10, KJV).

CHAPTER 8.
MEMORIAL STONE 5
WORK

So, where do we go from here? I am glad you asked. Ruth provided us another good example of our next stone as well. On our journey of walking, we will now set up our fifth stone of remembrance, "*work*." Yes, "work." Before you breathe a big sigh and say all I do is work, let us look at what the work of the Lord and the work of the ministry look like. If we are to look at Jesus, the author and finisher of our faith, we can ask the question, "Did He work?" In addition, if He did, what work did He do and why. We see and experience the work of God every day—the work of His hands in the newborn baby, the sun, the moon, the stars, the trees, the flowers, the birds! I have seen His wondrous work in creating and bringing forth our children, our first grandson, Josiah, and now, his brothers Isaiah and Azariah! How beautiful is the work of God! "I will praise thee; for I am fearfully and wonderfully made: marvelous are thy works; and that my soul knoweth right well" (Psalm 139:14, KJV). "Of old hast thou laid the foundation of the earth: and the heavens are the work of thy hands" (Psalm 102:25, KJV). God's way, His work, is perfect, and even though on God's timetable it is a short work, more importantly, it is a work He is right now endeavoring to finish. "But Jesus answered them, My Father *worketh* hitherto, and I *work*" (John 5:17, KJV) (emphasis added). "Jesus saith unto them, My meat is to do the will of him that sent me, and to *finish his work*" (John 4:34, KJV) (emphasis added).

God is always at work. Jesus came to "work the works" of God and to "finish His work." There is coming a time when no man can work. What is left? Is there a work for us, and if so, what is it? You may say, "All I do is work," and "I don't need any more work." On the other hand, maybe you think God does not need my help; let Him do it. However, trust me, my dear sister, this work of the Lord is not only needed and noticed but also recorded and rewarded! He has already prepared works for us:

> For we are God's [own] handiwork (His workmanship), recreated in Christ Jesus, [born anew] that we may do those good works which God predestined (planned beforehand) for us [taking paths which He prepared ahead of time], that we should walk in them [living the good life which He prearranged and made ready for us to live].
>
> Ephesians 2:10 (AMPC) (emphasis added)

As we continue to wait on God, worship Him, watch for Him, and walk with Him, He will lead us to endeavor and pursue the works He has prepared. God has prepared works specific to you, or deeds, to endeavor, perform, and complete. He created us to perform the works that we might produce fruit. In order to understand the full parameters of what "work" God has called us to and predestined us for, I would ask you to consider the following twelve pillars as the support for these endeavors. Once established, your work will stand the test of time and be for you an eternal reward and an established stone of remembrance.

1. Principle of Work

In discovering the principles that govern God's system of "work," we begin with its definition and its purpose. One of the best motivations for any undertaking is to understand the "why." However, before we can do that, let us look at the "what." These two go hand in hand and constitute the essential elements of God's immutable truths concerning "work." I would ask you to consider first, "what is work." The Scriptures refer to "work" as the "good" work, the "work of God," the "work of faith," and the "work of the Lord." What is "work"? Before you say, "Oh, I've got this," stay with me here and let us look at the full picture God paints.

The Bible uses several different definitions for the word "work." Whether we are using it as a noun or a verb, the idea is consistent: an act or a deed; labor; toil; producing an effect; ministry, or to bring about something, an accomplishment. The difference is not how we understand this but how God wants us to understand. If I am called to "work" producing, ministering, and accomplishing, then the One calling me and preparing the work has the right and the responsibility of how and what is the resulting product, ministry, or accomplishment. In essence, "work" is the outcome or effect the believer's life brings to bear on a given situation or person, whether good or bad. This outcome, referred to as "bearing fruit" or "producing," when good, glorifies God. "When you bear (produce) much fruit, My Father is honored and glorified, and you show and prove yourselves to be true followers of Mine" (John 15:8, AMPC).

In this, we show or reveal ourselves as true followers of His. A good root will produce good fruit. As such, this producing is not only part of everything we do, but also of whose we are, a "Christ-one." When we are rooted in the love of God, our lives are continuously productive. I hope to show you this. We understand living a productive life honors and glorifies God. In other words, by working, we accurately reflect God to the world around us. Because God is always at work, as we have stated, in order to reflect Him, we must work as He does. In working, we partake or participate in His divine nature and in turn, manifest or reveal God to an observing world. God is the Creator. He calls us to participate in His creativity by creating.

When we work, we create an effect, accomplishing or bringing something about. We can create by different means physically, mentally, or spiritually. Physically, with our body, commonly we think in terms of our fingers, hands, or arms, in other words, our strength, we can do and make. Scripture admonishes us in: "Let him that stole steal no more: but rather let him labour, working with his hands the thing which is good, that he may have to *give* to him that needeth" (Ephesians 4:28, KJV) (emphasis added).

Interesting here, though, we read the purpose is not as the world says, "I owe, I owe, so off to work I go." No! Rather, we work for a "giving," not a "living." When we begin to take on the purposes of God, our attitude toward our work will adjust. Think about that, "I work to give."

He already knows what needs we have and is fully prepared to meet those needs when we work for Him to be a blessing to others. When it is not about us gathering as much as we can but giving as much as we can, God accomplishes His work in us. If God can get it "through" you, He will get it "to" you.

However, speaking too, using our mouth produces fruit, either good or evil. We are created in the image of God. God's words work and create. "Through faith we understand that the worlds were framed by the word of God, so that things which are seen were not made of things which do appear" (Hebrews 11:3, KJV).

My mentor Vicki Kendrick once told me, "The miracle is in the Word He gave you, work the miracle!" Our mouths create more than we could ever realize. We are living today what we spoke yesterday. Jesus did likewise as we read: "Believest thou not that I am in the Father, and the Father in me? The *words* that I speak unto you I speak not of myself: but the Father that dwelleth in me, he doeth the *works*" (John 14:10, KJV) (emphasis added).

Jesus likened His words with the works of God. Jesus gave God something to do! Jesus spoke the words of God, which, in turn, brought God on the scene inviting Him to perform. Translated from the same Greek word "logos," the two words "words" and "works" join in accomplishing God's will. God's work is accomplishing His Word. God's Word works. His words are spirit and life; there is power in the Word of God. Do you see, the very words of Christ brought manifestation of the works of God? Words are works, so work the Word. The words out of your mouth work. "So will the words that come out of my mouth not come back empty-handed. They will do the work I sent them to do; they will complete the assignment I gave them" (Isaiah 55:11, MSG).

When we speak the Word of God, His promises, they immediately begin working and accomplishing the will of God! God is perpetually actively listening for His word to perform or bring it to pass. What He spoke in His word through the prophets is working today. What are you speaking? Look around and see the harvest of your words. If you like what you see, keep saying what you are saying; if not, find out what God's Word says, sow that seed in your heart, and begin to nourish that seed with your words and works of faith. "Then said the Lord to me, You have seen well, for I am alert and active, watching over My word to perform it" (Jeremiah 1:12, AMPC). Speaking God's Word is productive and effective, bringing about the will of God. Your words are as effective in accomplishing a matter as your hands or your mind. You have been creating with your words either good fruit that yields a good life or bad fruit that yields a bad life.

What you have said is either working to glorify God or not. The Bible makes it clear that we will eat what we say. You know the saying, "You'll eat your words?" Well, that is a biblical principle. In other words, my mouth produces a harvest of fruit, and it will taste either good or bad; it is up to me. Look at a few verses to see the power working in your words: "You are snared with the words of your lips, you are caught by the speech of your mouth" (Proverbs 6:2, AMPC).

> *A good man eats good from the fruit of his mouth, but the desire of the treacherous is for violence. He who guards his mouth keeps his life, but he who opens wide his lips comes to ruin.*
>
> Proverbs 13:2-3 (AMPC)

> *A man's belly shall be satisfied with the fruit of his mouth; and with the increase of his lips shall he be filled. Death and life are in the power of the tongue: and they that love it shall eat the fruit thereof.*
>
> Proverbs 18:20-21 (KJV)

In other words, when we indulge or engage our tongue, we will eat the fruit of what we have said. It will come back to us. Your words fill you. Are you satisfied? Do you like what you have been "eating"? Your words are working, and what you and I say is coming back to us. What you are living today is, for the most part, what you said yesterday. We like to blame God or our spouse, or our parents, or even the devil, saying, "The devil made me do it." What God is all the while saying, this is on you; you are living and eating your own words. The charge here is to keep silent until you know how to speak life and blessing and then yield, agreeing with God and His Word through confession and declaration. That's why David prayed: "Set a guard, O Lord, before my mouth; keep watch at the door of my lips" (Psalm 141:3, AMPC).

David understood the power of his words, and so it seems did his son, Solomon, who penned the previous verses in Proverbs. May we speak words of life, words that produce a harvest of good, tasty fruit that will satisfy not only ourselves but others as well, and fruit that in turn glorifies God. What better word to start with than "the Lord is My Husband?" This is God's word, and He watches over it to perform it. If I eat my words, then this would bring such a bountiful harvest I would never be hungry again, or for anything (or anybody) else.

I hope this expands your understanding of how much broader a scope "work," God's work, entails. However, this is just in the physical realm; the mental and spiritual realms also play a role in providing a source for "work." Mentally, with our minds, we can imagine, envision, process, record, and then fulfill that vision. In addition, spiritually, in our spirit, we can produce fruit through the spiritual sacrifices of various prayers, meditations, praises, thanksgiving, and supplications. Even the seeds you sow in tears praying can produce a harvest that God promises you will joyfully bring with you! "Those who sow in tears shall reap with joyful shouting" (Psalm 126:5, NASB).

When we "work" spiritually, we do the Lord's work in ministering to the spirits of humanity. Again, as in physically working to give, so too spiritually we work to give. If you have made Jesus your Lord, God entrusts you with His work in sowing the incorruptible seed of Jesus in your heart, and from that seed, He expects a harvest. God is a giver, and giving glorifies God. When we give, we glorify Him. What do you have to give? If you have no other reason to work, work so you have something to give to others and to God. Minister love, give hope, sow peace and righteousness; you will produce and reap an abundant harvest if you faint not! Work as unto the Lord will bring fulfillment not just in the physical realm but in the spiritual as well. God's kingdom advances in our life now and eternally. Start at home, sow into your family as unto the Lord. We will see how being sanctified wholly: spirit, soul, and body come together to make complete the work of God in us and through us.

Therefore, "work" is energy applied or exerted physically, mentally, or spiritually in accordance with the directives of the Spirit of the Lord and His word in order to produce or bear fruit. Ultimately, this "work" accomplishes the purposes of glorifying God and revealing the believer as His. This is the fundamental principle, and yet, obtaining the desired result requires additional values clarification according to God's perspective on "work."

2. Priority of Work

Once we understand the purpose, we can more clearly see the priority. The priority of work is where on your list of importance or urgency this exists. Yes, God prepared works for us; He called us to work and to glorify Him with our work in bearing fruit. Yet, you will notice this is not at the beginning of this book. God is a God of order, not confusion. He is not trying to trick us. However, He does want us to understand the truth in light of eternity with Him. With an eternal perspective, let's look at what Jesus told the disciples in:

> *Therefore I say unto you, Take no thought for your life, what ye shall eat, or what ye shall drink; nor yet for your body, what ye shall put on. Is not the life more than*

meat, and the body than raiment? Behold the fowls of the air: for they sow not, neither do they reap, nor gather into barns; yet your heavenly Father feedeth them. Are ye not much better than they? Therefore take no thought, saying, What shall we eat? or, What shall we drink? or, Wherewithal shall we be clothed? (For after all these things do the Gentiles seek:) for your heavenly Father knoweth that ye have need of all these things. But seek ye first the kingdom of God, and his righteousness; and all these things shall be added unto you.

Matthew 6:25, 26, 31-33 (KJV) (emphasis added)

Our purpose protects our priority, and our purpose will reflect in our priorities. If I am working to give and to glorify God, then I will not be distracted by self-serving. This is evident. I will trust God for my provision, as I desire the kingdom and seek it first. If I am to "seek first the kingdom of God," I need to know what that is. Seeking the kingdom is pursuing this: "For the kingdom of God is not meat and drink; but *righteousness*, and *peace*, and *joy* in the Holy Ghost" (Romans 14:17, KJV) (emphasis added).

Jesus says to seek first or pursue as our highest priority, the kingdom of God. Paul defines God's kingdom as *righteousness, peace, and joy in the Holy Ghost.* First, even though "I am the righteousness of God in Christ Jesus," there is a righteousness I am to pursue, right standing with God, living God's way through faith, believing God every minute of every day. Once I am born again and given positional righteousness in Christ, clothed in His wedding garment, I then work out or pursue practical righteousness through walking by faith like Abraham: "For what saith the scripture? Abraham believed God, and it was counted unto him for righteousness" (Romans 4:3, KJV).

Believing God at all times and in all things is the challenge and the call. The temptation to doubt looms; I must be prepared and proactive in seeking to believe God first. It took Abraham twenty-five years to get it right; may we learn that believing God is the priority. That means I trust His word first, and over any other word, I walk and keep walking as though His word is true. Learning to believe God is not instantaneous, as is birth. There is the practical pursuit of believing God in every situation for all my needs as I learn to trust His Word. To pursue righteousness, then, is simply to believe God.

Then, I seek and pursue "peace," that place of quiet confidence that comes from a complete trust in God, a place of rest and undisturbed composure where nothing is lacking, everything is in its place, in the hands of God:

> *Be careful for nothing; but in everything by prayer and supplication with thanksgiving let your requests be made known unto God. And the peace of God, which passeth all understanding, shall keep your hearts and minds through Christ Jesus.*
>
> Philippians 4:6-7 (KJV) (emphasis added)

"For we which have *believed* do enter into *rest*" (Hebrews 4:3, KJV) (emphasis added). "Let us labour therefore to enter into that *rest*, lest any man fall after the same example of *unbelief*" (Hebrews 4:11, KJV) (emphasis added).

Lack of peace helps identify when we are not trusting or believing God and His word. If I am to "labor" or "pursue" peace, then I must endeavor to release all concerns and worries to God in prayer and receive the hope and assurance from His word that gives peace. Peace manifests as strength found in a quiet and confident expectation of God. Peace is a place of rest where nothing moves you; you can be still, quiet, and confident in the face of the unknown or the ugly. Belief yields rest; righteousness precedes peace. As I receive God's truth believing, I can take life's challenges to Him in faith, and there, there alone, do I receive peace. My "work," therefore, is to believe God at all cost and receive my rest, lest I fall into unbelief and miss my Promised Land of rest.

Then finally, I seek and pursue "joy" in the Holy Ghost, joy unspeakable and full of glory! "Thou wilt shew me the path of life: in thy presence is *fullness of joy;* at thy right hand there are pleasures for evermore" (Psalm 16:11, KJV) (emphasis added). "Whom having not seen, ye love; in whom, though now ye see him not, yet *believing,* ye *rejoice with joy unspeakable and full of glory*" (1 Peter 1:8, KJV) (emphasis added). "And these things write we unto you, that your *joy may be full*" (1 John 1:4, KJV) (emphasis added).

God wants to bring us to a place of fulfillment that manifests in an abundance of joy. Peace makes a place for fullness of a joy unspeakable. I can only imagine what that might sound like, but God knows! To seek the kingdom of God is to seek righteousness, believing God; peace, resting in God; and finally, joy, enjoying God. Believing, resting, and enjoying, sounds like an abundant life! Seek first to believe God, rest in His Word, and enjoy His love, His blessings, His mercy, and grace. The world seeks these things: gods, rest, enjoyment, but to no avail. They look around for fulfillment in the kingdom of this world, but we look up to God and inward to Jesus, the kingdom of our God. "My voice shalt thou hear in the morning, O Lord; in the morning will I direct my prayer unto thee, and will look up" (Psalm 5:3, KJV).

Our priority is to seek first righteousness, peace, and joy, a living faith that believes God, rests in God, and delights in God. Do you believe? Then you are resting, and if you are resting, then you will have a calm delight, a lightness, and cheerfulness that can rejoice. Pursue them first. Put that on your vision board, believing, resting, and enjoying God! Are you confident all is right between you and God? Are you at peace? Do you have the joy of the Lord? Stop all other endeavors until you can answer a resounding "yes!" Just simply start the day with Him.

Challenge your purpose by discovering your priority. Do you have a clear vision of your purpose? If not, now is a great time to clarify that and to commit to seeking God's priority, pursuing the kingdom of God, His righteousness, peace, and joy. Know that through this, sowing the seeds of His kingdom, you can fulfill your purpose, glorify God, and bear much fruit. Why are you working? Is it for you or for God and others? If it is for God and others, you will stay at that hard job when you do not want to until God releases you. If it is for God and others, you will work when you have plenty, so you have more to give. If, however, I am working to amass a great fortune or, on the other hand, just to get by, I will miss the blessing of the harvest from sowing seeds of the kingdom of God. If glorifying God is my purpose, then believing, resting, and enjoying Him will be my priority. With my purpose settled and my priority right, God can cause me to be productive in every good work, bearing much fruit.

Can you imagine the powerful impact of a believing, restful, joyful spirit flowing through you into your spouse, your children, your family, and friends? God says this is our highest priority; it will yield the most fruit in our lives. A woman at rest exudes an air of calm confidence that is very attractive not because she is lazy but because she is led by the Spirit. You draw people to you as you practice believing, which rides on hope, resting, which is Spirit-led activity, and enjoying, which is thanking God. A hopeful, restful, thankful Christian spreads life and attracts hungry hurting people, just like Jesus. Start with this word, "The Lord is my Husband." Believe that, rest in it and rejoice in it. That takes all the pressure and anxiety off man; now you can enjoy people because your expectation is on God. The count is over; let him up off the mat. Quit trying to nail him down on everything, believe, rest, and enjoy God. "Now the God of hope fill you with *all joy and peace in believing,* that ye may abound in hope, through the power of the Holy Ghost" (Romans 15:13, KJV) (emphasis added).

Now for the third Pillar of Work, preparation.

3. Preparation for Work

Now that you have settled the purpose and priority of your life, it is time for preparation. It is time to "make ready" or "get fit" for kingdom purposes, for every good work. "If a man therefore purge himself from these, he shall be a vessel unto honour, sanctified, and meet for the master's use, and prepared unto every good work" (2 Timothy 2:21, KJV).

Preparation begins with purging. Purging is the picture of emptying, as in detoxing or cleansing from impurities or toxins. We have toxins that must go in order to do the "good work."

> But in a great house there are not only vessels of gold and silver, but also [utensils] of wood and earthenware, and some for honorable and noble [use] and some for menial and ignoble [use]. So whoever cleanses himself [from what is ignoble and unclean, who separates himself from contact with contaminating and corrupting influences] will [then himself] be a vessel set apart and useful for honorable and

noble purposes, consecrated and profitable to the Master,
fit and ready (prepared—KJV) for any good work.

2 Timothy 2:20-21 (AMPC)
(emphasis added) (parentheses added for clarity)

This passage describes a home with different containers, some used in an elegant, lovely dining room like crystal, china, and silver, and those used to take out the trash. They are all desired and have purpose in a well-appointed home, but God is charging us to be the "vessel" or "container" that is used for the nobler purpose that can be used to present blessings to any of God's guests. Think how we treat these items; our silver often comes in a beautiful, velvet-lined wooden case. Special storage protects them from the scratches of everyday utensils, the tarnish from exposure to air and moisture, and separates them for special use. The same with our china and crystal, we store or house them in cabinets specially designed with mirrors, glass, and lights to display and admire their beauty. I am not saying to wrap yourself in velvet and hide out in a cabinet. No, rather, the point is to separate yourself from the things of this world, the lust of the eyes, the lust of the flesh, and the pride of life that tempt us and draw us away into an earthly lifestyle. Jesus said we are "in the world not of it," and He prayed not that God would take us out of the world but that the Lord would keep us from the evil. As God sent Jesus into the world, He now sends us.

When I expose myself to contaminating and corrupting influences, I limit my desire and preparedness to minister. Have you ever just felt like you were not in a place to pray for someone? To be prepared for any opportunity, Paul is telling Timothy here the answer is to separate from those influences that contaminate your faith. Think of things in which we might expose ourselves that corrupt our spirit. Things such as people, places, the internet, games, television, movies, music, literature, and the list could go on.

Interesting, though, supernatural wisdom that gives perspective and discernment is required here to make the tough choices. Then, once you make the choice, endure the persecution that comes when we separate ourselves, not concerned what men may say. Think of the seed you have sown in the garden of your heart. The contaminating influences are like "weeds," they choke out the life of faith and take the nourishment needed for the seed. "Weeds" like unforgiveness, bitterness, rebellion, and disobedience must be removed or released from our hearts and replaced with the nourishment of love, peace, and joy. How can we do the "good work" of God as a "noble vessel" if we are filled with the contamination of unforgiveness? God is calling for His people to be "cleansed, set apart, useful, consecrated, fit, ready, and prepared." Paul tells Timothy to separate and cleanse himself, to purge himself from uncleanness and corrupting influences. Why is this? He wants fruit; He wants us to be productive, to accomplish what He calls us to do, a vessel prepared for the filling of the "holy." Now is the time to separate and set yourself apart, to consecrate for preparation. Paul encourages us in: "And your feet shod with the *preparation* of the gospel of peace" (Ephesians 6:15 KJV) (emphasis added).

God desires a people ready for the work of the Lord, prepared to share and to show the gospel of Jesus Christ, that is, forgiveness and love that brings peace, reconciliation with God.

> But all things are from God, Who through Jesus Christ reconciled us to Himself [received us into favor, brought us into harmony with Himself] and gave to us the ministry of reconciliation [that by word and deed we might aim to bring others into harmony with Him].
>
> 2 Corinthians 5:18 (AMPC)

That by "word," everything we say, and "deed," everything we do, we are endeavoring or working to bring others into relationship with Jesus Christ. The relationships in your life have supernatural significance. God calls you as a minister to your spouse, your children, and others as a minister of reconciliation. The work God has for us accomplishes a divine mission. How do we prepare? If I am to be separate, cleansed, and purged in order to be a "vessel unto honor," where do I start? Through looking into, learning, receiving, and doing the Word, we prepare. The Word of God is the plumb line.

> *Every Scripture is God-breathed (given by His inspiration) and profitable for instruction, for reproof and conviction of sin, for correction of error and discipline in obedience, [and] for training in righteousness (in holy living, in conformity to God's will in thought, purpose, and action), So that the man of God may be complete and proficient, well fitted and thoroughly equipped for every good work.*
>
> 2 Timothy 3:16-17 (AMPC) (emphasis added)

Bring every thought into captivity to the Lord Jesus Christ and allow every deed to be directed by His Holy Spirit. For us to know His will and His ways, we must know Him. His Word is the revelation of Himself through Jesus. If we allow Him to, the Lord will wash us with His Word.

> *That he might sanctify and cleanse it with the washing of water by the word, That he might present it to himself a glorious church, not having spot, or wrinkle, or any such thing; but that it should be holy and without blemish.*
>
> Ephesians 5:26-27 (KJV)

The Word of God washes and cleanses the impurities of our flesh, the world, and the devil from our mind, will, and emotions. Then we are prepared to receive and understand His thoughts, His purposes, and His plans. With His thoughts, I can then discern and determine what pleases Him and builds my relationship with Him and what grieves or saddens and pollutes my relationship. As we choose this separated life, we are prepared to produce! We will then produce fruit that remains. We will be a blessing, reconciling people to God. Our fruit will not burn up but will be fruit that endures God's judgment, fruit that receives a crown!

Recorded for us in the book of Esther is a beautiful and powerful story of preparation for a divine work. Let us learn to prepare by the example of how preparation set up one young girl for her destiny.

Written, most likely, by a Jew named Mordecai, we have a story of the culmination of hatred toward the Jews and the providence of God in keeping His covenant with His people. Still celebrated today by the Jewish people, the two-day Feast of Purim lives on as the story of victory through the power of God's intervention. This book, called the "Megillah," is read and passionately acted out in its entirety during the Feast, as a memorial and celebration of God's deliverance, as well as of the vessels He used for "honor and dishonor" and for "noble and ignoble" purposes.

The saga starts with a very wealthy king, King Ahasuerus, also known as King Xerxes. Ahasuerus is his title, meaning "venerable king," and Xerxes the Great of Persia was his name. He reigned over a great kingdom from Ethiopia to India, including one hundred twenty-seven provinces. In the third year of his reign, the King was having a great feast for all the nobles, princes, and servants from all the provinces for one hundred eighty days. Then he began a feast in the palace showing all his wealth and majesty, drinking wine and eating. The queen, Vashti, was also having a feast for all the women in the royal house of the king.

On the seventh day, the king commanded the chamberlains to bring Queen Vashti before him and his guests to show her beauty. However, the queen refused to come. The king was angry. The royal princes advised the king that this was wrong, not only to the king but also to all the people in all the provinces. Then Memucan stood and recommended removing Queen Vashti and replacing her with another better than her, lest all the women hear of her contempt and act similarly. Therefore, the king agreed and forbade Vashti from ever coming before him again. The decree went out that every man should bear rule in his own house; that wives were to give honor to their husbands.

This seems an unusual beginning to a story of God's providence to His people. Enter a pagan king and his wife having feasts and banquets, drinking and carrying on. Meanwhile, the Jewish people, after freedom from their Babylonian captivity, dispersed and remained among these provinces, called the Diaspora, under the rule of King Xerxes. Instead of going back to their homeland of Israel, they integrated with the people so much that they were not distinct, not separated. Imagine how God felt, His own special people not even recognizable as a nation.

After a time, however, the king regrettably remembered his queen, and in an effort to please him, the servants suggested fair young virgins be brought to the palace from all the provinces to be prepared to bring in to him. The one that pleased him should take Vashti's place as queen.

Families brought many young, beautiful virgins to the palace, where servants gave them beauty treatments for a year. Mordecai, a Jew, brought up his lovely adopted daughter to the king's palace. Her name was Hadassah, meaning "star" in Hebrew, but he named her "Esther" to hide her Jewish nationality. Both her parents had died, and Mordecai, her cousin, raised her as his own daughter. She gained favor in the house of women and, as a result, received seven maidens as well as the best rooms. After her time of preparation, which lasted over a year, she went in to the king. Imagine a whole year of spas, massages, oils, perfumes, and fine food! Now that is some preparation. (I might mention that my husband complains about two hours at the hairdressers.) In addition, to think she was already young and beautiful, and it still took a year! The king was pleased, and she found favor with him, so he put the royal crown on her and made her queen. In honor of the new Queen Esther, the king held a feast, gave gifts, and even suspended taxes for a whole year! It seems the king was very pleased. Imagine a Jewish queen over a very Gentile, heathen nation. God is working.

While she was in the palace, her cousin/father Mordecai worked at the king's gate. Because Mordecai would not bow according to a decree as the king's right-hand man, Haman, walked by, animosity arose between them. Haman, a descendant of Agag from the Amalekites, was a long-time enemy of the Jews. Had King Saul fulfilled his orders, Haman likely would not have even existed. God was angry with them for committing violence on the weaker ones when they were in the wilderness and told King Saul to destroy them. In His disobedience, God removed him from the throne and replaced him with a young shepherd boy named David.

Likely, Haman and Mordecai were aware of this history. Discovering Mordecai's nationality, Haman is even more enraged, realizing that all the Jews may likely follow suit by disobeying the king's command to bow at Haman's presence. Meanwhile, Mordecai overhears of a plot to kill the king and tells Queen Esther, who tells the king, who, then, in turn, investigates and finds it to be true. The King ordered the culprits hung, and the matter recorded in the chronicles of the king how Mordecai saved the king.

Haman, however, has had enough. He plots to kill Mordecai and his people by slyly manipulating the king to issue a decree to "destroy, kill, and cause to perish" all peoples in all the provinces who will not obey the king's commands, specifically the Jews, young and old, women and children, and to spoil their goods. The king gives Haman his ring, his signature or stamp of approval, and sends the decrees across the land. Haman secures free course to do as he pleases. Fear then strikes the land, but in the palace, Haman and the king drink with delight, most likely to their supposed superior wisdom and rulership.

This decree, like the one of putting out Queen Vashti, is irrevocable, unalterable. Imagine the news of this decree spreading throughout the land. Weeping, wailing, and fasting in sackcloth and ashes became the order of the day. Mordecai would not allow his public weeping silenced, even though Queen Esther sent a change of clothes to hide his "burial" clothes of sackcloth. Ignorant of this decree, though, she would soon find out all the enemy had planned.

Mordecai sent word to Esther, giving her a copy of the decree, encouraging her not to think that even though now safe in the palace, she would be saved, but that she needed to go ask for the king's mercy. She was fearful of what might happen, though, since the king had not summoned her in thirty days. In addition, she knew that anyone going in uncalled for faced the possibility of death unless the king extended the golden scepter. But Mordecai's challenge was powerful:

For if you keep silent at this time, relief and deliverance shall arise for the Jews from elsewhere, but you and your father's house will perish. And who knows but that you have come to the kingdom for such a time as this and for this very occasion? Then Esther told them to give this answer to Mordecai, Go, gather together all the Jews that are present in Shushan, and fast for me; and neither eat nor drink for three days, night or day. I also and my maids will fast as you do. Then I will go to the king, though it is against the law; and if I perish, I perish. So Mordecai went away and did all that Esther had commanded him.

Esther 4:14-17 (AMPC)

Convinced by Mordecai's words, she, her maidens, and all the Jews now set themselves apart, consecrating themselves for the plan of God. Notice how this preparation comes before they have a plan. Why is it we get in such a hurry to concoct a plan? Before this fast, Esther is fearful of the king and embarrassed for Mordecai. Now she and her people would set themselves to seek the Lord through calling a time of consecration and separation.

With the fast over, the time is now come. She has a plan and starts it rolling. She prepares herself in all her royal robes to go before her husband, the king. Will he extend the golden scepter to her? The time to find out has come. She approaches the court. From the throne room, the king sees her, and she immediately finds favor in his eyes so that he extends the golden scepter to her. Relieved yet purposeful, she approaches and touches the tip of the scepter. He asks, "What will you have?" He then offers her, "Up to half the kingdom."

Esther was up to something. Prior to this meeting, she had prepared a banquet. She did not have a plan prior to the fast, but now she invites the king to bring Haman and come and join her at the banquet. Imagine the beauty of this setting; she serves all the best food on the best china, crystal, and silver. During the wine course, the king once again asks her what this is about and what she wants. To which she then invites them both again to another banquet the next day, at which time she will give him her request. What an interesting delay tactic! What patience, considering her and her people are facing extinction, no panic, and no desperation! Her fear has turned to faith, as she trusts God's leading; she is a vessel of honor, purged and prepared for "such a time as this."

Think about this for a moment. She did not run in his office or call him running on about the problem. No! Quietly, calmly, she prepared his meal and then presented herself. The phrase "the way to a man's heart is through his stomach" comes to mind, yet first, she dressed to the "nines" and presented herself in all due reverence and respect. She cleaned up, fixed up, and dressed up in her royal robes, identifying with her husband as she willingly and bravely presents herself as his Queen. The exact opposite of Queen Vashti, who would not even come when called upon. Sometimes we despise the very beauty that attracted our husbands. We may even be prone to anger as to why we should go "out of our way" to fix up for them, much less why they should need or want to look at us. Then we wonder why they get angry. You may have taken on the attitude "he should love me like I am." Loving him means giving him your best, not your leftovers.

This may not be a gospel message, yet we can still receive a message on the power we have as women to minister to our husbands and bring the best out of them. Esther ministered first to her husband and his basic needs of pride in his wife, respect, and hunger. Think about how this may look in your relationship; the first step may be making the most of yourself when in public with your spouse. This starts with an honest look in the mirror. Maybe it is time for a new hairdo, a gym membership, a spa treatment, or some new clothes. How you feel about yourself affects the confidence you exude. We are not talking about perfection here; beauty is in the eye of the beholder. What we are talking about, though, is being the best you can be because he is looking. Men "do" look on the outside, and before you get mad about that, God made them that way!

Take some time to evaluate, take inventory of yourself, even open up and be vulnerable without getting mad, and ask him. Maybe you already know what he likes, and you have not been willing to please him. Why not go all out for him and show him you really do care what he thinks by endeavoring to adjust to his wishes. The very thing you have been wanting from him may come flooding in on the heels of your efforts. Yes, it takes courage and bravery, set your own ideas aside, and put on your royal robes for your king. It will be worth it!

Back to our story, curiosity and imagination have time to build in both the king and Haman. Haman is elated, feeling very privileged to be the only guest invited by Queen Esther to this special banquet with the king. His mind fills quickly with exalted thoughts of himself until, just as quickly, the thought of Mordecai at the gate not paying him honor steals all his jubilation. To comfort him in his pity party or just to shut him up, his wife, Zeresh, suggests he make gallows on which to hang Mordecai. Great idea! All night long, Haman's men built gallows fifty cubits high right in his front yard. He plans to ask permission from the king to hang Mordecai the very first thing in the morning. All is well, or so it seems.

In the palace, however, the king is not so restful. In order to pass the time, he calls for the chronicles of his reign read to him. While reading, they come across the story of how Mordecai revealed the plot to have him killed. The king then asks if they did anything to show gratitude and honor for this deed of loyalty, only to find out that they did nothing for him. No promotion, no raise, no distinction, nothing was done to show gratitude to Mordecai for saving the king's life! About that time, early that morning, in comes Haman. However, before Haman could ask for Mordecai's life, the king asks Haman what we could do for the man the king "delights to honor." Thinking that the king would not delight to honor anyone more than himself, he suggests giving that man the royal robes, the royal crown to wear, and the royal horse to ride while a royal prince proclaims before him while parading him in the square. The King likes it, "Thus it shall be done to the one in whom the king delights to honor." Tall order, he now tells Haman to do it all for Mordecai! What a coincidence, or not!

The mighty, providential hand of God has intervened and come to exalt the humble servant who not just a few days before was in sackcloth and ashes in this very square, refusing the temporary comfort sent by Esther to hide his weeping and mourning over the decree of death for his people. God was silent but present. The preparation has made a place for the omnipotence of God. No man could have orchestrated what God, in His perfect timing, has brought to a crescendo! Imagine Haman's embarrassment before his family and all those who worked on the gallows, even the whole city.

The Scripture "pride goes before a fall" comes to mind. I imagine they all knew by now whom Haman had the huge gallows built for the night before. Humbled, he runs home with his head covered, greeted by his wife, who now tells him he will "not prevail against Mordecai if he is a Jew in whose eyes you have begun to fall." Great, thanks, now you tell me!

Suddenly, the king's horses come to take him to the palace for the queen's banquet. At the end of the meal, the king once again asks Queen Esther, "What is your request?" The time is right; the "pump is primed." She answers with skill and boldness, asking for her life and the life of her people. The king asks, "Who did this? Where is he? Who would dare presume in his heart such a thing?" (Unfortunately, he did, but she wisely knows better than to point the finger at the king.) The true source of the motivation for the decree was sitting across the table from them both, and she points him out, "That evil and wicked Haman!" The timing is perfect! The king rises in rage to go out of the room while Haman, struck with fear, seeks forgiveness from the queen and, overstepping his politically correct boundaries, falls on the couch where she is reclined. As fortune would have it, the king returns at that moment and accuses Haman of forcibly assaulting his queen. What outrage! Quickly the attendants cover Haman's head and inform the king of his evil plot to hang Mordecai on gallows built in his own front yard. The king commands, "Hang him there instead!"

With Haman gone, what becomes of the decree? The king goes on to give the estate of Haman to Queen Esther. In addition, after she reveals her relationship with Mordecai, the king gives the signet ring he had taken from Haman to Mordecai. Then Esther puts Mordecai over Haman's estate. Nevertheless, even after this goodness, Esther begs the king to avert the decree against her people, asking, "How can I live knowing they are sentenced to death?" Because the law forbids reversing this decree, the king tells them that they may write a new royal decree, as they please, in his name and seal it with his ring. Sent throughout all the land, the new decree allowed the Jews to gather and defend themselves and their families against any attack and take whatever spoils they find. Wow, what a complete turnaround; they could now fight and defend themselves! The Jews rejoiced! God has taken what the enemy meant for evil and turned it into a way to bless His people. Only God could do this! They could have never dreamed of a plan like this...but God!

Mordecai's faith challenged the fearful young Esther to rise to the occasion, but first, they had fallen on their knees and done battle in prayer. The cleansing and purging of fasting and prayer strengthened and purified them from fear to faith. Esther, who was not willing to approach her own husband, the king, was not only able to enter his presence boldly but also willing to confront her archenemy face to face and hold her tongue until the moment was right! That might even be more of a miracle!

What a beautiful story of the power of preparation. Prepared as a young girl with the graces to charm her way through the competition to win the King's side, and then through the encouragement of her stepfather, Mordecai, prepared to fight for the salvation of her people. How different this story would be if they had not taken the time to wait on the Lord, to see how He would lead them. Three days of fasting and praying paved the way for the power of God to lead them in confidence, taking back what the enemy was endeavoring to steal, kill, and destroy.

The fruit of this work stands forever in time as the nation of Israel lives on. They defeated those that hated them and gained favor with all the king's men. Preparation in prayer and fasting, yielding patience and wisdom, brought about a complete work, not only saving God's people, defeating the enemy, and spoiling their goods, but also adding to their nation. You see, the fear of the Jews fell on many of the people so that they became Jews! God even added to His own family. Now there is the work of the Lord, producing much fruit.

That is what He wants for us if we will slow down long enough to seek Him and receive His plan. The world has it backwards, saying to plan first, then prepare. I believe this shows us clearly to prepare ourselves first by seeking the Lord, and then we can receive God's plan. His ways and His thoughts are higher than ours are. We cannot even imagine what God has in store for His people. Why settle for our plan?

The Jews had rest from all their enemies; their sorrow turned to gladness, their mourning into celebration. Now by the decree of Queen Esther, they could celebrate Purim. Annually, they would fast one day and celebrate two days in remembrance of their deliverance with feasting, sharing food, and giving to the poor. Mordecai, highly favored and loved by all the people, advanced from the gatekeeper to second in command to the king. Read each year in its entirety during the Purim celebration; the "Whole Megillah" remains as a powerful testimony to the impact of one young little orphaned girl and her stepfather willing to risk everything and prepare as "vessels unto honor" by the power of God.

What a turnaround! From weeping in the town square with a death decree over his head to governing in the king's palace wearing the king's ring. Taking a young girl to the King's side for the salvation of His people, something only God could do. Oh, my dear sister, is there anything too hard for the Lord? Your situation and relationships may not include gallows (although you may wish they did) or the future of a nation, and yet still seems as insurmountable. But God, without even a word, ordained and moved on the heart of this woman to trust Him and courageously yield to His plan. In like manner, He is moving on your heart now. Will you trust Him and believe? Nothing is too hard for the Lord!

He can turn it around. The place to start is on our face. You may have to fast. This is a very powerful spiritual discipline. Fasting is depriving the body of nourishment or abstaining from food. Literally, it means to "cover your mouth" and to afflict yourself. There are many other instances in the Bible about fasting, David, Daniel, Elisha, Jesus, the disciples, Paul, and others. Upon learning of the deplorable state of the wall of Jerusalem, Nehemiah fasted and prayed, asking God for mercy and favor with the king. Then he went to work repairing the wall.

There are different kinds of fasts. The Esther fast was a complete three-day fast, not even water. There is the Daniel fast as recorded in Daniel 10:3, that is no meat or sweets, and mostly fresh fruits, vegetables, and beans for twenty-one days. God gives specific promises to fasting, not given to anything else. In Isaiah, we find a powerful passage on fasting.

> *[Rather] is not this the fast that I have chosen: to loose the bonds of wickedness, to undo the bands of the yoke, to let the oppressed go free, and that you break every [enslaving] yoke?*

Isaiah 58:6 (AMPC)

The supernatural power of God is at work in us and in others, breaking bondages (even addictions) and setting captives free. According to this passage, the fast by Esther and her people wrought the work of God first in the supernatural realm by removing the oppression and breaking the decree of destruction off the Jewish people. Fasting accomplishes works of the Lord we may never even imagine. Maybe your spouse is blind as King Xerxes was to the outcome of his actions, and maybe you tried to no avail to help him see. God may be calling you right now to a fast. God can do more with a surrendered soul He can flow through than a team of mules dragging your husband. But look, God continues to give additional promises if during our fast we do this:

> *Is it not to divide your bread with the hungry and bring the homeless poor into your house—when you see the naked, that you cover him, and that you hide not yourself from [the needs of] your own flesh and blood? Then shall your light break forth like the morning, and your healing (your restoration and the power of a new life) shall spring forth speedily; your righteousness (your rightness, your justice, and your right relationship with God) shall go before you [conducting you to peace and prosperity], and the glory of the Lord shall be your rear guard. Then you shall call, and the Lord will answer; you shall cry, and He will say, Here I am. If you take away from your midst yokes of oppression [wherever you find them], the finger pointed in scorn [toward the oppressed or the godly], and every form of false, harsh, unjust, and wicked speaking,*

Isaiah 58:7-9 (AMPC)

God promises prosperity, speedy healing, righteousness, and protection as His response to one who opens up their breadbasket, home, and closet to the poor during the fast. Notice during the annual Purim celebration the Jewish people fast, feast, and give food away to the poor. Is it any wonder they are so blessed? These principles of God work. Who would ever say you are "working" when you are fasting? Nevertheless, more is happening than we realize or than we could ever make happen on our own. Joel 2, verses 15 to 32 tell of God relenting and restoring provision and time to our life as a result of corporate prayer and fasting, weeping and mourning over sin. The spiritual changes the natural. You may be trying and trying in vain, or to no avail, to change things, but if you would just stop the natural and engage the supernatural first, change will come.

Maybe you would say, "Oh, I prayed and skipped a meal." No! That is not it. It is a position of humbling ourselves before God, sincerely asking Him to search our hearts and see if there is any wicked way. Allow God to remove everything that is not of Him, all impurities that pollute your faith, and to replace it with "all" of Him. Many times, we just need to get rid of things in our hearts to make room for God. Just as fasting detoxifies our body physically, I believe it detoxifies our faith spiritually. Our faith is refined and purified so we can boldly walk in the work God has prepared for us. We can then become full of His spirit of power and wisdom. Then God can get the job done. Prepare for His presence. Make as much room in your heart for Him as you possibly can; give it all to Him. Like Mordecai, who would not be comforted, and Esther, who put her life on the line for her people, God wants all of us. That is preparation. Once you have prayed, fasted, and prepared yourself, now you are ready. Let us get going with God and look at the fourth Pillar of Work.

4. Pursuit of Work

Pursue work; why would I want to pursue work when work seems to pursue me, chase me, and even hunt me down! Have you ever felt like you had a tracking device on you when you just wanted to run and hide? In our quest for life, we search or pursue many things, people, and places. Maybe you or someone you know has said, "I just want to 'find' myself." However, how can we spend our time "finding" ourselves if God says to "lose" ourselves? Our house will surely fall if built on "finding" ourselves; we are empty. No, our house will expand, enlarge, and flourish when we purposely pursue the work God calls and prepares for us.

What of Esther, Mordecai decreed failure and death if she withheld her influence:

> For if thou altogether holdest thy peace at this time, then shall there enlargement and deliverance arise to the Jews from another place; but thou and thy father's house shall be destroyed: and who knoweth whether thou art come to the kingdom for such a time as this?
>
> Esther 4:14 (KJV)

Mordecai gave powerful words of rebuke, destruction to her now seemingly safe house if she were to "remain silent." Her "work" involved speaking on behalf of her people. She may have wanted to run and hide, but the magnitude of the moment would not allow her to do it ignorantly. The decision is set before us destruction or deliverance, will we engage. Scripture admonishes us to engage zealously, enthusiastically, and eagerly:

> Who gave Himself on our behalf that He might redeem us (purchase our freedom) from all iniquity and purify for Himself a people [to be peculiarly His own, people who are] eager and enthusiastic about [living a life that is good and filled with] beneficial deeds.
>
> Titus 2:14 (AMPC)

God invites us to join Him in His work, which that alone should cause us to be eager and enthusiastic! Our eagerness to work will be so peculiar in our culture that people will take notice or take offense. Have you ever noticed how intimidated people get when someone with passion becomes involved? I have seen the fire of young believers be squelched by the mediocrity or "lukewarmness" of "seasoned" Christians. Passionate pursuit of the work of the

Lord is in itself a testimony! Think about it, what gets you excited? What makes you "boil over" is enthusiasm. God wants us to be "hot or cold," none of this in-between, lukewarm, "Okay, if you want me to" attitude. He wants us to run back to Him and say, "What's next, God?" Can you imagine when you give your child a chore, how great it would be if, instead of finishing it and going to their room, they come to you and say, "What else can I do for you?" What a wonderful attitude! Maybe you have experienced this. On the other hand, maybe, you yourself know the satisfaction that comes from a job well done. The Amplified says it this way:

> *Therefore, my beloved brethren, be firm (steadfast), immovable, always abounding in the work of the Lord [always being superior, excelling, doing more than enough in the service of the Lord], knowing and being continually aware that your labor in the Lord is not futile [it is never wasted or to no purpose].*

1 Corinthians 15:58 (AMPC) (emphasis added)

"Doing more than enough" or "going above and beyond" what is expected gets God's attention. My mom said it this way, "leave it better than you found it." That always made her happy and makes good biblical advice. God wants us clearly to slow down long enough, availing ourselves to look for opportunities actively and enthusiastically where we might accomplish, produce, and be on mission with Him. The scripture tells us we are "co-laborers." "For we are fellow workmen (joint promoters, laborers together) with and for God" (1 Corinthians 3:9, AMPC).

When we work, we work with God and for God. Some people make the mistake of thinking God has to do it or that He has to make them do it, like a puppet. Not at all; working with God is our highest call. However, God challenges our desire to pursue working with Him until we consider it a privilege and an honor. Think about a time you did a project or task with someone you didn't know well. What happened? By the time the project is over, you usually get to know that person very well. You see this all the time on TV or in the movies. Actors and actresses work on a project together, and by the time it's over, they are getting married! That is how it is with God; we get to know Him intimately when we go on mission with Him. Wow, we can actually work on a project together with God, imagine!

He is always at work, and He desires us to join Him and enjoy the work, knowing it is not in vain. In other words, it is not pointless, but powerful! It produces a harvest, fruit that is eternal, not just temporal. Look around, see where God is working, and join Him. Ask Him what you can do. In what way has He gifted you? What are your talents, skills, and abilities? Ask the staff at your church what they need or how you can help them. Maybe God has given you a vision. Begin to cultivate that. Look for ways to develop in your gifting through work. Remember, one thing always leads to another, be faithful in the little things, and God will make you ruler over much. God records, and God rewards the faithful. "For a day in thy courts is better than a thousand. I had rather be a doorkeeper in the house of my God, than to dwell in the tents of wickedness" (Psalm 84:10, KJV)

Like the psalmist, we can enjoy even being a "doorkeeper" when compared to being in the wrong place. You may be thinking, "What can I do?" If you are a believer, you are a member of the body of Christ, and He has made you His finger, toe, or knee, or maybe something you cannot see. There is something for you; that is part of the adventure. Find something, and do it heartily as unto the Lord, faithfully. God holds us responsible for what we have, not what we do not have. Think of the things you can do, not what you cannot. Your work may or may not bring a monetary result, but either way, it can and should produce an eternal harvest. Be a blessing to someone today. Start a Bible study or a prayer group in your home, join the worship team, choir, or band, help prepare materials for classes at the church, work on the grounds of the church or at the homes of some of the elderly people in your church, take food to the shut-ins, or visit the sick or the imprisoned.

Look for God at work and join Him. When you do, you will enjoy an intimacy with Him that alone satisfies the longings in your soul. Look for ways to give of yourself. The enthusiasm in sharing the heart of God into the unknown is the life of faith, the adventure. Just like Abraham, whose work was to obey the call to worship with his son, we, too, will experience the reward of our faith. In a moment of sacrifice, God provided a substitution, and Abraham became the father of our faith. Maybe you already have a sense or a passion for some work you know God has put in you. When we yield to that, no matter the challenge, we know and experience God. We see the manifestation of His glory, just as Abraham saw the ram! God wants to reveal Himself and the manifold wisdom of His grace. He will do it through you and me—the church. Let's pursue together, sister, and if I fall, will you pick me up? If you do, I hope and pray someone is there to pick you up and encourage you to continue!

5. Pattern of Work

God is a God of order, and He gives us a "blueprint," as it were with which to work. That "blueprint" is a pattern for others to see and duplicate. Does the repetitive nature or habit of your work glorify God? Is it consistent with what you say? How do you reveal

God in your work? Are you consistently late, or do you seem to always have something else, somewhere else, or someone else on your mind? Faithfulness, instant in season and out of season, steady, whether we feel like it or not—that is the pattern to emulate. We carry out the will of God, enduring what may come. What would the pattern of your life make? If all the church looked closely at your life and imitated you, what kind of church would it be? Paul told Titus to be a "pattern," someone worthy of imitation.

> *And show your own self in all respects to be a pattern and a model of good deeds and works, teaching what is unadulterated, showing gravity [having the strictest regard for truth and purity of motive], with dignity and seriousness.*

Titus 2:7 (AMPC) (emphasis added)

On the island of Crete, the spiritual temperature was low, and the moral climate was bad; Paul encourages Titus to set the pace. He was to be "a pattern of good works" in all things. The word translated "pattern" is tupos, from which we derive our English word "type." A type is a divinely planned illustration. It literally means to make an impression with a die, to mold or form, to strike an impression. To be a "pattern" or "type" is to model your life as an open book. To be this example, one must practice what they preach. One's behavior must match their teaching. We are to be a "mold," duplicated in others, inspiring them not only to good works but also as a divine illustration of the work of God in us and among men. Would you like others to examine you so intimately in order to duplicate your every thought, word, and deed? Ask yourself, what "impression" does my life make?

We pattern our life well when as a type of Christ, we make a lasting impression of the power of God to work and to love through us. That is why we are called "Christians" or "Christ—ones." We glorify God when we are the accurate reflection of God in Christ for the world to see and know that He is God. As ambassadors of a heavenly kingdom, sojourners, and pilgrims passing through, our mission, as His, is reconciling men to God. We have been given this ministry of reconciliation:

> *…hath given to us the ministry of reconciliation; To wit, that God was in Christ, reconciling the world unto himself, not imputing their trespasses unto them; and hath committed unto us the word of reconciliation. Now then we are ambassadors for Christ…*
>
> 2 Corinthians 5:18b-20a (KJV)

God was in Christ our pattern, now He is in us, having given us the same word, and now we represent Christ. How well do you represent Christ in your life and your words? Are you exemplifying a pattern for the heavenly kingdom or this earthly kingdom? Children provide an amazing picture of following an example. Just listen, and you will hear the very words and phrases of the parents or caretakers come right out of their mouth, even if they do not know what they are saying. You can even observe that actions and mannerisms among family members are similar. A pattern forms and, in turn, is duplicated. People watch and duplicate others they admire. God desires our work to be a pattern in word and deed of truth, purity, and dignity so that those around us, our family and church, may duplicate and thereby reveal or reflect Christ to the world. Truth or honesty in all things at all times; purity, a life separated to God; and dignity, a sober realization of the mission to reconcile the world to God, these model the "good works."

The work God does in us and through us will be honorable and remembered. Think how we remember the works of faith of Rahab, Ruth, Esther, and Mary. Good works stand the test of time, giving life and hope to future generations. Every Christmas, millions around the world remember and give honor to Mary, the virgin mother of Jesus. Every spring, Jews around the world celebrate Purim, remembering and honoring Esther's work of faith in keeping the Jews from annihilation. We celebrate "Mother's Day," "Father's Day," "President's Day," "Memorial Day," etc., in remembrance of the good these people have done for their families and their country. What about you, what will people remember about you? I pray God gives us faith to work the good works through love honestly, purely, and soberly. "He hath made his wonderful works to be remembered: the LORD is gracious and full of compassion" (Psalm 111:4, KJV).

How do you know if your work is memorable? In Psalm 111:2, 3, David tells us the work of God is "great, honorable, and glorious," and in Proverbs 20:11, "even a child is known by his doings, whether his work is pure and right." This speaks to the motive if it is on the "up and up." In other words, if I am trying to meet my own needs of significance, the work will not stand the test of time. Esther received the challenge to move outside of her comfort zone. At the right time, led by the *Lord*, she did the brave work to save her people. If she had opted to save herself, Mordecai said she would lose, but salvation would arise from somewhere else without her. Because of her pure, right, and timely work, the Jewish people memorialize her annually. The motive energizing me to good deeds is to bring honor and glory to God, to share His love. God even says there is a "time for every purpose and for every work." When God impresses you, move spontaneously, adjust quickly to follow these promptings; time is of the essence.

Once you have determined your work, do it, do it now, and do it with all your strength.

The conclusion of the pattern of our life's work is found in: "Whatsoever thy hand findeth to do, do it with thy might; for there is no work, nor device, nor knowledge, nor wisdom, in the grave, whither thou goest" (Ecclesiastes 9:10, KJV). May you, with quiet confidence, be established in every good work God directs, and may the pattern of your work be worthy of following or emulating.

6. Plenteous in Work

"Now there was at Joppa a certain disciple named Tabitha, which by interpretation is called Dorcas: this woman was *full of good works* and alms deeds which she did" (Acts 9:36, KJV) (emphasis added). This woman is a wonderful example, or pattern, as we just explained, for us. The Greeks in the local church there in Joppa knew her as Dorcas. She spent her life in acts of kindness and compassion. In the end, her works of sewing and making coats spoke so loudly of her love for the Lord and the people, that Peter upon hearing this, prayed at her deathbed, and God raised her up! Her works were such a powerful evidence of her salvation that God gave her additional time to continue. Can you imagine being so full of good works that God will raise you up to keep you going? I am inspired just writing this. I want that, don't you?

> *That they do good, that they be rich in good works, ready to distribute, willing to communicate; Laying up in store for themselves a good foundation against the time to come, that they may lay hold on eternal life.*

1 Timothy 6:18-19 (KJV) (emphasis added)

Paul encourages Timothy to teach this principle of doing good, being rich in good works, that the work of giving and sharing of not just our physical resources but our spiritual as well, would be abundant. In other words, our daily employ is that of looking for a place to minister to those in need of our help, finances, or encouragement. In so doing, we are preparing a solid foundation for our future. You may think you do not have anything to give, but you do. Ask God to show you what you have. You are accountable for only what is in your hand and to provide for your own family. "But if any provide not for his own, and especially for those of his own house, he hath denied the faith, and is worse than an infidel" (1 Timothy 5:8, KJV).

Then for widows:

> *Honour widows that are widows indeed. But if any widow have children or nephews, let them learn first to shew piety at home, and to requite their parents: for that is good and acceptable before God.*
>
> 1 Timothy 5:3-4 (KJV)

And also for elders, "Let the elders that rule well be counted worthy of double honour, especially they who labour in the word and doctrine" (1 Timothy 5:17, KJV).

The Scripture teaches us to give to those who are in need, those who cannot give back. God desires to find us as a faithful steward of all He entrusts us with, including our time, talents, and treasure. Be plenteous, abundant, and rich in good works, ready to distribute and willing to communicate as God calls upon you. When we are going about doing well and looking for ways to help, we will not have time for "pity parties" or "petty nitpicking." You just do not have time or energy to waste on the little irritations with which the enemy wants to trip you up. Working for the Lord encourages your own soul as well as others. It actually lifts you up. Be a blessing to someone today. Ask God to show you who and how you can help. God wants to increase our capacity and enlarge our influence to love and bless others. Simply ask God to enlarge your heart with more love; you then will be plenteous in good works for Him. "And God is able to make all grace abound toward you; that ye, always having all sufficiency in all things, may abound to every good work" (2 Corinthians 9:8, KJV). Grace, God's favor, blessing, and power, will not only be your sufficiency but will also come to you in abundance for every good work. That is abounding in the grace of God! We are plenteous because there is no end to the grace of God! We can take the example of Jesus: "I must work the works of him that sent me, while it is day: the night cometh, when no man can work" (John 9:4, KJV). What God has put in you to do, do now, do not delay. Now is the time. To delay is to disobey. It is never too late to begin. What you sow grows, so sow good seed of good deeds generously. Begin, continue, and end in abundantly working for the glory of God, plenteous in work: "Therefore, my beloved brethren, be ye steadfast, unmovable, always *abounding* in the work of the Lord, forasmuch as ye know that your labour is not in vain in the Lord" (1 Corinthians 15:58, KJV) (emphasis added).

7. Power of Work

The power of work, or we could say, the influence. One of the most valuable effects of work outside of provision and example is light. "Let your light so shine before men, that they may see your good works, and glorify your Father which is in heaven" (Matthew 5:16, KJV).

When we work in such a way as to allow the light of God to shine through us, onlookers will take notice and glorify (doxazo) our (notice it says "your") Father. He may not even be their Father, but because of the obvious light in your "good works," they will see "your" God. Are you looking for the pat on the back or gold plaque? On the other hand, are you rather content seeing others glorify God as they see the light in your works? Work has powerful influence to point others to Christ. Does the light of Jesus Christ, The Light, shine through your work so much that others glorify God? Help us, Lord, to seek not our own but God's glory, and may people praise, giving glory (doxazo) to God.

In the words of Thomas Ken from "The Doxology" of 1674, may all who see our work:

> *Praise God from whom all blessings flow;*
> *Praise Him all creatures here below;*
> *Praise Him above ye heavenly host;*
> *Praise Father, Son, and Holy Ghost. Amen.*

Thomas Ken

Good works have the power to bring people to a place of glorifying God. Even though people may speak despairingly, the eyewitnesses of your good works will, by the mercies and calling of God, give Him praise and glory for your honest work and conversation (conduct). God be praised, and His kingdom advanced!

> *Having your conversation honest among the Gentiles:*
> *that, whereas they speak against you as evildoers, they*
> *may by your good works, which they shall behold, glorify*
> *God in the day of visitation.*

1 Peter 2:12 (KJV) (emphasis added)

Jesus gave reference to the power of work(s) in: "If I do not the works of my Father, believe me not. But if I do, though ye believe not me, *believe the works:* that ye may know, and believe, that the Father is in me, and I in him" (John 10:37-38, KJV) (emphasis added). "Believe me that I am in the Father, and the Father in me: or else *believe me for the very works' sake*" (John 14:11, KJV) (emphasis added).

Jesus' life was consistent; His works fulfilled His words. So much so that He could confidently encourage faith in God through the mere observation of His works. Your work and the attitude with which you work either show people Jesus and His salvation or not. If you go the extra mile, show mercy, keep silent, come in early, stay late, and solve problems, you will get people's attention and usually favor with the boss. People are watching and listening. How we conduct ourselves personally and professionally will lead others either to Christ or away from Him. Let us receive the challenge to prepare, pursue, and abound in the "good works" of power that others will remember and glorify God in the day He visits them. The power of work will evangelize! Just like Esther and Mordecai, whose work of faith gave powerful testimony to the sovereignty of God and yielded numbers of converts to the Jewish faith. Think of it; your works today can bring someone to faith in Christ. Imagine your work may win the lost. Praise be to God for good works that result in the salvation of others today.

8. Prove Our Work

Let us consider our work in light of God's perspective. "And the work of righteousness shall be *peace*; and the effect of righteousness *quietness* and *assurance* forever" (Isaiah 32:17, KJV) (emphasis added).

When God calls us to work, and we respond by the power of His Spirit accomplishing His will, then God blesses His children with the gift of peace. God's peace brings a wholeness that alone not only produces in us a calm confidence of eternal reward but also keeps us in a fruitful place. As a pilgrim and sojourner, the believer knows this is not home; we are only passing through. We work not for earthly reward or accolade but for the glory of our heavenly Father. To Him, we live and move and breathe and have our being. As He is glorified, His peace floods our souls. In the midst of turmoil, insults, hatred, and confusion, God gives the worker of righteousness peace.

Esther continues to provide a beautiful example through her work; yielding to the call, she moved forward in each step with a quiet, confident posture that left Haman and Xerxes so inquisitive. The peace of God enveloped her as she carried out His plan to expose the enemy and save the nation. The resulting victory brought the blessing of rest, a quiet, calm confidence in the renewed kingship of Xerxes. I remember the one elusive night of sleep that no money in the world could buy for Michael Jackson, one of the world's most famous icons—leaving this world overdosed on drugs to help him sleep. His work did not produce the peace of God. Oh yes, it brought financial prosperity, but that alone could not give him one simple night's sleep nor put him in a fruitful place. How grateful we can be to lay our heads down at night to know we have done the work of God. By His grace, He empowers us to fulfill His Word and His will in our work. In this, we prove our faith. We show through our work whether we are believers.

> *What doth it profit, my brethren, though a man say he hath faith, and have not works? Can faith save him? Even so faith, if it hath not works, is dead, being alone. Was not Abraham our father justified by works, when he had offered Isaac his son upon the altar? Seest thou how faith wrought with his works, and by works was faith made perfect? Likewise also was not Rahab the harlot justified by works, when she had received the messengers, and had*

sent them out another way? For as the body without the
spirit is dead, so faith without works is dead also.

James 2:14, 17, 21-22, 25-26 (KJV)

Abraham proved he was justified by revealing his faith through what he did the work of faith. By obeying God and offering Isaac on the altar, believing that God could raise him from the dead, Abraham confirmed his faith, his trust in God. He showed a true, genuine faith, living faith that completes and finishes its course. James pronounced Rahab just and saved because she worked on mission with God in hiding the Israelite spies. God even included her in the lineage of Christ. This faith proves to be living and active. Without the works, our faith is dead, lifeless, and worthless because it is not accomplishing the will and work of God. Let us work as unto the Lord, completing our faith, fulfilling the good pleasure of His goodness, and the work of faith with *power!* In so doing, the name of our Lord Jesus Christ is glorified in us and us in Him according to His grace. Like Esther, Abraham, and Rahab, prove your faith through your work. Just do it!

9. Praise for Work

Remember the story of the woman with the alabaster box, how she poured her perfume out upon the Lord and then endured ridicule by the disciples for not giving them the perfume to sell and then, in turn, give the money to the poor? Jesus stepped in and intervened on her behalf, bringing correction.

> *When Jesus understood it, he said unto them, Why trouble*
> *ye the woman? For she hath wrought a good work upon*
> *me. Verily I say unto you, Wheresoever this gospel shall be*
> *preached in the whole world, there shall also this, that this*
> *woman hath done, be told for a memorial of her.*

Matthew 26:10, 13 (KJV) (emphasis added)

The sacrifice and depth of devotion of this woman for Jesus before an audience of dissenting men brought her honor. Through this good work, she honored Jesus, and He did, in turn, honor her. Imagine wherever man preaches the gospel in the whole world; what she did will be remembered and admired. Now that is "good work." The works we do will either bring the praise of God or not. If we, through our works, showing our love and devotion, do them personally to Him and for Him, then we, too, will receive a reward.

According to the grace of God which is given unto me, as a wise masterbuilder, I have laid the foundation, and another buildeth thereon. But let every man take heed how he buildeth thereupon. Every man's work shall be made manifest: for the day shall declare it, because it shall be revealed by fire; and the fire shall try every man's work of what sort it is. If any man's work abide which he hath built thereupon, he shall receive a reward. If any man's work shall be burned, he shall suffer loss: but he himself shall be saved; yet so as by fire.

1 Corinthians 3:10-15 (KJV)

The eternal result of our work is either reward or loss. Ask God to search your heart to purify the motive for all you do. Out of a pure heart, our work will abide through the test of fire and receive a reward. As this woman, who gave nearly a year's wages to pour ointment on the head of Jesus, may we, too, give honor to Jesus by making such a bold, courageous offering of our love and devotion through our work.

Will your work stand through the fire? Will Jesus call it "good work?" Sometimes our work will be so extravagant as to be outside of the realm of common sense. It may have been common sense for her to sell this ointment and give to the poor, but Jesus would soon be gone, and she needed to show Him honor and love right then. If the Spirit of God is prompting you to do something right now, do it! Do not let an opportunity pass. Put aside the temporal for the eternal reward. The only other option found in verse 15 is suffering loss. God actually says we will not get by with a single thing that is not right. The fire of God will examine our work, and if it does not pass the test of fire, it burns up, and no reward is given. Mary's work of pouring out the oil on Jesus' feet passed the test and received His praise. Do the work well with honesty and purity that God lays on your heart. I pray you, too, like Mary, experience the joy of God's honor and His reward. "Behold, I am coming soon, and I shall bring My wages and rewards with Me, to repay and render to each one just what his own actions and his own work merit" (Revelation 22:12, AMPC).

> *For God is not unrighteous to forget or overlook your labor and the love which you have shown for His name's sake in ministering to the needs of the saints (His own consecrated people), as you still do.*
>
> Hebrews 6:10 (AMPC)

Are you working for the rewards of the here and now or the hereafter? All this will pass away; it is temporal. The work done, as unto the Lord, will reap (render) eternal rewards, and it will stand throughout eternity. God sees and knows every little daily thing you do for Him in ministering, especially the things that go unnoticed by man, and He promises to repay and reward you. May our rewards be eternally great for His glory!

10. Provoke to Work

"And let us consider one another to *provoke unto love and to good works*" (Hebrews 10:24, KJV) (emphasis added). With your heart, your mind, and your mouth, filled with the faith of God in His Word, you then show, or reveal, this faith in your work. We are, in turn, to stimulate or provoke our brothers and sisters to these good works. The Amplified says it this way:

> And let us consider and give attentive, continuous care to watching over one another, studying how we may stir up (stimulate and incite) to love and helpful deeds and noble activities,
>
> Hebrews 10:24 (AMPC) (emphasis added)

We are to actually "make a study" of how to stir, stimulate, and incite each other up. You may think, "Oh, I'm good at inciting," and inciting may seem easy at first, but to good works not bad; calling on the Spirit within each other to fulfill our call and bless others. As iron sharpens iron, so we are, as we provoke each other to noble activities. Consider those with whom you worship—your own family. What are their gifts, talents, personalities, and abilities? What did God make them do? Maybe their gift is to teach, to administrate, to help, or maybe pray. The gifts of the Spirit are many, and their function is as varied as the creativity of God. Yet, God instructs us, as our brother's keeper, to provoke by calling, inciting, and stimulating each other to join in the work of the kingdom, sowing seeds as deeds of righteousness, being full of good works. If we do not come together, how can we do this? Based on God's faithfulness to us, we faithfully, boldly, and confidently stimulate the body of Christ to be actively and energetically involved in the work of the kingdom.

Christians are like coals of fire—

together, they glow;
Apart, they grow cold.

~ Our Daily Bread 9/9/98

When we separate ourselves from those God placed in our lives to help us, the fire or light of our salvation begins to dim. Until left alone, it goes out or turns into ashes. Many Christians have left the church through laziness, bitterness, or busyness only to become discouraged, depressed, lonely, and hardened. Confused as to the reason for their present state and taking no responsibility, they continue until their once-thriving life becomes completely fruitless and lifeless. This self-imposed state of isolation only seeks to eat away at the faith and love God has for His body. This is how the writer of Hebrews said encourages the believer in the next verse: "Not forsaking the assembling of ourselves together, as the manner of some is; but exhorting one another: and so much the more, as ye see the day approaching" (Hebrews 10:25, KJV).

Making a commitment to serve in some area of the work of the Lord will give you the accountability for someone to come alongside you and encourage you. Remember how Mordecai so intently provoked Esther to step up to the plate as it were and stand in the gap for her people. He did not leave any room for ambiguity; if she went and hid in the palace, she would be destroyed. The times and the days prior to the second coming will become more and more evil and tempting. The power is in the corporate unity and assembly of the body, where we not only give exhortation but we receive it. Keep yourself connected and open to a sister in the Lord, to a teacher, a pastor, someone in the body of Christ who can speak into your life the truth of the Gospel. This should be someone who encourages you to demonstrate your faith and love through good deeds. You might even need to start a small prayer group or bible study to create a safe environment where encouragement can take place. If you have faith in Christ and love for the Father, you will love of necessity the body of Christ, the broken, the hurting, and the hungry. The love of God so envelops your being that you must have an outlet for it. Through prayer for each other and knowledge of each other, we can then help to promote, provoke, and stir up these noble activities in the body.

11. Prosper in Work

> *They shall not build, and another inhabit; they shall not plant, and another eat: for as the days of a tree are the days of my people, and mine elect shall long enjoy the work of their hands. They shall not labour in vain, nor bring forth for trouble; for they are the seed of the blessed of the LORD, and their offspring with them.*
>
> Isaiah 65:22-23 (KJV)

If you are a child of God, you are the seed of the blessed of the *Lord*. As the people of God, His elect, you will enjoy the work of your hands. God has decreed and declared this blessing over our work; how awesome, will you receive this? Thank God I will "long enjoy the work of my hands." James also brings this into the New Testament.

> *But he who looks carefully into the faultless law, the [law] of liberty, and is faithful to it and perseveres in looking into it, being not a heedless listener who forgets but an active doer [who obeys], he shall be blessed in his doing (his life of obedience).*
>
> James 1:25 (AMPC)

The blessing begins in the doing and continues because of the doing. How blessed to know I am in the will of God going about doing well! That alone blesses my soul as I fulfill the purpose to which God created me. The Amplified says as the blessed of God, we will be happy, fortunate, and to be envied. We enjoy a life of God's blessing in the "doing." God cannot help but watch over His Word; He will perform this in your life. As you do unto others sowing seeds of love, God will return back to you a harvest of blessing. The principles of the kingdom again at work, what you sow you reap.

The person who hears and does the Word of God is blessed. Note that James refers to the Word of God as the perfect "law of liberty." This means that the Word of God will set a person free from the bondage of sin and death. The Word of God will free a person from all the temptations of this life and give him the full and victorious life for which his soul longs—a life that will continue on and on eternally with God. A person who does and lives the Word of God will find that freedom from all that enslaves his soul upon earth. He will discover love, joy, and peace—a soul that just soars with a sense of...

- ... freedom and liberty;
- security and safety;
- victory over temptation;
- assurance and confidence;
- purpose and meaning;
- deliverance from sin;
- joy and rejoicing;
- life over death.

The Word of God is the law of liberty, the law that sets one free to know and fellowship with God forever and ever. This is true prosperity. However, note a critical point: we must continue in the Word of God. We must continue to live just as it says. If we do, then we shall be blessed, made abundantly, and eternally happy. Now, the final and twelfth pillar of work.

12. Prayer for Work

> *Wherefore also we pray always for you, that our God would count you worthy of this calling, and fulfil all the good pleasure of his goodness, and the work of faith with power: That the name of our Lord Jesus Christ may be glorified in you, and ye in him, according to the grace of our God and the Lord Jesus Christ.*
>
> 2 Thessalonians 1:11-12 (KJV) (emphasis added)

I, too, along with Paul, pray for you: may you purpose to glorify God; seek Him first; prepare for every good work; zealously pursue the work of the Lord; pattern your work to exemplify a practice of honesty, wisdom, and diligence; and be plenteous in good works. May you lead others to Christ through a good example of work, prove the faith, and hope that lies within you with work as unto the Lord. Finally, may you receive praise for your work that will abound with eternal rewards; provoke others to work by your example and your care of the church; and, that in so doing may you prosper and be blessed to long enjoy the work of your hands.

Once these pillars are settled, you will look at work in light of eternity, from God's perspective, weighing everything you do as to its eternal weight. Remember, as you are working, the miracle is working. If, as Jesus says, God glories in fruit, then may your work and your life bear much fruit and fruit that will remain to the glory of the Lord! Emptying your life of the wood, hay, and stubble that burns up easily and fulfilling this "good work of the Lord" will provide the much sought-after satisfaction in your life, and before you know it, you will arise higher and higher to new heights of living.

Prayer ~

Lord, may I work as unto You. May there be none of me and all of You. Energize and empower me with Your Spirit to seek and pursue the work You have prepared for me. May I be a vessel unto honor, ready and prepared for Your work. May I glorify You in how I work and how much I work, and may that work lead many to a saving knowledge of Jesus Christ. I ask that You would forgive me for works of the flesh, seeking to meet my own needs through my work. May my work be a blessing to my family and others and bring eternal rewards. I believe, declare, and thank You that I complete and fulfill all the work of faith with power that you have prepared for me. In Jesus' name, amen.

Chapter 9.

Memorial Stone 6

War

*"Be strong and courageous, be not afraid nor dismayed,
with us is the Lord our God, to help us, and to fight our
battles".*

(2 Chronicles 32:7a, 8a, NKJV)

You are waiting and watching, worshipping God, walking in His ways, and working the miracle, and all of a sudden, *bam*! Seemingly, out of nowhere comes this attack, as if you have an X on your back. You feel like everyone or everything is against you. Is this really the case? Could it be that you are just now realizing you have been in a battle all along? Now, for the first time, you realize the enemy has noticed your newfound faith and resolve and is endeavoring to thwart you on every front and in every work and every relationship. Have you noticed any resistance to the work God has for you? Take heart, my dear sister, be of good courage, the Lord has sent us and set us in the midst of evil, and it is *game on*! "Behold, I send you forth as sheep in the midst of wolves: be ye therefore wise as serpents, and harmless as doves" (Matthew 10:16, KJV).

This sixth stone will take some boldness to set up, so join me and set up the memorial stone of *war* in your life. There is no turning back now; to do so would mean utter destruction. It is time to press in, press on with strength and fervor, and take back all that is yours! Yes, the promises and blessings in the kingdom of God have an enemy and have always had an enemy, but God has given us a command to take them and seize them as a precious prize. So welcome to the war sister, a woman's war.

So, what war? If God is for me, then why am I in a war? Moreover, why do I have to war? You might be thinking, "There's really a war?" On the other hand, you might be saying, "Yea, I know, I live in a war-zone every day!" What do we mean when we say "war"? How and what do we need to war? Who or what is the enemy, do I fight him or it, and if so, how?

Okay, I can hear some of your answers, and yes, if you said Satan is the enemy, he does play his role in it, but there's more. Knowing the enemy is part of the wisdom God intends for us to have in order to gain the advantage. How easy for an enemy to gain access and take his prey if said prey is totally ignorant of his enemy's presence and methods or even goes so far as to disavow the very existence of an enemy.

> *There are two equal and opposite errors into which our race can fall about the devils. One is to disbelieve in their existence. The other is to believe and to feel an excessive and unhealthy interest in them. They themselves are equally pleased by both errors.*
>
> C.S. Lewis

This is really where the faith journey gets adventurous. When I began to war in the spiritual realm, fighting "for" my marriage, so many things started to change around me. Unhealthy attachments and bonds started falling off our marriage. Watching God defeat the enemy is so rewarding and encouraging; you will never again let him get an advantage. There is a "thrill" in victory when you know how to war. God is awesome!

So let us shine the light of knowledge on this and gain understanding necessary to set up the stone "*war.*" To do so, we first break it down with the investigative approach asking these questions: who, what, when, where, why, and finally, how.

Who?

The first question, "who," identifies all the involved players, "who wars." If I am not aware of the involved parties, then I could be quickly deceived, distracted, or divided from my mission and thereby defeated. As in most team training, we learn who is on our team and what they bring to the table, and then who we are facing. Scripture identifies three persons or entities: a) the Godhead, including Father, Son, and the Holy Spirit along with angels; b) the devil and his angels; and finally, c) you and me. Recognizing who is at war will help us discern our strategy.

1. *The Godhead*

First and foremost, God, that is to say, "*Elohim,*" plural God including the Father, the Son, and the Holy Spirit, otherwise known as the Trinity or Triune God. Also, in Hebrew, Jehovah Tsebaoth as found herein: "*The LORD is a man of war: the LORD is his name*" (Exodus 15:3, KJV) (emphasis added). Identified as the Lord of Hosts, or the Lord of Armies, a "man of war" in this title indicates the great powers by which God defends, punishes, or governs His creation and also indicates that He invokes the assistance of an army of two-thirds of the heavenly angels. "Are not the angels all ministering spirits (servants) sent out in the service [of God for the assistance] of those who are to inherit salvation?" (Hebrews 1:14, AMPC).

The reasons God the Father thus sent His Son, Jesus, reveal His involvement. 1) To bring a sword, signifying the presence of an enemy; and 2) to destroy the works of the devil: "Think not that I am come to send peace on earth: I came not to send peace, but a sword" (Matthew 10:34, KJV). "He that committeth sin is of the devil; for the *devil sinneth* from the beginning. For this purpose the Son of God was manifested, that he might *destroy the works of the devil*" (1 John 3:8, KJV) (emphasis added).

Jesus also serves as Commander, or Captain, of the Lord's army: "And the *commander* of the Lord's army said to Joshua, 'Take off your sandals from your feet, for the place where you are standing is holy.' And Joshua did so" (Joshua 5:15, ESV) (emphasis added). He is the "Almighty" in Revelation, the "Deliverer" in Romans, the "Most Mighty" in Psalms, and the "Power of God" in Corinthians—Jesus, the true "Lion of the tribe of Judah," Revelation 5:5.

And then when Jesus ascended on high, He sent the third person of the trinity, the Spirit of God, the gift of His Holy Spirit, to take His place: "Wherefore he saith, When he ascended up on high, he led captivity captive, and gave gifts unto men" (Ephesians 4:8, KJV). "Then Peter said unto them, Repent, and be baptized every one of you in the name of Jesus Christ for the remission of sins, and ye shall receive the gift of the Holy Ghost" (Acts 2:38, KJV). "But you will receive power when the Holy Spirit has come upon you, and you will be my witnesses in Jerusalem and in all Judea and Samaria, and to the end of the earth" (Acts 1:8, ESV).

Participating individually yet corporately, the Godhead or Trinity, God the Father, the Son, and the Holy Spirit maintains complete involvement engaging at every level in the war along with the two-thirds of the host of heavenly angels. They cannot deny who they are, Jehovah Tsebaoth, the *Lord* of Armies, Christ Jesus the Messiah, our conqueror, and the gift of God, His Holy Spirit, the source of power. The angels, too, are sent to serve under the Lord's command on behalf of the saints. Knowing God is the most important first step in warring. Confidence comes not from knowing the enemy but from knowing the victor. Knowing God encourages boldness in believers as the scriptures say, "But the people that do know their God shall be strong, and do exploits" (Daniel 11:32, KJV). God is who He says He is!

2. Satan

The second entity or involved player, Satan, literally meaning "adversary," wars with one-third of hierarchy of demonic angels:

> *For we wrestle not against flesh and blood, but against principalities, against powers, against the rulers of the darkness of this world, against spiritual wickedness in high places.*
>
> Ephesians 6:12 (KJV)

Paul here gives us some insight into the depth of the sophistication and power of our enemy. He is a formidable foe with hierarchy and order. Satan is the leader of one-third of the heavenly angels who fell with him, wielding power and authority at several levels. Although he is not omnipresent, he has positioned rulers, demons, and princes over specific areas. Although these spirits or demons may work through people, you are not fighting with flesh and blood. He works through the ranks of his kingdom to exert his power and authority, looking to influence and take control where he "may." "Be sober, be vigilant; because your adversary the devil, as a roaring lion, walketh about, seeking whom he *may* devour" (1 Peter 5:8, KJV) (emphasis added). "Keep *a cool head. Stay alert.* The Devil is *poised to pounce,* and would like nothing better than to catch you napping" (1 Peter 5:8, MSG) (emphasis added).

Our opponent is "poised to pounce!" He is constantly seeking the unaware soul. Has the devil caught you sleeping? Have you ever felt "pounced" upon? It is time to wake *up*! He is seeking whom he "*may*" devour, the one who is easy prey, off by themselves, daydreaming, thereby allowing him access.

The sad truth about Satan is, as we see in Ezekiel, God created Satan to be at home in heaven. He was the worship leader of heaven, full of wisdom, perfect in beauty, the "king of Tyrus" he is called, the "anointed cherub that covereth." God set him as the guardian angel of His throne, perfect in all his ways until God found iniquity in him.

> *...the workmanship of thy tabrets and of thy pipes was prepared in thee in the day that thou wast created. Thou art the anointed cherub that covereth; and I have set thee so: thou wast upon the holy mountain of God; thou hast walked up and down in the midst of the stones of fire. Thou wast perfect in thy ways from the day that thou wast created, until iniquity was found in thee.*
>
> Ezekiel 28:13b-15 (KJV)

Have you ever thought about that? Did you realize sin began in the heart of Satan? Angels were the first to sin. Isaiah tells us here that "Lucifer," meaning brightness, or morning star (from the Greek root word "halal," meaning to praise, boast, celebrate, and even marry) was cast down out of heaven. Is it any wonder he likes to "party" or, for that matter, attack marriages? You see, he perverts every purpose God created for him. It seems he lived up to his name, but instead of praising God, he praised and uplifted himself.

> *How art thou fallen from heaven, O Lucifer, son of the morning! How art thou cut down to the ground, which didst weaken the nations! For thou hast said in thine*

heart, I will ascend into heaven, I will exalt my throne
above the stars of God: I will sit also upon the mount of
the congregation, in the sides of the north: I will ascend
above the heights of the clouds; I will be like the most
High.

Isaiah 14:12-15 (KJV) (emphasis added)

No wonder Satan wants to trip us up with pride, so we fall as he did. Note the five "I will" statements, "pride goes before a fall," came to fulfillment the day God cast him out of heaven. He wanted to take God's place and be like Him, then and now. John's revelation reiterates this:

And the great dragon was cast out, that old serpent,
called the Devil, and Satan, which deceiveth the whole
world: he was cast out into the earth, and his angels were
cast out with him. And I heard a loud voice saying in
heaven, Now is come salvation, and strength, and the
kingdom of our God, and the power of his Christ: for the
accuser of our brethren is cast down, which accused them
before our God day and night.

Revelation 12:9-10 (KJV)

Devil, Satan, serpent, and *dragon* are certainly ominous enough names, but his true agenda is exposed here as the *"accuser of the brethren."* His name "devil" means false accuser, slanderer. He approached the throne of God, as in Job, to bring accusation against the family of God.

Satan endeavors at every turn to blame, through lies, judgments, and misrepresentations, to lower, disgrace, mock, violate, and betray. The enemy is behind the attacks and temptations on your character. By lowering or debasing us, he attempts to destroy and cut us off from all fruitfulness, faithfulness, and forgiveness of others and ourselves. Jesus witnessed this fall from heaven, where Satan, cast down, consumed with indignation, concentrates his efforts in a race against the clock. Satan became the enemy of God, opposing the sovereignty and omnipotence of God. "And he said unto them, I beheld Satan as lightning fall from heaven" (Luke 10:18, KJV).

> *Therefore rejoice, ye heavens, and ye that dwell in them. Woe to the inhabiters of the earth and of the sea! For the devil is come down unto you, having great wrath, because he knoweth that he hath but a short time.*
>
> Revelation 12:12 (KJV)

Satan is mad! He not only knows he has lost, but he knows his time is short, and the fulfillment of his judgment is soon. He is on a mission to take as many with him as he can. He is the archenemy of all that is of God, from God, and for God, including you and all that pertains to the life God has for you.

He is the "*tempter*" in Thessalonians, the "*evil one*" in Matthew, the "*murderer*" and "*father of lies*" in John chapter eight. He tempts us with his evil desires, motives, and methods to destroy our life at any possible level, including but not limited to our families, homes, dreams, passions, futures, ministries, and influence. He is not playing for fun but for keeps. As a liar, he employs every possible tactic to deceive his prey into believing he is "for" them, has a "better" way, gives "life," "knows best," and he only can be trusted, not God. He laughs at fighting fair, demanding it of you but is under no obligation to do so since he is judged already. That's why we get mad so often, and he loves it. Nevertheless, he is not only a liar, endeavoring to deceive and blind his victims; he is the "*father of lies*," which means he gives seed to every lie. That is why

God puts such an emphasis on truth. He sent the embodiment of truth in His son, Jesus, the complete antithesis of the deceiver.

3. *The Church*

And finally, yes, the church actively participates in this war, knowingly or unknowingly, willingly or unwillingly, as we will see. We are told in Ephesians 6:12 that "we wrestle" or rather, as the Amplified puts it, "we contend" with the enemy. In 1 Timothy 1:18, the church is told to "war a good warfare." In 1 Timothy 6:12, we are told to "fight the good fight," and in 2 Timothy 2:3, we are called to be a "good soldier." The church is reminded in 2 Corinthians 10:3 that "we do not war after the flesh," in other words, we are engaged in a spiritual or supernatural fight. Paul tells us to "be strong" and use every weapon the Lord has made for us to defeat the enemy. We enforce the victory Jesus won on the cross over the enemy.

We find the history of the involvement of the people of God, the church, from the beginning in the Garden of Eden. Anytime we participate in deception or lies, we give voice and life to the enemy's tactics. We, thereby disavowing the truth, open ourselves to loss brought on by following the deception. Satan can never birth truth, but he can pervert or twist it; this is the supernatural war. He is so subtle, but by learning his tactics, we can recognize the lie. The first and most notable lie was in the Garden of Eden; through it, he successfully gained power and control over the earth by overthrowing mankind. Notice how he weaves the conversation:

> *Now the serpent was more crafty than any of the wild animals the Lord God had made. He said to the woman, "Did God really say, 'You must not eat from any tree in the garden'?" The woman said to the serpent, "We may eat fruit from the trees in the garden, but God did say, 'You*

must not eat fruit from the tree that is in the middle of
the garden, and you must not touch it, or you will die.'"
"You will not surely die," the serpent said to the woman.
"For God knows that when you eat of it your eyes will be
opened, and you will be like God, knowing good and evil."
When the woman saw that the fruit of the tree was good
for food and pleasing to the eye, and also desirable for gain-
ing wisdom, she took some and ate it. She also gave some
to her husband, who was with her, and he ate it. Then the
eyes of both of them were opened, and they realized they
were naked; so they sewed fig leaves together and made
coverings for themselves.

Genesis 3:1-7 (NIV) (emphasis added)

Satan engaged Eve in a conversation, which was her first mistake! Why do we want to talk so much? He got her! By questioning her understanding of God's instructions, he got her ear, then the "hook," the twist, the lie, "You shall not surely die." This was followed by the "the line," "God knows you will be as gods," the very sin that caused him to lose his place. Finally, the sinker, "God's holding out on you; you cannot trust him." She listened, looked, pondered, and ate. Gotcha! She heard the lie, believed the lie, acted upon it, and died.

Death came to all humanity through Adam and Eve's simple act of unbelief in God and belief in the lie. Satan plays for real and for keeps. When Satan comes in, sin comes in! All of his deceptions are an effort to steal, kill, and destroy the plans of God for our lives. Adam and Eve lost forever their place in the Garden of Eden, their possessions freely provided, and their power over the enemy. That fateful day they handed the authority of this world over to Satan and brought death to mankind. Thank you guys, great job! Since we were in Adam, the seed of man after its own kind, we died too.

Have you ever thought what the stakes might be if we do not wake up? Maybe you have experienced this loss in your own life. Satan can steal your *place*, your *possessions*, and your *power*, either by subtlety as with Eve or blatantly as he tried with Jesus in the wilderness. He boldly attempts to entice and distract as he did when he said to Jesus, "If you will bow down and worship me, I will give you all the kingdoms of the world." Whatever works, he will try.

Your place could be a position of ministry or work, even a physical location. Adam and Eve lost forever the Garden of Eden. Worse than that, they sacrificed the closeness and intimacy of their daily communion with The Lord. Your possessions may not be the whole world as in this case, but he can still take the provision God intended for you. In addition to your place or position and possessions, Satan can also steal your power. They had power over the enemy, but because Eve thought there might be some "good" in the evil, she relinquished her power. Adam and Eve had power over Satan, and he knew it; the problem was they did not. By getting them to yield to sin, he took the authority and dominion of this world that was given to them by God.

And God said; Let us make man in our image, after our likeness: and let them have dominion_over the fish of the sea, and over the fowl of the air, and over the cattle, and over all the earth, and over every creeping thing that creepeth upon the earth. So God created man in his own image, in the image of God created he him; male and female created he them. And God blessed them, and God said unto them, Be fruitful, and multiply, and replenish the earth, and subdue it: and have dominion over the fish of the sea, and over the fowl of the air, and over every living thing that moveth upon the earth.

Genesis 1:26-28 (KJV) (emphasis added)

They had power and authority over Satan, but he was not going to have it if he could do anything about it, so he did just that and stole their power, dominion, and authority. That is why Satan is called the "ruler of this world" and the "god of this age." Adam handed it over to Satan through disobedience, yielding to him the control, authority, or power of this world. It was Adam's to lose. You have heard that expression before; it means "it's yours if you want it." Adam's sin was rebellion; he chose his will over God's, Eve was deceived. They both lost, relinquishing their place and giving Satan a temporary victory, including all the spoils of territory and power. We know this is true when we read of the temptation of Jesus in the wilderness. Satan offered Him all the kingdoms of the world if Jesus would bow and worship him. Jesus did not deny his right to offer them; because they were legally Satan's to give. The good news, though, is he is not all-powerful or omnipotent, as God. Jesus said, "And Jesus came and spake unto them, saying, All power is given unto me in heaven and in earth" (Matthew 28:18, KJV).

However, one of the more challenging ways Satan comes is as the "*angel of light*." For many unsuspecting people who think they are Christians, and even those that are, Satan is hard at work mixing enough truth with lies to deceive "even the elect, if possible." For non-Christians, what a great deception to make them think they have salvation, whether through good works, generosity, church attendance, you name it. On the other hand, for Christians, he seduces them into believing a powerless "social" gospel that brings in doubt and despair. As a result, Christians depart from the church, making them ineffective and fruitless, stealing their place, possessions, and power. You can see how Satan could advance if he keeps believers, the church divided, distracted, defeated, and disengaged. We have families, provisions, healing, ministries, miracles, and souls at stake. God calls it our inheritance:

> *To open their eyes, and to turn them from darkness to light, and from the power of Satan unto God, that they may receive forgiveness of sins, and inheritance among them which are sanctified by faith that is in me.*

Acts 26:18 (KJV) (emphasis added)

Satan does not want us to see, know or understand how gloriously rich and abundant is the inheritance of the saints. Adam and Eve did not appreciate that they had it all. Now, we join with Paul's prayer for the church at Ephesus that God would open our eyes to the wisdom and revelation of the power of the truth of our inheritance. Lies blind and lies bind, but truth helps us see and sets us free. The lies of the enemy keep us from seeing and taking what is ours. Truth exposes lies and deception. No longer can the enemy hold you as his captive when you fully comprehend the truth. Moreover, no longer will you hold to the lies of darkness when you see the light. The light of the gospel exposes the darkness. Then the church can walk in all God has for her.

We have some worthwhile valuables at stake here, and he knows it! We oftentimes forget that the devil believes and trembles. Remember, Satan quoted scripture to Jesus in His temptation. My husband, Pastor Ken, said, "He's a bad devil, but he's not a stupid one." Remember, the devil has been at this a long time, although he usually exposes himself by overplaying his hand. God already has an answer for any move he makes. The only problem is, if we do not know Scripture or the truth, Satan can pervert and twist it all day long, and we will never suspect any foul play.

Satan, the great dragon, the old serpent, has nothing new, and he is not alone. The angels that fell with him have been placed in strategic areas the Bible calls "principalities." They actually have been given specific assignments and locations to work their evil plans. He has also assigned "rulers" or "master spirits" of the darkness and engages with spirit forces of wickedness in the heavenly realm. Have you noticed the flood of interest and exploitation in the entertainment world of the supernatural? If we are not careful, we will fall victim to paralyzation and blindness as a soldier through unbelief to the reality of this war.

His game is old, and his tactics, subtle or not, should be obvious to the believer. So why, then, do we struggle? If he is so obvious, and we know his tactics, why has the church taken such a hit? Confusion! With all the insight God gives on our enemy, the church still is not convinced there is a war. Many pretend, deny, or are, at best, vague about it. Whether out of fear, ignorance, or indifference, confusion paralyzes its soldiers.

Some confusion continues over who the enemy is when some blame God for their problems, while others blame each other or their leaders. Still, others may blame Satan or God for what is actually our part. Surely, somebody, anybody else, should take responsibility for the attacks and losses in our life. We should not have to be responsible for our response; they (anybody else) should fix it. Think about it; he is only being and doing what he is: a liar, he lies; a murderer, he kills; a thief, he steals; an accuser, he accuses; and, a tempter, he tempts.

The question is, with Eve as our example, why do we continue to listen to his lies. Are we letting him destroy the gifts and blessings of God? Do we give him access or entrance to accuse and tempt? Even though we may understand the enemy, we still can struggle in this warfare, feeling defeated and destroyed. Confusion in any of these areas, including what is at stake, leads to defeat, depression, division, and ultimately, captivity. Maybe you have already experienced this. You may be saying, "You don't understand; it's too late for me!" To which I say, "It's never too late! You are alive, aren't you? And you are reading this book!" Praise the Lord!

What War?

Now that we know who the players are, let's clarify what we mean when we say "war." The Bible realistically describes warfare and bloodshed from the time of the entrance of sin into the human race (Genesis 3). Nevertheless, what is "war" for the New Testament believer, the church? Are we talking bloodshed? Until the "Day of the Lord" comes, there is a conflict, a fight, active and aggressive hostility with the lives and the faith of every man, woman, and child. "Simon, stay on your toes. Satan has tried his best to separate all of you from me, like chaff from wheat" (Luke 22:31, MSG). God gives life, and the enemy, Satan, seeks separation from God today just like He did with Adam and Eve and the disciples. Still distracting, dividing, and denying our relationship with the Lord, he ultimately and actively seeks our demise, and even to the point of death. "The thief cometh not, but for to steal, and to kill, and to destroy: I am come that they might have life, and that they might have it more abundantly" (John 10:10, KJV). Just on this statement alone, whom do you think has been behind the massive slaughtering of millions of unborn children in the world. Many Christians around the world have suffered intense persecution, torture, and death for their faith in Jesus Christ. Yes, we are talking bloodshed; Satan plays for keeps; just look at the suicide rates. God has even ordained the very soldiers and "peace" officers, men and women who serve in law enforcement as sheriffs, deputies, police officers, FBI agents, etc., to protect this great nation and others to work as "ministers of God" to keep the peace! The peace we enjoy is a gift from God.

> *For he is the minister of God to thee for good. But if thou do that which is evil, be afraid; for he beareth not the sword in vain: for he is the minister of God, a revenger to execute wrath upon him that doeth evil.*
>
> Romans 13:4 (KJV)

Oh, how we need a renewed respect for these heroes. God has ordained these powers to protect the society against many evils. If one resists, then a conflict ensues. Each of these "ministers" operates under specific jurisdiction and laws or guidelines. Unless you are designated as one of these official "ministers," you have your own personal jurisdiction for not only yourself but also your family and your property, whereby you may seek to protect and guard against attack or assault. "For though we walk in the flesh, we do not war after the flesh" (2 Corinthians 10:3, KJV).

We are talking about a physical and spiritual war, but not warring in or after the ways of our flesh or the world. The world does not fight fair; that is the way of the flesh. Paul tells us that the believer, though walking in the flesh or in the world, does not war as the world does. We do not fight according to our emotions, our passions, or the ways of the world, "dog eat dog." How many times are we tempted, and how many times have we fallen, thinking that fighting on the same level as the world would give us what we want, whether satisfaction or success, only to find out, in the end, it doesn't work? James explains further what this "war after the flesh" looks like:

> *Where do you think all these appalling wars and quarrels come from? Do you think they just happen? Think again. They come about because you want your own way, and*

fight for it deep inside yourselves. You lust for what you do not have and are willing to kill to get it. You want what is not yours and will risk violence to get your hands on it. You would not think of just asking God for it, would you?

James 4:1-2 (MSG)

So we see, this is the lust of the flesh, striving for what we see and feel, fighting to get or keep what we want and do not have. This is the world's war, fighting in the natural or in the "flesh." The enemy would just love us to stay on this plane or level because as long as we do, he wins, and we lose. We not only lose the battle, but you can lose your mind, your peace, and everything warring in the flesh. So then what war?

We, God's girls, are called to a holy war, a woman's war. War as a noun, a literal conflict, struggle or battle, and war as a verb, active engagement or participation as in combat, wrestle or fight in the supernatural, the realm of faith. Paul says it this way, "Fight the good fight of faith, lay hold on eternal life, whereunto thou art also called, and hast professed a good profession before many witnesses" (1 Timothy 6:12, KJV). The implied subject is "you," you "fight," first, in a "good" fight, and then, secondly, "of faith." God calls this holy war good or worth everything, and then He informs us that it is all about our faith. This is not for the faint of heart, the weak, the insecure, or the confused. This war is very real; it is a good fight and one that is worthwhile. Here we learn this is a war of words; our faith begins with a good profession. And now the challenge is to speak or not to speak, and the wisdom to know the difference. And when and if we do, what words? God not only invites women to the war but appoints and anoints us for the fight. You may think, I'm a woman; does God really mean for me to fight? I want you to remember how God has called on women all throughout the Bible. We have talked about Rahab and Esther already. There is another wonderful story about a woman known for her courage, wisdom, and strength, whose name is Deborah, meaning "honey bee." Her name has come to be associated with hard work, persistence, and importance in light of the contribution of the "honey bee." Even in this simple little creature, we see the beauty and miracle of God. A bee is not aerodynamically supposed to fly, but it does anyway. See how a woman, Deborah, flies right into the middle of a battle.

Let us here take encouragement to set up this stone from two women whom God used to "war," Deborah and a woman named Jael, one a leader and one a housekeeper. Beginning in Judges 4, we find the Israelites caught again in the cycle of compromise and chastisement. They had left the ways of God and did evil, so God allowed King Jabin, along with his Captain Sisera, to take them captive. Suffering cruel bondage for twenty years, they cry out to God. How faithful is God to even listen to us! He knows us best and loves us the most. Enter Deborah, a very unusual situation where God raises up a woman as not only a prophetess but also a judge. "And Deborah, a prophetess, the wife of Lapidoth, she judged Israel at that time" (Judges 4:4, KJV).

This is the first and only time we find this dual role in Scripture, held specifically by a woman and interestingly in the Old Testament. Nonetheless, God can and will use women to accomplish His purpose all the while bringing even more glory to Himself. God, by His divine Spirit, gave her knowledge of His will by which she became His mouthpiece. She was in a position of authority to give insight and direction in matters both in the civil arena, as the Judge, and in the spiritual, as the prophetess.

Now, at the same time, God had placed a military leader by the name of Barak over all the men of war of Israel. God evidently had spoken very clear instructions to Barak, but he was slow in responding to the call. So Deborah calls for him,

> *And she sent and called Barak the son of Abinoam out of Kedesh Naphtali, and said unto him, Hath not the Lord God of Israel commanded, saying, Go and draw toward mount Tabor, and take with thee ten thousand men of the children of Naphtali and of the children of Zebulun? And I will draw unto thee to the river Kishon Sisera, the captain of Jabin's army, with his chariots and his multitude; and I will deliver him into thine hand.*

Judges 4:6-7 (KJV)

In fact, she was right, the Lord had told him, but he was afraid, even when God gave him assurance of winning. Listen to his response, "And Barak said unto her, If thou wilt go with me, then I will go: but if thou wilt not go with me, then I will not go" (Judges 4:8, KJV).

Wow! You expect to hear that out of your kids, but not a captain in charge, and especially to a woman. She obviously came to be very trusted. She must have been amazed, but, while agreeing, she had to let him know that God would give the glory of the victory to a woman. The lesson, don't delay, obey. Have you ever imagined that if your covering, the one God sets up to deliver you and your people, does not fight for you, God will raise up someone else? That someone might be a woman. He may be saying to you, "You are this woman!" You may be the one God says, "Okay, if they won't get me the victory, I will give it to you."

So, Deborah goes with him into battle, and as they wait, God gives her the go-ahead. She calls for Barak to lead the army into battle, and the enemy is defeated. However, the commander, Sisera, realizing his army was defeated, escapes in fear and flees for his life. Thinking he may find safety at an acquaintance's tent, he agrees to the offer of his friend's wife Jael to go in her tent and hide. After she gave him food and drink, he fell asleep. Then, while he was sleeping, Jael took advantage of the opportune moment and drove a tent peg through his temple into the ground. When Barak came looking for Sisera, Jael came out to bring him in and show him the death of his enemy. Wow! That is staying focused and alert until the victory is won! But please, do not try this at home! God gave the victory to this woman, Jael. Sometimes you just have to wait and let God bring the victory to you by the hand of someone else!

The next chapter is a song of victory by Deborah and Barak of how God used a woman to get Himself this win. "Blessed above women shall Jael the wife of Heber the Kenite be, blessed shall she be above women in the tent" (Judges 5:24, KJV). A simple "tent-keeper," or we might say today a "homemaker," receives the glory for the victory. We, fortunately, are not called to drive tent pegs, but in a real sense, the church of God continues to face an enemy. Jesus said, "If they hated me, don't be surprised when they hate you." Could it be that God is looking to use you? Maybe you are in a very strategic location to give God the victory. Maybe you feel alone in the desert-like Jael, or maybe you feel like God has set you up to call a man to the battle. Either way, God wants to use you if you will humble yourself before Him and let Him exalt you in due time.

Deborah stayed courageous, spoke the challenge boldly and confidently, yet at the same time, remained sensitive to the voice of God, listening and heeding His word and instructions. We must exercise our sensitivity to the Holy Spirit so much so that in the heat of the battle, we only say and do exactly as God leads and instructs. She kept it simple and to the point without bringing any demeaning or insulting language. God honored her humility by giving the glory of the victory to a woman. Without any fear, doubt, or unbelief, she willingly engaged in the war, confident of her God. Our next question is:

When?

The enemy, knowing his time is short, is always going about seeking, looking actively for his next victim. When the enemy is on the move, we must be ready to go. All our armor and weapons which we will cover are of no value if we do not know how, when, and where to use them. You may know there is a reason to fight, and you may even see the battle looming, but until you learn to hear from God for His instructions on when, or how, or who, you will either not be ready and miss the call, or you may jump in too soon and be ahead of God. Still practically, however, the battle rages on without ceasing, and we are encouraged to be alert, on guard, sober, watching. And, as Paul encourages, "Praying always with all prayer and supplication in the Spirit, and watching thereunto with all perseverance and supplication for all saints" (Ephesians 6:18, KJV).

You may see the battle raging, but like Esther, we begin in prayer. Not until we have our marching orders or clear instruction do we engage. Only then are we fit for battle. When Jesus resisted the devil three times in the wilderness, angels came and strengthened Him, reviving, renewing, and fitting Him to carry on. Although we, too, may have seasons or times of respite, the battle continues to rage until: "The Lord said unto my Lord, Sit thou at my right hand, until I make thine enemies thy footstool" (Psalm 110:1, KJV).

The Lord is waiting for "the precious fruit of the earth" until all His children come to Him, then the final war rages where the enemy of our soul faces his final defeat and destiny. Fortunately, we can read the end of the book!

Where?

So now the question is, where is the war, or where do we war? "For, when we were come into Macedonia, our flesh had no rest, but we were troubled on every side; without were fightings, within were fears" (2 Corinthians 7:5, KJV).

Two places the war is fought: within and without. Within our soul, our flesh, that is to say, our mind, will, and emotions, we contend with thoughts, decisions, and feelings that must be brought under the control of the Holy Spirit. What we think leads to what we feel; what we feel fuels our passions which ultimately leads to our choices. This is the battleground where the enemy likes to wage war, and this truly is where victory or defeat is framed. Then without, the war without is all around, activities presented in the world and influences by the devil. We are to "be in the world, but not of it," or given to its influences. Significant to remember here again is that this war takes place in the supernatural realm first, "against principalities, against powers, against the rulers of the darkness of this world, against spiritual wickedness in high places." We war in the supernatural, not the flesh (Ephesians 6:12). While we may experience confrontations, attacks, assaults, insults, or temptations physically, emotionally, or mentally, the true battle is first spiritual, not physical. These attacks serve only as a distraction. Understanding where the war is will help us not only fight well but also stay protected. The victory is sure on God's battleground.

Are you where God would have you be? If not, come out, and at once, for you certainly ought not to be there. If you are, then be afraid to complain of circumstances which God has ordained on purpose to work out in you the very image and likeness of His Son.

Mark Guy Pearse

"Come out at once" or as the scripture says, "flee!" Paul's instruction is to "flee" or to run as fast as you can back to God, and He will lead you back to the highway of holiness. There is no shortcut, no back road. There is just one way, God's way, repentance through Jesus His Son, who is "the Way."

This will take some retraining. First, recognizing we have an enemy, that we are in a war, that he is constantly maneuvering, and then that this war takes place in the unseen world should raise the question, so how do I win? First, to run away is certain defeat, but to run to God and His Word will give us the tools for certain victory. The underlying reason helps give encouragement...

Why?

Why war? Why or for what reason do I or should I engage in this war is a fair question. The answer helps set the stage for the strategy. We have talked about what is at stake: our position, possessions, power, peace, and particularly people, but the root of this is our faith. Because we appropriate these gifts, blessings, and fruit by faith, the enemy knows, if he can steal our faith, he can deliver a devastating blow to not only our life, our family, and the church, but to the kingdom of God. Paul told Timothy about this fight of faith that we were "called" to it.

We war because God has literally "called" us to this fight, a "good" fight of faith in every area of my life. To lay hold or firmly grasp and appropriate for myself all that God has for me. Knowing

God actually called me, literally chose me for this fight gives a great sense of confidence in expecting victory. Yes, the battle is the Lord's, and He is calling you as an enlisted soldier, that is who we are:

> *Thou therefore endure hardness, as a good soldier of Jesus Christ. No man that warreth entangleth himself with the affairs of this life; that he may please him who hath chosen him to be a soldier.*
>
> 2 Timothy 2:3-4 (KJV) (emphasis added)

So why? To please God as a good soldier, faithful to the end, knowing He chose me, and in so doing, we as women, like Deborah, will give God all the more fame and glory. We literally make Him proud, like when He bragged about Job to the devil, God brags about you.

Also, we see our purpose in the words of Nehemiah, who encouraged the Israelites as they were rebuilding the wall of Jerusalem in the face of their enemies:

> *And I looked, and rose up, and said unto the nobles, and to the rulers, and to the rest of the people, Be not ye afraid of them: remember the Lord, which is great and terrible, and fight for your brethren, your sons, and your daughters, your wives, and your houses.*
>
> Nehemiah 4:14 (KJV)

Fight for people, their lives, possessions, positions, power, and ultimately, to establish, maintain and advance the kingdom of God and His glory. We fight for, not against, our marriages, for our families, not against them. "For" means I know and understand that the Almighty God empowers me, His hand is upon me, He strengthens me, and stations angels to not only stand guard all about me but fight when necessary. Upholding me is the Almighty

God who is for me and for giving me an abundant life, or life to the full. That includes so many things, and not the least of which is our families knowing, loving, and serving God. You can waste a lot of time and energy fighting in your marriages and families, accomplishing nothing, enduring, and even losing ground for the kingdom. Fighting for them is the higher purpose. When we do this, we connect with all of heaven's glory and power to bring the kingdom of God to our homes.

Finally, the *Lord* gives us this promise as our purpose:

> *He that overcometh, the same shall be clothed in white raiment; and I will not blot out his name out of the book of life, but I will confess his name before my Father, and before his angels.*

Revelation 3:5 (KJV)

For the overcomer, she is promised a glorious reception, clothed in a spotless robe of gladness, treated as more than a conqueror, given the priestly array to in turn offer the glory back to the Father. With our purpose heavenly, the glory divine, and the reward worthy, we engage all our faculties with all His energy. This is the high calling of God in Christ Jesus. May His kingdom come, in you, in me, in our homes, our churches, our communities, and around the world until the day of the Lord.

Acknowledging that (1) we have an enemy, (2) who that is, (3) when and where he operates, and (4) why we are to engage helps us prepare, strategize, war, and win. With that in mind, let us now look at how we war.

How?

How do we wage war in the 21st century as a soldier, a warrior in the army of God? Great question! With the following seven principles as a framework, we launch into a biblical perspective to acquire tools that will develop and strengthen our spiritual muscles. With these, we may war well, fighting fair in order to please our Captain, the Lord, when we win! In this war, we come out with more than just a win; we come out above and beyond what we can imagine.

Principle 1. War with Confidence:

First, and foremost we begin preparations by taking the hand of the Lord, our Husband, while breaking up with doubt. Let that old, dead, lifeless defeated relationship with fear and doubt go, and embrace the Lord. In the arms of our Lover, we gain all the assurance and confidence necessary to know without a doubt that God is for us.

> *What then shall we say to [all] this? If God is for us, who [can be] against us? [Who can be our foe, if God is on our side?] (Psalm 118:6) Yet amid all these things we are more than conquerors and gain a surpassing victory through Him Who loved us.*

Romans 8:31, 37 (AMPC)
(emphasis added) (parentheses added for clarity)

What possible defense could be mounted against one who is safely held in the arms of the Almighty God? The *Lord* is on my side; I will not fear: what can man do unto me? We are more than conquerors, which means as overcomers, we go out with more than the victory; we take the spoils as well. "Be strong and courageous. Be not afraid nor dismayed with us is the Lord our God, to help us, and to fight our battles" (2 Chronicles 32:7a, 8a, NKJV).

In Romans, Paul asks, "If God is for you, who can be against you?" What can man do? What man can stand against the omnipotent, all-powerful defense, protection, and aid of heaven? Think about it, who do you see as against you, your spouse, your in-laws, your children, a coworker, maybe your boss? Maybe your teacher or even a leader at your church is putting up resistance or even attacking you. Or, maybe, like Deborah, there may be someone who is not necessarily against you; they are just apathetic, not fulfilling the call of God on their life, and it effects you. Paul rhetorically asks because his point is no matter who is against you, well-meaning as they may seem, their power against you is not to be compared to the power of God who is for you! If God, who? The question here is, do you know, understand, and, more importantly, believe God and believe He is for you? Take a minute and say that to yourself, "God is for me," then out loud, "*God is for me*!" Believe that, sister! "Ye are of God, little children, and have overcome them: because greater is he that is in you, than he that is in the world" (1 John 4:4, KJV).

He is in you and for you, to have life and life more abundantly! He loves you, sees you, and hears you; He knows, understands, sympathizes, and has a plan for battle. My job is to keep believing, keep the dream alive, dream the impossible! Chase it, even go so far as to eagerly seize it.

> And from the days of John the Baptist until the present time, the kingdom of heaven has endured violent assault, and violent men seize it by force [as a precious prize—a share in the heavenly kingdom is sought with most ardent zeal and intense exertion].
>
> Matthew 11:12 (AMPC)

Seize the kingdom, go after it, chase it with an intensity, a zeal assured of victory. Chasing the prize, the victory of the kingdom of God, righteousness, peace, and joy in the Holy Ghost. This kingdom is our Promised Land, a confidence in God: believing, resting, and enjoying victory with God. War with assurance, confidence in the promises of God, His ability, and His desire to give us the kingdom. If a doubt comes, doubt it! Doubt the doubt, and believe God. No more stressing, fuming, manipulating, arguing, only believing, resting, enjoying. God has got this! Believe! He may not do it the same every time, it may look different and sound different, but with confidence, I am assured and know that no matter who the foe or what the circumstance, the Lord is the Captain of the Angel Armies. "Cast not away therefore your confidence, which hath great recompense of reward" (Hebrews 10:35, KJV).

In this confidence, I know He is mine, and I am His. I now receive, know, and understand my territory and boldly accept the challenge to take, protect and defend all God has given me. This is my mission, and with God, nothing is impossible, and His word will never self-destruct but, on the contrary, stand forever!

Principle 2. War with Silence:

And Joshua had commanded the people, saying, Ye shall not shout, nor make any noise with your voice, neither shall any word proceed out of your mouth, until the day I bid you shout; then shall ye shout.

Joshua 6:10 (KJV)

"To every thing there is a season, and a time to every purpose under the heaven: A time to rend, and a time to sew; a time to keep silence, and a time to speak" (Ecclesiastes 3:1, 7, KJV).

Before the praise, before the shout, war with silence. There comes a time to cease all noise, to cease from speaking and even shouting, to wait and listen through the silence for the voice of one calling us to "stand still and see the salvation of the Lord."

Our temptation is to tell the story and then tell it over and over again. Stop! Hold your peace. Sometimes we have too much to say, but God says when you are talking, He is silent, but when we are silent, God can do the speaking. I have heard some women say, "I just have to give him a piece of my mind." No, you don't! You will need that piece. Trust me on this and try it; you will see change. People know, especially men, how hard it is for women to hold their tongue, so just the silence alone is a sign that God has showed up. We errantly think we need to discuss everything with people, especially our husbands, but God is saying, "Silence, stop talking!"

> *Likewise, wives, be subject to your own husbands, so that even if some do not obey the word, they may be won without a word by the conduct of their wives, when they see your respectful and pure conduct.*
>
> 1 Peter 3:1-2 (ESV)

Silence wins your husbands' submission to the word of God. Amazing! You may ask, how does silence work? Shouldn't I point out where he is missing it? *No!* Our silence is counted as respect when it is done in sincerity, with a pure heart, not as punishment as in giving them "the silent treatment." This is a husband's love language, respect. He will probably wonder what happened to you when you do not give reaction to his foolishness. The next time you are tempted to tell your side of the story or to explain everything, or try to discuss a problem, be silent. God just may be waiting on you to trust Him through your silence to let Him speak for you. Sometimes, just change the subject, and talk about something totally unrelated. Just for fun, throw something totally off base and "out there," so to speak, just to throw them a really good curveball. Keep them guessing, "What has gotten into her?"

Remember, if we believe God is our Advocate, our lawyer, our defense, then we both cannot talk about the issue at the same time. When you stop talking, God will tell your story, your side better than you. What He has to say will be delivered and articulated in just the right way to cut through and make the point, and yes, even yield the desired result. Think of Esther and her silent patience in waiting for the right moment to speak without accusing Xerxes. What about Rahab, keeping her secret to herself and not telling of the spies. Then there is Sarah, who we did not hear from for thirteen years while they waited for the miracle of Isaac? Their silence was broken with laughter by the son of promise, Isaac, meaning "laughter." Remember Hannah, who told her story to the Lord and then left the priest "no more sad" after she received her word from the Lord? Now, only faith in action was needed to bring forth the baby, no talking or complaining, only serving and sex! No wonder her husband Elkanah let her offer the boy to the priest; he was stunned into silence. The silent, faith-filled, hopeful, sexual pursuit of his wife revealed the glory of the Lord.

Silence and fear can, and will, position you to allow the mighty power of God to move on your behalf. Talk to God. We women sometimes just talk too much. If you must talk, talk the Word of God in prayer. God wants to hear you! Your husband may not listen or want to hear you, but God does. And actually, the devil is waiting to hear you too. Silence to man, words to God. Hopefully, you see the power in silence, and maybe now it is your time, war with silence. "The Lord shall fight for you, and ye shall hold your peace" (Exodus 14:14, KJV).

Principle 3. War with Words:

We begin our new life in Christ with our confession and profession of Jesus as our Lord, and that before many witnesses. We confess Him before men even in our baptism at the beginning, and then we continue, or keep on confessing and professing Him in the face of certain persecution or temptation with words first of praise.

Of Praise ~

> *When he (Jehosaphat) had consulted with the people, he appointed singers to sing to the Lord and praise Him in their holy [priestly] garments as they went out before the army, saying, Give thanks to the Lord, for His mercy and loving-kindness endure forever! And when they began to sing and to praise, the Lord set ambushments against the men of Ammon, Moab, and Mount Seir who had come against Judah, and they were [self-] slaughtered;*
>
> 2 Chronicles 20:21-22 (AMPC)
> (parentheses added for clarity)

Now, on the other hand, there is a time to open our mouths, but with a praise, not a complaint. Praise will raise you; praise brings God on the scene. Complain, and you remain; complaints open the door to the enemy. Who do you want on the scene? Who do you want working for you, God and His angels, or the devil and his demons? When they began to sing, God moved! When you begin to sing and to praise, Heaven moves. War with praise, words of thanksgiving to God.

David was a man of great victories, and he praised the Lord seven times a day. That is stopping to give God praise about every other hour. Give thanks to the Lord for His mercy, His loving kindness, His justice and righteousness, His protection, His faithfulness. Give thanks; He is not a man that He should lie; He never changes! He is the same yesterday, today, and forever. Praise His Holy name! Give thanks; He is the Lord, your Husband. He has called you to His banqueting table, and over you, He flies a banner of love. "He brought me to the banqueting house, and his banner over me was love [for love waved as a protecting and comforting banner over my head when I was near him]" (Song of Solomon 2:4, AMPC).

In the valley, sing:

> *And I will give her her vineyards from thence, and the valley of Achor for a door of hope: and she shall sing there, as in the days of her youth, and as in the day when she came up out of the land of Egypt.*
>
> Hosea 2:15 (KJV)

When it seems like all is lost, sing. When it seems like you are at the end of yourself sing, the victory is at hand. The victory of faith is nigh thee, even in your mouth. Your victory is as close to you as your mouth. Open it up and give thanks always, in all things. Offer the fruit of your lips, that is, giving thanks to His name. To the King of Kings, the Lord of Lords, and God Most High be praise continually. Yes, it is a sacrifice when marching into battle, but it is this sacrifice that God desires, not the blood of bulls and goats. "By him therefore let us offer the sacrifice of praise to God continually, that is, the fruit of our lips giving thanks to his name" (Hebrews 13:15, KJV).

He wants to hear the voice of victory, the voice that gives God the glory before, during, and after the battle. Praise God now; you are a victor. "But thanks be to God, Who gives us the victory [making us conquerors] through our Lord Jesus Christ" (1 Corinthians 15:57, AMPC).

Of Testimony ~

"And they *overcame* him by the *blood* of the Lamb, and by the *word of their testimony;* and they loved not their lives unto the death" (Revelation 12:11, KJV) (emphasis added).

John, the revelator, shares how he sees the church overcoming our accuser. The words of your testimony literally overcome the enemy. We begin with confessing Jesus as Lord. Then, we continue with what we attest to as true and accurate, either agreement with God through His testaments and will by faith or agreement with the natural, the seen world as the truth. If you, as a woman of faith, want to experience success in defeating the enemy, you must set your conversation aright in honoring God's word, His truth, above any reality you face. Then declare the goodness of God in your life, giving Him glory for all He has done. Remember, give God glory, not the devil, in your testimony.

The word of your testimony, your declaration is powerful, life-giving, and victorious. When by faith you believe and confess the Lord and His word in the midst of every situation and circumstance in your life, God enters, invades, and changes things. When I testify that He is Jehovah Jireh in my finances, Jehovah Rapha in my body, Jehovah Shalom in my home, Yahweh, the Great I am that I am, my Shield, and Buckler, my Strong Tower, and a very present help in time of trouble, I give the devil a stab with my sword and gain ground. I declare He is my Comforter when I mourn, my Counselor when I am confused, my way-maker when I am lost, my bread when I hunger, my living water when I thirst, and my strength when I am weak. He is the Lord, my Husband, in security and safety, in righteousness and judgment, and in loving kindness and tender mercies. He says I am an overcomer, not a failure; I am a forgiven saint, not a sinner; I am His child, an Heir, not alone; and I am washed, cleansed by His blood, not dirty.

My words of agreement with God overcome the attack on my mind, emotions, body, spirit, finances, family, etc. No one can speak for you; you must give voice to your faith. Faith is voice-activated! When I feel bound, He says I am free; when I feel unloved, He says I am loved; when I feel forgotten, He says I am chosen; when I feel alone, He says I am family; and when I feel dirty, He says I am Holy. Agree with God now, add your "Amen," declare His truth as your testimony in the face of doubt, fear, and attack. A confident testimony, words of life spoken boldly, open the door for the entrance of the King of Glory to come into every area of our life and war on our behalf. Speaking words of truth and life into the dead places paves a path for God to come in all His glory into your life. Just like when Paul and Silas offered praises, God came in and opened the prison doors. Overcome sister by the word of your testimony. Lift up your voice and testify of God! Take these words and testify His Word is true.

Principle 4. War with Authority:

> *And Jesus came and said to them, "All authority in heaven and on earth has been given to me. Go therefore and make disciples of all nations, baptizing them in the name of the Father and of the Son and of the Holy Spirit,"*
>
> Matthew 28:18-19 (ESV)

Next, we war with authority. The same power that raised Jesus from the dead lives in me, and with that, He bestows His authority to continue the ministry, carry out the commission, and conquer the enemy. We are sent to do the bidding of the King, in the King's name. Jesus has done all that was necessary to give us everything we need on the cross.

> *Behold, I have given you authority to tread upon serpents and scorpions, and over all the power of the enemy: and nothing shall in any wise hurt you. Nevertheless in this rejoice not, that the spirits are subject unto you; but rejoice that your names are written in heaven.*
>
> Luke 10:19-20 (ASV)

He gives us authority or power over all the power of the enemy! Helps word studies describes this authority from the Greek word "eksousia" as authority being conferred power; delegated empowerment ("authorization"), operating in a designated jurisdiction. Eksousía, "delegated power," refers to the authority God gives to His saints—authorizing them to act to the extent they are guided by faith in His revealed word. So the question is, what is my designated jurisdiction? The area under my authority, responsibility, or control is my focus. That alone will keep me busy, so best to leave the areas, not under my control alone.

For example, remember Jael, she was at home in her tent minding her own business when along came the enemy. She could handle this now that Sisera came into her tent; that was her "designated jurisdiction." She defeated him, and God blessed her with the glory of the victory. On the other hand, we mentioned how Queen Esther, after three days of fasting with her handmaidens, used her position as Queen and boldly offered herself in humble submission, trusting God for the favor and goodness of the King interceding on behalf of a whole nation. She, defeating the enemy, paved the way for victory and gained the greater renown for her people, and more importantly, for God.

God gives us wisdom to exercise authority in our homes, through the blood covenant in our marriage, over our children, and over all our property when we stay in order, in a position of submission. When you are a woman properly positioned under your head, you will be in submission to your husband if you are married or to your pastor or parent if you are single. From a position of submission, you are in order, and the power of God can flow to you and through you defeating the enemy and gaining the victory.

This authority is ours through the crediting of the blood and the name of Jesus to our account. When we overcome by the blood, we recognize the shedding of Jesus' blood as the covering for our sin, representing the new covenant. No other blood needs to be shed; He did it once and for all. There is power in the blood of Jesus. His blood overcame then, and His blood still speaks today on our behalf. By the shedding of His blood, He defeated death, hell, and the grave. As I stay submitted and surrendered to the Lord, I am protected and hidden by His victorious blood. Then, in the victory of His death and resurrection, I authoritatively testify as a covenanted one who has been redeemed, released, and revealed as a child of God that He is my Lord, my King, my protector, provider, lover, and Husband. Through agreement, my words take on the authority of heaven. Whatever area the enemy attacks, God has already been there and made provision in Himself through His Word. Jesus is the Word made flesh. When I testify, I simply agree with Jesus that His word is mine. "This is the third time I am coming to you. In the mouth of two or three witnesses shall every word be established" (2 Corinthians 13:1, KJV). All the promises of God are "yes" and "amen" in Christ Jesus; when I declare them, He has already answered an emphatic "Yes!" That is exercising authority. Boldly take your position of submission, knowing that in your place, this same mighty power flows to you.

Principle 5. War with Fasting:

"And he said unto them, This kind can come forth by nothing, but by prayer and fasting" (Mark 9:29, KJV).

Jesus, instructing the disciples on how to successfully overcome the enemy, has just cast out a demon that they could not. The difference he explains is fasting along with prayer. When we war with fasting, we simply "put our hand over our mouth." Covering your mouth, as in abstinence from food and drink, helps to focus our faith through denying our flesh. If you are looking for change and change quickly, add the spiritual discipline of fasting to your prayer life and watch God work on your behalf. Fasting with prayer makes a place for the manifestation of God's power. When I began to fast for my marriage, long-standing soul ties began to break off, and after some time, I knew I finally had one hundred percent of my husband. There are good books on fasting; however, the following explanation offers a brief overview.

The purpose of the fast is to set myself aside for the work of God in my life. Fasting creates a place in my heart for forgiveness, freedom, and filling with the Spirit of God. My faith undergoes a spiritual detox or cleansing. Fasting provides a purification to my spirit as it does a detox to my body. Doubt, insecurity, fear, unbelief are removed and replaced with the love, truth, and Spirit of God. Fasting inspires fervency. I become more "spirit" sensitive than "flesh" sensitive. If you sense apathy toward sin, a lack of faith, or need for more of God, then like Esther, like Moses, like Daniel, like Jesus, and like Paul, fast. Fasting says less of me and more of you, God. The question really never was "if" the disciples of Jesus would fast but "when":

*But thou, when thou fastest, anoint thine head, and
wash thy face; That thou appear not unto men to fast,
but unto thy Father which is in secret: and thy Father,
which seeth in secret, shall reward thee openly.*

Matthew 6:17-18 (KJV)(emphasis added)

It is somewhat of a lost discipline in the church, although some churches declare a congregational fast after the beginning of each new calendar year. The bible, however, records on many occasions where not just a personal fast was called, but also a national fast, in some places, referred to as a "Solemn Assembly." That is when a nation gathers together for the purpose of fasting and praying on behalf of their country, turning back to God. Ezra, Joel, Esther, Nehemiah, and others declared fasts.

Preparation is needed and helpful before beginning a fast. For example, begin to remove addictive food and beverages like sugars and caffeine from your diet. This is a good first step because of the side effects of detoxing. Once you have broken these addictions, you can safely set a time to fast. Then, determine the specific purpose of the fast and compile scriptures to focus and build up your faith. The Bible offers many examples of fasting, from Esther's three-day fast for the Jewish nation to the forty-day fasts of Moses and Jesus. The most popular is the twenty-one-day fast of Daniel, where he fasted meat, bread, and dairy products and ate fruits, vegetables, legumes, nuts, and grains. The important part is to set the time aside, usually spent on meal preparation and eating for praying. Usually, water is not fasted or, if so, only for a brief time. Endeavor to drink a gallon of water a day during a fast.

The fast that God favors is the secret fast that moves me with compassion to generosity through the giving of food, clothing, and shelter to the poor and outcast. Not an outward religious fast, but a fast that calls for soul searching in order that my heart will align with the generous, just heart of God. This is the fast accepted with promise of God hearing and healing "speedily."

> *Is not this the fast that I have chosen? to loose the bands of wickedness, to undo the heavy burdens, and to let the oppressed go free, and that ye break every yoke? Then shall thy light break forth as the morning, and thine health shall spring forth speedily: and thy righteousness shall go before thee; the glory of the Lord shall be thy rearward. Then shalt thou call, and the Lord shall answer; thou shalt cry, and he shall say, Here I am. If thou take away from the midst of thee the yoke, the putting forth of the finger, and speaking vanity;*
>
> Isaiah 58:6, 8-9 (KJV)

War with fasting defeats the enemy in ways you could never imagine. Remember Esther, before her fast, she could not envision herself going in to the King, much less confronting the enemy Haman face to face over a meal! Fasting replaced fear with faith, and the Jewish nation was saved. The annual Jewish festivities of Purim begin with fasting and then banqueting and giving of food. Is it any wonder the Jews are so blessed! May you begin to experience the victory and breakthrough of healing and deliverance through fasting in your life. Maybe begin with just one meal or one set day a week, but either way, set it aside for prayer.

Principle 6. War with Keys:

> *And I will give unto thee the keys of the kingdom of heaven: and whatsoever thou shalt bind on earth shall be bound in heaven: and whatsoever thou shalt loose on earth shall be loosed in heaven.*
>
> Matthew 16:19 (KJV) (emphasis added)

War with the kingdom keys. When we wage war and begin to do battle, we can quickly gain an advantage with these spiritual keys: binding and loosing. Keys give access or entrance, opening doors, but closing them as well. Kingdom keys give access to the working of the heavenly kingdom through allowing or forbidding spiritual activity. The power of the kingdom of heaven is available, and that power can be "bound" or "loosed" through the application of authority. Why would I need to "bind" or "loose"? Remember, God has given us authority here; we enforce the victory of the cross of Christ until His return.

What I bind or forbid to operate here is bound in heaven. Satan can only operate where he is given access or ground, forbid or bind him in your life, your family, and your home. These are under your jurisdiction or authority. If you allow him entrance, he can operate; without it, he is resisted. On the other hand, what I lose, or allow entrance, like the Spirit of God, has authority and influence. So bind the enemy and loose the presence of God in you and around you. Use your keys, open the door for the King of Glory, and kick the enemy out!

Ask God for discernment in this area so that you are not kicking him out one door and letting him in another. Satan is allowed entrance through all types of entertainment that are seemingly "innocent" but can have serious spiritual implications. For example, games, music, movies, and shows that do not glorify God, and some that even brazenly exalt the kingdom of darkness. Steer clear, stay away, flee, and do not set any wicked thing before your eyes. If you have, stop, repent, renounce Satan and his work, bind him and send him packing. You may need to throw out some things, do it! Begin to worship the Lord and give him all your property.

Then, loose God and spiritual blessings in heavenly places, and you will see a change.

Principle 7. War with Armor:

"Put on the whole *armour* of God, that ye may be able to stand against the wiles of the devil" (Ephesians 6:11, KJV) (emphasis added).

Our final means of defeating the enemy in our life is given by God and put on by us, that is, our armor. It is now time to get dressed for battle. God intends for us to engage in the warfare by getting dressed for battle and then standing against the "wiles," that is, the deceptions, attacks, and strategies the devil throws at you. So when it is all said and done, you will be the one still standing. With God's armor, we fight a "clean" fight, and when those that fight fair win, they keep their rewards. In order to be a "good" soldier, one must fight by the rules, just like an athlete in any competition. God laid out the rules through Jesus' life, and their culmination is revealed here in our armor.

God has thought of everything and given us everything to assure victory. We have covering from head to toe if we will put it on. Paul reminds us before we put it on, though, to be strong in the Lord and in the power of His might. It is the power and strength of God that will enable us to compete; otherwise, we would fall apart and lose the battle. Be strong in the Lord, my sister; you cannot do this on your own. You might be good, but you are not that good. You need Him. Remember, we were deceived by the enemy when we thought we could do it on our own. Ouch! We've paid the price long enough for that one, so give in to God's strength; trust me, you will need it for this.

Stand therefore, having your loins girt about with truth, and having on the breastplate of righteousness; And your

feet shod with the preparation of the gospel of peace;
Above all, taking the shield of faith, wherewith ye shall
be able to quench all the fiery darts of the wicked. And
take the helmet of salvation, and the sword of the Spirit,
which is the word of God:

Ephesians 6:14-17 (KJV)

The Belt of Truth~

The soldier's first item, as the Amplified Version calls it, is her belt. Seems a bit strange; neither my husband nor I put our belts on first. Typically, we think of a belt as an accessory, not a necessity, going on last. However, when you see so many young men walk around holding their pants up, you suddenly realize how nice a belt works and looks. In this, you see its purpose, to hold things up or together, to support. Think of how a police officer's belt holds so many things, bullets, clubs, mace, gun, handcuffs, etc., or the tool belt of a carpenter. In much the same way, a soldier's belt held the other armor in place, the breastplate and the sword. The other items, surrounded with the belt, could stay secure.

So too, for us, our spiritual armor depends on the strength and security of our belt. Paul calls it the "belt of Truth." For truth to be truth, it cannot be subjective. It does not change with the circumstance, the country, or the calendar. God is truth. "Jesus said to him, I am the Way and the *Truth* and the Life; no one comes to the Father except by (through) Me" (John 14:6, AMPC) (emphasis added). "Sanctify them [purify, consecrate, separate them for Yourself, make them holy] by the *Truth*; Your Word is Truth" (John 17:17, AMPC) (emphasis added). "Wherefore putting away lying, speak every man *truth* with his neighbor: for we are members one of another" (Ephesians 4:25, KJV) (emphasis added).

If Jesus is the Truth, then Paul is telling us in order to put Him on, we must surround ourselves with the truth. He, Truth, gives strength and support and holds everything together, literally our very life. He further explains His Word is Truth. Jesus, the Word who became flesh, is Truth. When nothing and nobody else can be trusted, God's Word can and will hold you up and hold you together. How do we put truth on? "But his delight is in the law of the LORD; and in his law doth he meditate day and night" (Psalm 1:2, KJV).

What are you looking at, thinking on, and listening to for direction? In other words, surround and fill yourself with the Word of God. Meditate, run over and over again in your mind, memorize and speak the word. Let the word of God dwell in you richly. Make a commitment to be a person of the Book, the Good Book. Read it, study it, learn it, memorize it, and listen to it. The world does not have this truth, and they are forever searching. This is your armor, put it on like a good soldier, prepare for the battle. Then, be a woman of truth. Determine you will speak truth. Live upright and honest in all things. Take responsibility for yourself. Without Truth, anything goes. With Truth, we are set free, free from bondage to peace.

Truth gives us stability and produces strength. We go from the milk to the meat as we develop in applying the Word to every area of our lives relationally, socially, physically, emotionally, and financially. God is calling for His children to grow up, gear up, and get in the fight! Flee evil and be free from deception by surrounding yourself with truth. Ready? Stand tall and buckle yourself up with the strength, security, and stability of the Belt of Truth, your "Bible Belt."

The Breastplate of Righteousness~

Next, we put on the breastplate. If you or someone you know has ever carried a gun, you may know about bulletproof vests. They are worn either hidden under your clothes or over them. Its purpose is obvious, to protect your vital organs, that is, your heart and your lungs. One direct shot can take you out instantly, rendering the victim either dead or completely harmless. We, too, in the same way, are told to protect our heart, to guard it, for out of it are the issues of life. Your heart is the place of your communion with God, the seat of your being, mind, will, and emotions. Satan had this and lost it, and oh, is he jealous of you having the beauty of the peace of that relationship. The breastplate that protects is righteousness. God gave His Son, Jesus, that we may live unto righteousness: "And be found in him, not having mine own righteousness, which is of the law, but that which is through the faith of Christ, the righteousness which is of God by faith" (Philippians 3:9, KJV). "Even as Abraham believed God, and it was accounted to him for righteousness" (Galatians 3:6, KJV). "For with the heart man believeth unto righteousness; and with the mouth confession is made unto salvation" (Romans 10:10, KJV).

Our heart is the seat of our faith where we believe unto righteousness. Once you get something in your heart, you will act on it; that is faith that works by love. The righteousness of God through faith in Jesus Christ protects and guards our heart by filling it with love. God is love. To be righteous is to be full of the love of God through faith in the goodness of God. "But let us, who are of the day, be sober, putting on the breastplate of faith and love" (1 Thessalonians 5:8a, KJV).

A bulletproof vest is stiff, and so is our breastplate of righteousness. It strengthens us to stand tall, straight, upright. Why?

We know we are loved not because of anything we have done to be right or to be right with God, but it is the power of faith in the gospel, the death, burial, and resurrection of our Lord Jesus Christ that gives us this standing. Confidence in the work of Christ as our righteousness is critical. "For he hath made him to be sin for us, who knew no sin; that we might be made the righteousness of God in him" (2 Corinthians 5:21, KJV).

When we submit to the work of Jesus Christ, we put on His righteousness or "right-wiseness." It is in believing we are right with God. When our faith is sure, the enemy cannot deceive us into thinking we are separated from the love of God. In the Old Testament, the High Priest wore a breastplate as a "memorial" to God of the chosen tribes of Israel. Now, in the New Testament, our breastplate is a memorial to the work of the cross of Jesus. God sees us covered with the righteousness Jesus earned. As I stay close to the cross through confession, repentance, and faith, love shines forth. In that is our strength to resist and to stand against the attack on our hearts. We are saved and secure through faith in the finished work of the cross of Calvary.

Our heart, filled and protected by the love and forgiveness of God, is now freed to commune with the Holy Spirit. How Satan wants to prevent you from the love of God, to keep you from giving and surrendering completely your heart to His embrace. Once we fully believe He loves, forgives, frees, and fills us, we are untouchable! That is why anything outside of faith is sin. It is impossible to please God without it. We must "believe God is," or that He actually, literally exists as God "and that He is a rewarder of those who diligently seek Him" (Hebrews 11:6, KJV). Abraham believed God. He believed! That faith was counted or credited to him as righteousness. Every time you take God at His Word, every time you stand on His promises, every time you believe Him, you hold your ground and thwart an attack on your heart. Let every step be a step of faith. Today declare, "God *is*" all that He reveals Himself to be.

Maybe you have never put on the armor, now is a good time. Or could it be that yours has been sitting in the corner for some time, unused, collecting dust. Give God your heart for the first time or once again, and put on your breastplate of righteousness. Start believing now. Now, then, always, and until; keep the faith. It is by faith that our heart keeps pumping; the just shall live by faith! Let faith in God's goodness fill your heart. Receive His love right now and rejoice forever. You are loved, highly favored, and blessed of God! Walk in that, my dear sister! Put on His righteousness, His "rightwiseness," in other words, His way of right thinking, being, and doing. His way is love. Pursue it, and your heart will stay protected. Righteousness wards off the wounds. Staying right with God yields a heart bubbling over with joy, issuing forth rivers of living water and producing a harvest of fruit. "But seek ye first the kingdom of God, and his righteousness; and all these things shall be added unto you" (Matthew 6:33 KJV).

Righteousness, positionally in Christ, covers me, and then practically through Christ, the breastplate of righteousness protects me. A heart open to God, surrendered, softened, and submitted to His will is the heart that is protected. When we harden our hearts, they are unprotected and easily broken. This is the paradox of the kingdom of God. The way up is down. The way of protection is not hardness; it is a tenderness toward God and people. A tender heart does not easily break; its softness makes it resilient. "A new heart also will I give you, and a new spirit will I put within you:

and I will take away the stony heart out of your flesh, and I will give you an heart of flesh" (Ezekiel 36:26, KJV).

Let God soften your heart and fill it full of His presence. Knowing God intimately stirs the desire and passion to protect the place of love. Put on the breastplate of righteousness; believe God now. His love is real, and He loves you. This love is unstoppable.

Shoes of Peace~

Next, we put on our "Peace Pumps," the preparation of the Gospel of peace. This means it is time to get ready to go. If God asked you right now to go share the Gospel with a stranger, would you know how? God says prepare to share! How well can you articulate the faith that lies within you? The charge here is to tell your faith story. Be ready to make peace or share your experience with the Lord. It may inspire someone to accept the Lord or maybe make things right with someone. "But sanctify the Lord God in your hearts: and be ready always to give an answer to every man that asketh you a reason of the hope that is in you with meekness and fear" (1 Peter 3:15, KJV). "For I am not ashamed of the gospel of Christ: for it is the power of God unto salvation to everyone that believeth; to the Jew first, and also to the Greek" (Romans 1:16, KJV).

What is the "gospel"? Very simply, the gospel is reconciliation with God through the death, burial, and resurrection of Jesus Christ, the Son of God, for the salvation of man. Death for our death, that if in Him we die, then in Him we live forever with God. That is the power the enemy cannot deny, the power of the resurrected Christ. God accepts us in the beloved, His Son, Jesus, when we accept Him as our Lord and Savior. God came to give us life and life more abundantly. Good news! We can be saved from our sins and have peace with God. With our "Peace Pumps" on, we are ready to go and humbly share why we have hope. Hope lights up your face in an otherwise dark world. Light draws attention. When you have the Light, people will want to know where or how to get it. Be prepared to share. We are ministers of reconciliation, reconciling men to God. We are peacemakers; seek peace. Start the day with your spiritual shoes of peace on, and you will be ready when the call comes.

Shield of Faith~

Now we are ready to pick up our "shield of faith." The word "shield" does not mean the small round shield which the soldier held in his hand to fight off the weapons of the enemy. It means the great oblong shield, much like a door, worn by the soldier to protect his/her body from the fiery darts thrown by the enemy. The darts were dipped in pitch or some other combustible material and set afire. When they struck, they served the purpose of small incendiary bombs. Satan has his fiery darts—those things that cause the believer:

- To question salvation;
- To question calling;
- To question if she is worthy;
- To question if she can really serve;
- To question if the project can really be done;
- To question, doubt, and wonder;
- To become discouraged, depressed, and defeated;
- To burn with passion and desire.

Such fiery darts are sent to strike at the core of the believer, her heart and mind. The sign of the Christian soldier, however, is the shield of faith, faith in God—a complete and perfect trust that God will quench the darts of doubt and evil that attack her, that God will help her control her mind and emotions, conquering the evil doubts and thoughts. The Christian soldier's defensive shield is her conscious reliance on God's presence all around and within her. "After these things the word of the LORD came unto Abram in a vision, saying, Fear not, Abram: I am thy *shield*, and thy exceeding great reward" (Genesis 15:1, KJV) (emphasis added). "For the LORD God is a sun and *shield*: the LORD will give grace and glory: no good thing will he withhold from them that walk uprightly" (Psalm 84:11, KJV) (emphasis added). "Our soul waiteth for the LORD: he is our help and our *shield*" (Psalm 33:20, KJV) (emphasis added).

God is our shield, our help, our exceeding great reward. He is our protection. God may call you to a place, a person, or a people group that is attacking you. Remember, our enemy is not flesh and blood; Satan's influence is supernatural. So too, your shield lifted supernaturally protects your heart and mind so you can continue to believe and love. Your faith in God's love and presence guards and protects your heart as a shield. Do you see why the enemy so desperately wants us to doubt God? If we do, we drop our shield. Trust, believe, and be fully persuaded God is who He says He is.

The command here, though, is to "take it up" or "lift it up" over all the other armor. Faith helps us to go even when we don't know. You may not have all the answers; that's okay; you may not be able to explain all the mysteries but, put up your shield of faith and keep trusting God. The enemy hurls these fiery darts as fast as he can, but no worries! Put up your shield; you do not have to defend God; He wants to defend you! Think about this shield. It is rather large, hard to see around, and meant to hide behind. Remember, it is faith. "Faith is the evidence of things not seen."

You trust without looking. God is your defense when you lift up the shield by trusting God. He is quenching the darts of the evil one. Like Jesus said, "Only believe, and you will see the glory of God." Not you fighting for your needs or your rights or even respect. Relax, lift up your shield, guard your heart; God's got it! Put up your resistance to the enemy, and he will flee. Thank God we can trust Him and know He is a God who sees, hears, and cares. You can trust God and move forward to take your ground and stake claim to all that God has for you. A woman with her shield of faith up knows God is who He says He is, and He can do what He says He can do. Faith perceives as real all God says in His Word. This truth supersedes any present reality, thereby affecting change in the natural. This is the power that is working in me, God's Word. "Now unto him that is able to do exceeding abundantly above all that we ask or think, according to the power that worketh in us" (Ephesians 3:20, KJV).

Keep lifting up your shield of faith. Let God see it; let the enemy see the shield. He cannot touch you behind the shield. One interesting component of an ancient Roman shield was that of leather. Not only was a shield made of wood, but also of leather. Oftentimes, they would soak the leather in water so as to quickly quench the fiery darts. How interesting that Jesus refers to Himself as the source of "living water."

> *Jesus answered and said unto her, If thou knewest the gift of God, and who it is that saith to thee, Give me to drink; thou wouldest have asked of him, and he would have given thee living water.*

> John 4:10 (KJV)

"He that believeth on me, as the scripture hath said, out of his belly shall flow rivers of living water" (John 7:38, KJV).

When we are hydrated, having drunk of the water of the Word, the living water, the only drink that truly satisfies, our protection is greater. Our shield is soaked as we drink freely of the water of life and let the words that are spirit and life flow out of us in giving glory to God. How much more efficient our shield is now in quenching those fiery darts. We will not get burned! Get your shield wet, drink of the living water, and let the rivers of life flow from your heart and life. Satan's fiery darts are of no consequence to the woman flowing in the spirit. Sometimes we just need to "soak" in the presence of God, "marinate," so to speak. "And he said unto me, It is done. I am Alpha and Omega, the beginning and the end. I will give unto him that is athirst of the fountain of the water of life freely" (Revelation 21:6, KJV).

If you are dry and thirsty, maybe even dying of thirst, come and drink freely of the water of life, the living water. Take in the person and the presence of Jesus; only He can truly satisfy. When you are satisfied, filled with the living water, out of your belly will flow rivers of living water. This is the life-giving water that quenches the enemy's fiery darts. Oh, taste and see that the Lord is good! Only He can satisfy. Lift up your cup, poured out and emptied of all the poisonous toxins of the world, the flesh and the devil, and drink of His living water, the glory of His presence. Fill my cup, Lord, fill it up and make me whole.

Imagine the power and protection of a door-sized shield soaked in water covering you. God's Word is amazing! These shields usually had an identifying mark of whose side the soldier was on as well. When the soldiers came together with the shields, they made something like an armored tank. Now God calls His church to be "built together for His habitation." When we stand together behind our shields of faith, we have greater protection. May we lift up the shield of faith, identify with God, and trust God to defeat the enemy and to protect us while we stand rejoicing!

Helmet of Salvation~

Next, we must protect our heads by putting on the "helmet of salvation." With the assurance and confidence, knowing Jesus will one day return and take us home to be with Him, we can stand against Satan's attacks of doubt and confusion. As a blow to the head could be deadly, salvation by grace through faith in the finished work of the cross of Christ is a sure defense. A person without the hope of salvation will certainly fall prey to the empty and evil thoughts of the enemy and eventually yield to the discouragement of hopelessness. Salvation fills our mind with the mind of Christ and enables us to bring into captivity every thought that exalts itself against Him. "But let us, who are of the day, be sober, putting on the breastplate of faith and love; and for an helmet, the hope of salvation" (1 Thessalonians 5:8, KJV).

The hope of salvation through Jesus keeps our minds from despair and error. This hope gives confidence for safety in battle and a victorious win. Hope in the grace of God gives strength to our courage as we walk with our heads held high as a child of God. The hope of salvation delivers us from the kingdom of darkness into the kingdom of light. The hope that gives the confidence we are on the winning side. We are to "hope against hope" as Abraham, the father of faith, did when he believed for a son. When hope is alive, faith can work. The hope of impenetrable protection is the blood of the Lamb, our salvation, the delivering, preserving, saving power of God. With the helmet of salvation securely in place, we identify with the victory of our Savior. It is the signifying element of the army of God.

In modern days, it is much like the helmet of your favorite football team, each having an individual symbol or logo in which to identify them. Ours is the blood of the Lamb, the cross, and hope. That is why it is so important to "keep your hopes up!" Let the hope of salvation, by grace alone, through faith alone in Christ alone, fill your thoughts today, reviving the goal God has set before you of victory. "For the grace of God that bringeth salvation hath appeared to all men" (Titus 2:11, KJV). "For consider him that endured such contradiction of sinners against himself, lest ye be wearied and faint in your minds" (Hebrews 12:3, KJV).

When we put on our helmets, we signify whose side we are on while at the same time protecting our thoughts from defeat and despair. Once you set your mind on things above and settle the questions that whether you know it all or not, you will stay focused in battle, knowing clearly who the enemy is and who the enemy is not. Deceptions will not confuse you into giving up the fight. So put on the surety of your deliverance, "Therefore He is also able to save to the uttermost those who come to God through Him, since He always lives to make intercession for them" (Hebrews 7:25, NKJV).

We are saved from sin and condemnation to sit as children with Him in heavenly places. Jesus is the only mediator between God and man; it is He who saves. Because He lives, we also live when we receive Him as our Lord and Savior. Without Him, we are still in the enemy's camp. Receive Jesus not just as your Savior but as your Lord. Make Him Lord of every area of your life; His thoughts becoming yours. Truth, Jesus, brings freedom, salvation, and deliverance everywhere He is received. The Truth sets you free! If you doubt, you have not embraced Truth fully. Let go of the self-protection that fails you and put on the only sure defense, hope in the saving grace of Jesus Christ, the Son of God. As God raised Him, He, too, will raise us. Praise be to the One who holds the future in His hand. He is the Alpha and the Omega, and He will have the final word in your life. Only believe!

The Sword of the Spirit~

And finally, we take up our offensive weapon, the Sword of the Spirit:

> *and the helmet of the salvation receive, and the sword of the Spirit, which is the saying of God, through all prayer and supplication praying at all times in the Spirit, and in regard to this same, watching in all perseverance and supplication for all the saints—*

> Ephesians 6:17-18 (YLT)

Notice here the punctuation from the Young's Literal Translation; verse 17 ends with a comma, the thought continues and includes verse 18. What is the sword of the Spirit? The "saying of God," or as the KJV says, the "Word of God," is our sword. But when read together, we receive insight into our instruction as to how to wield this sword. Paul tells us, "Through all prayer and supplication praying at all times in the Spirit." If you put this together, you will "pray the Word." This is where the battle is fought, in prayer. That's why Paul said our warfare is not carnal or fleshly but spiritual, and we do not war against flesh and blood. When we take the Word of God into the heavenlies, we give God something with which to work. God gives us the means to bring about the victory. He does not need to hear us recite the problem; He wants to see and hear the answer, the Word. He sees us covered by the blood of Jesus and hears our testimony, our agreement, or confession of His Word. If we truly believe His Word, we will confess it, thereby giving testimony and validating its truth over our lives. We speak the promises, the truth, into the midst of the storm. This sword, or word, is spiritual and given by the Spirit. He then watches over His Word to perform it. The only guarantee He gives is for His Word, not our word. If we want God to work, we must speak His Word to grant Him access: "Then said the Lord to me, You have seen well, for I am alert and active, watching over My word to perform it" (Jeremiah 1:12, AMPC).

> *So shall my word be that goeth forth out of my mouth: it shall not return unto me void, but it shall accomplish that which I please, and it shall prosper in the thing whereto I sent it.*
>
> Isaiah 55:11 (KJV)

> *For the Word that God speaks is alive and full of power [making it active, operative, energizing, and effective]; it is sharper than any two-edged sword, penetrating to the dividing line of the breath of life (soul) and [the immortal] spirit, and of joints and marrow [of the deepest parts of our nature], exposing and sifting and analyzing and judging the very thoughts and purposes of the heart.*
>
> Hebrews 4:12 (AMPC)

Get your sword out! The angels respond to His Word. God's words are alive and active, and they are working the will of God; God sees to it that they work. When we speak or confess them in agreement, we send forth the very power of God. The sword protects us through resisting and exposing the deceptive words of the enemy, thus warding him off. Remember how Jesus defeated Satan in the wilderness with the Word. The devil tried to misapply it, twisting it for his gain, but Jesus did not fall for it. He came back with the right word each time until the devil left. Jesus said:

"It is the spirit that quickeneth; the flesh profiteth nothing: the words that I speak unto you, they are spirit, and they are life" (John 6:63, KJV). "But he answered and said, It is written, Man shall not live by bread alone, but by every word that proceedeth out of the mouth of God" (Matthew 4:4, KJV). "Bless the LORD, ye his angels, that excel in strength, that do his commandments, hearkening unto the voice of his word" (Psalm 103:20, KJV). The sword is powerful! When we release God's words through agreement, confession, and declaration, we invite the heavenly hosts to work on our behalf. They can only hearken to the voice of God's Word. Do you know how to appropriately apply it in each situation? If not, then it is time to get in the Word and start meditating and memorizing until it becomes your confession. Isaiah declares, "And he hath made my mouth like a sharp sword; in the shadow of his hand hath he hid me, and made me a polished shaft; in his quiver hath he hid me" (Isaiah 49:2, KJV).

Your mouth is like a sharp sword, for good or for evil. Paul is telling us to pick up our sword by filling our mouth with the Word of God and speak the answer, not the problem. You may not always be in the heat of the battle confronted with temptations, but have your sword ready to pick up at a moment's notice. You might think of it like being called up off the bench into the game; you are already dressed, but now, grab your shield and your sword. Jesus, the Word is the truth in every situation, circumstance or problem. He is our shield, our defender, a very present help in time of trouble. He is our peace, our comforter, our counselor, our deliverer. We can declare, "You are my peace," and then receive the peace of God. When preparing for battle, the Israelites were given this instruction: "Beat your plowshares into swords, and your pruninghooks into spears: let the weak say, I am strong" (Joel 3:10, KJV).

If you are weak, declare strength. This is not lying; this is raising the truth of God and declaring it above your present reality. Does your sword work for you or against you? Remember, this is the "sword of the spirit," not the "sword of the flesh." Your victory begins with God's Word sown into your heart and coming out of your mouth in prayers of confession, thanksgiving, and declaration. Be sure you only use the "Sword of the Spirit," not the "sword of the flesh." Remember, your tongue can be used for good or evil, for blessing or cursing. Which sword are you using, one that cuts people down or one that agrees with God and defeats the enemy? "There is that speaketh like the piercings of a sword: but the tongue of the wise is health" (Proverbs 12:18, KJV). "Death and life are in the power of the tongue: and they that love it shall eat the fruit thereof" (Proverbs 18:21, KJV).

Do your words cut like a knife, wounding the victim, or do they bring health and life? When you speak life, you wound the enemy! Remember, this battle is not physical, so do not get tricked into speaking doubt and unbelief out of fear, hurt, or anger. The devil loves that when we fall for it. Any time he can make us feel unappreciated, unloved, or unnoticed, we are more likely to indulge our tongue and come out with all kinds of negative jargon. Proverbs says if we do, we will eat those words. Did you know that's where the phrase comes from, "You'll eat your words?" Think about what you have been saying about yourself and your circumstances. Who have you been handing the power to, God or the devil? Fill your heart and mind with the Word, and out of that well will flow the living water. Here is powerful treatise Jesus gave on the tongue:

O generation of vipers, how can ye, being evil, speak good things? for out of the abundance of the heart the mouth speaketh. A good man out of the good treasure of the heart bringeth forth good things: and an evil man out of the evil treasure bringeth forth evil things. But I say unto you, That every idle word that men shall speak, they shall give account thereof in the day of judgment. For by thy words thou shalt be justified, and by thy words thou shalt be condemned.

Matthew 12:34-37 (KJV)

Words are power. They can turn a whole nation from cowering fear mongers to courageous soldiers, as in the case of Great Britain before and after the famous speech of Winston Churchill during World War II, where he is quoted as saying: "We shall take them on the beaches…we shall not surrender!" These words charged the air with faith and changed the tide of defeat into victory. How you use your words determines your future, the direction of your life. Let your mouth be full of the praises and of the promises of God. Speak life into that dead relationship, life into your body and mind. Determine now that your mouth and tongue will give fresh, living water.

Out of the same mouth proceedeth blessing and cursing. My brethren, these things ought not so to be. Doth a fountain send forth at the same place sweet water and bitter? Can the fig tree, my brethren, bear olive berries? Either a vine, figs? So can no fountain both yield salt water and fresh.

James 3:10-12 (KJV)

Maybe you have been sending forth bitter water, cursing the very things that are meant to be a blessing. Repent and renounce those words. Plead the blood of Jesus over them and begin to wield the Sword of the Spirit. War with the Word of God, sending His promises into every situation in your life and waiting for that Word to work.

> *Then they cry unto the LORD in their trouble, and he saveth them out of their distresses. He sent his word, and healed them, and delivered them from their destructions. Oh that men would praise the LORD for his goodness, and for his wonderful works to the children of men! And let them sacrifice the sacrifices of thanksgiving, and declare his works with rejoicing.*
>
> Psalm 107:19-22 (KJV)

Our praise is not rooted in our situation; it is rooted in the goodness of God! He is good all the time; His mercy is from everlasting to everlasting. His mercies to you are new every morning! Praise Him! Begin now to give God thanks for sending His Word to you of healing, deliverance, and blessing. Praise God for "Who He is," Jehovah Raphe, my Healer, my Deliverer, my Shepherd, Jesus my Savior, and so on. God has not only been merciful in not giving us what we deserve but also gracious in giving us what we do not deserve, eternal life and abundant life! Oh, praise the Lord now, His saints; give Him glory, and you will see the salvation of the Lord!

Thank God for a powerful weapon guaranteed to accomplish all that God sent it to do. I boldly declare as I "enter into His gates with thanksgiving and into His courts with praise" that "I am who God says I am, and I can do what God says I can do!" Strength comes in the declaration. See how the sword works. Let's take another name of God and lift it up. God's Word tells us He is Jehovah Jireh, meaning "His provision is seen." So, since this is true, I can declare, "God is my provider, He provides for me, I am provided for in Him." I can take the sword of the spirit and receive provision by faith with His Word working in me and through me. Thank you, Lord, that Your provision is seen in me, that You prepare a table before me in the presence of my enemies! This is the power that is working in me, God's Word.

What amazing armor—Truth, Righteousness, Peace, Salvation, Faith, and the Sword of the Spirit. Put it on, take it up, and prepare for victory. Where is your armor, standing in the corner collecting dust or shined, sharpened, polished, and ready for action? Receive God and trust Him, confident of God's forgiveness and love, so prepare, and then, when the time is right, lift up the sword and boldly speak His Word. War my dear sister as a good soldier and see the Salvation of the Lord.

He wants us to trust Him, put on our armor, that is, our confidence in Him, who He is, and who we are in Him, and stand, resisting the devil. Maybe you had your armor on, and you've taken it off, sat down, and given up. God is saying, "Put Me on, My yoke is easy, My burden is light." This armor is specially designed to fit and lift. Nothing else was as custom made for you than Jesus Christ! We are made in His image and so clothed with Him, His salvation, truth, righteousness, and message. Lift up the shield of faith, believe God at His Word, taking the sword, and declaring it as your confession. "Praying always with all prayer and supplication in the Spirit, and watching thereunto with all perseverance and supplication for all saints;" (Ephesians 6:18, KJV)

Once we are dressed for success, we go into prayer ready to resist, stand and defeat the enemy. This prayer, motivated by the Spirit of God, wars in the heavenlies, bringing our inheritance into the natural realm. Our power is on our knees, bowing before an Almighty God. Scripture teaches the way up is down. When we invite God, He fights for us. "Submit yourselves therefore to God. Resist the devil, and he will flee from you" (James 4:7, KJV). Maybe your resistance has been down, and you are defeated; take heart, my fellow soldier, be encouraged, sister, you are not alone. We shall overcome if we do not give in. We shall rise because God has not fallen, and He will lift us. He will bring us through into the light with joy and rejoicing.

> *When thou passest through the waters, I will be with thee; and through the rivers, they shall not overflow thee: when thou walkest through the fire, thou shalt not be burned; neither shall the flame kindle upon thee.*
>
> Isaiah 43:2 (KJV)

Take heart and take courage, rouse yourself; the Lord Sabaoth, the Lord of the angel armies, is with you. Stake your claim, stand your ground, and war with all of heaven on your side from a place of victory. You, your marriage, your family, ministry, and posterity are worth the fight.

Let this be your song and prayer:

> *A mighty fortress is our God, a bulwark never failing;*
> *Our helper He, amid the flood of mortal ills prevailing:*
> *For still our ancient foe doth seek to work us woe;*
> *His craft and power are great, and, armed with cruel hate,*
> *On earth is not his equal.*
> *Did we in our own strength confide, our striving*
>   *would be losing;*
> *Were not the right Man on our side, the Man of God's*
> *own choosing:*

Dost ask who that may be? Christ Jesus, it is He;

Lord Sabaoth, His Name, from age to age the same, And He must win the battle.

And though this world, with devils filled, should threaten to undo us,

We will not fear, for God hath willed His truth to triumph through us:

The Prince of Darkness grim, we tremble not for him;

His rage we can endure, for lo, his doom is sure, One little word shall fell him.

That word above all earthly powers, no thanks to them, abideth;

The Spirit and the gifts are ours through Him Who with us sideth:

Let goods and kindred go, this mortal life also; The body they may kill:

God's truth abideth still, His kingdom is forever.

Martin Luther
(All grammar and spelling has been left unedited.)

This song, "A Mighty Fortress is Our God" by Martin Luther, has been called "the greatest hymn of the greatest man of the greatest period of German history" and the "Battle Hymn of the Reformation."

Chapter 10.
Memorial Stone 7
Well

*"Say ye to the righteous, that it shall be well with him:
for they shall eat the fruit of their doings".*

(Isaiah 3:10, KJV)

I hope this chapter finds you still standing after the battles. You have exercised tremendous fortitude in going with God and staying in the fight. Now I pray your aim is still high and your hopes are up. If so, you will show it with a face of trust, and you will sound like it with a voice of thanksgiving. Lift up the sacrifice of praise—the fruit of our lips—giving thanks to His name. As Joyce Meyer says, "Stop thinking and start thanking!" Be specific with your thanks. When you receive a gift, you give thanks specifically. For example, if it is a sweater, you might say something like, "Thank you for this lovely sweater; it will keep me nice and warm and go great with my new pants." So too, with God, He daily loads us with blessings and benefits. He is just looking for a grateful heart. Give Him thanks for the roof over your head. If you have ever lost a roof in a storm or catastrophe, you would be thankful now.

Now before, during, and after the battles, we need our next stone to remind us, it shall be "*well*" with you. To help us set up this seventh memorial stone, we turn our attention to a "great woman." In this Bible account found in 2 Kings chapter 4, we are never given her name, only these two things: that she was a "great (wealthy or notable) woman" from the town of Shunem, a "Shunamite." Her location and her status remain as her identifiers. She and her husband were very gracious in receiving the prophet Elisha on his travels back and forth to Shunem. One day she asked her husband to make an extra room for him and furnish it, which he did generously. She always fed him and his servant Gehazi, well. Then on one visit, the prophet, desiring to bless her for her hospitality, said for Gehazi to ask what they could do for her. He asked her if she would like him to speak on her behalf to the king or the commander of the army, much like offering position, power, and influence. She replied that she lived among her own people and was perfectly content, not desirous to change or move. She would not sacrifice her peace, her friends, or her comfort for more things or an elevated position. How quick are we to give up our local church family, our peace, our friends, and yes, maybe even our God for prestige, honor, or riches? This woman was truly rooted in her identity with family and God, a great woman. So Gehazi told Elisha that her husband was old and she was without child. Enough said that was it. Elisha told Gehazi to call for the woman. He told her she would have a son "about this season according to the time of life." But given her situation, this alarmed her, to which she replied: "...Nay, my lord, thou man of God, do not lie unto thine handmaid" (2 Kings 4:16, KJV).

She wanted him to know not to take this lightly, don't mess with her, as she would hope in this prophecy. Likely, he spoke to the traditionally deep-laden desire of every woman in that culture of which she probably had already given up. As the man of God had spoken though, she indeed bore a son. Later, when he was grown, he went into the field to help his father. While there, he cried to his father, "My head, my head!" Likely, some sort of heat stroke. His father told a servant to take him to his mother. While she held him on her lap, he died. All the comforts could not save him. She took him up and laid him on the prophet's bed there in the house, and shut the door behind her. Immediately, she asked her husband to send her quickly with a young man and a donkey to see the man of God. He did not understand and questioned her reasoning, "Why? It is neither the New Moon nor the Sabbath." To which she replied, "It shall be well." Note the focused, hope-filled prophetical declaration, "It shall be well."

So she saddled up the donkey and told the servant to take her as fast as he could to see the prophet. When they were yet a distance away, Elisha saw them, and he told Gehazi to go and meet her and ask, "Is it well with you? With your husband? And with the child?" Her response was simply, "It is well!" How can this be? Here she is riding as fast as she can to see Elisha because her son is lying at home dead! This is a woman of not only great strength but great wisdom. May God grant us this same spirit of wisdom and faith.

There are several things worth gleaning from the text. She recognized and had respect for authority; first, the authority of her husband and, secondly, the authority of the man of God. It is of particular significance that she asked her husband instead of telling him. In this moment of intense emotional upheaval, she maintained an appropriate level of respect, understanding she needed her husband's permission. When was the last time you asked your husband, instead of telling him what you were going to do? I mean, really, giving him the right to say "yes" or "no" and abiding by his answer? Are you willing to trust God like this? We see here even though her husband may not have been a man of faith; she trusted God enough to make a way for her.

When we stay under our covering, the authority God places over us; we maintain a position of spiritual power. When we do not recognize God-given authority, we yield place and power to the enemy. What if she left without her covering? Would that have put her in a position to ask God for a miracle? How could she have respect for the power of God to raise her son without respect for the covering He put over her? By this simple act of asking, she made room for the power of God to work in her life.

And then she had respect for the man of God, Elisha. As quickly as she could, she got herself face to face with the man God had placed in her life to bless her. What if she had just stayed at home and had a panic attack, or a pity party, or gotten mad at God? Could she just have accepted this, giving up her son? What an inspiring example for us of strength and courage. She went directly to Elisha. But what could he do? Whatever the outcome, she would be much more willing to accept it at the hand of the man God used to prophesy and bless her with this son.

What could have been another response? What about blame? Do we not just as easily and quickly kick it into blame mode? "It's all his fault; I was just fine without a son, now you gave me one just to take him away!" Because we get so mad and upset, how much of the miraculous plan of God do we miss out on? Where is the faith in that? People in churches are so accustomed to getting mad at the pastor or at some other thing or person; they do not think anything of just leaving a church. The very message you hate is very likely the message sent to bless you and save you. Stop running from God's man and run to him, like this woman. She did not stop on the way to discuss, complain, or cry to anyone, not even her husband. She had to get to the one she hoped could reverse her fortune.

But you can see a deeper level of hope and respect here when she laid her son on Elisha's bed. She believed so much in the miracle-working power of God that maybe the residue of that power on Elisha would be enough to raise her son from the dead. This was a simple act of giving him back, remembering Elisha's prophecy of the birth of her son. Indeed a humble act of hopeful surrender. She had most likely heard of the story of the resurrection of the women of Zaraphath's son that Elijah raised. That would be enough to inspire her to believe if God could do it for her, He could do it again now. Would she dare speak against the possibility of that miracle?

How many times do we just go along with circumstances before we check with the Spirit and Word of God? We just run off at the mouth without any thought of the miraculous creative power possible when we speak. Stop, and like this woman, guard your mouth and say, "It is well." Until you have heard from God, do not speak against the possibility of a miracle. It is well! It is well! She was willing to wait long enough until she could get to the prophet, there she would speak. Let's pick back up and see what she said.

> And when she came to the man of God to the hill, she caught him by the feet: but Gehazi came near to thrust her away. And the man of God said, Let her alone; for her soul is vexed within her: and the Lord hath hid it from me, and hath not told me. Then she said, Did I desire a son of my lord? did I not say, Do not deceive me?
>
> 2 Kings 4:27-28 (KJV)

When she finally reaches Elijah, she falls down at his feet, grabbing hold. Gehazi tries to pull her off, but Elijah says, "No, let her alone; she is sore vexed." He could see something was wrong. But God had not given Elisha a word, and the matter was hidden from him. She left her son lying on the bed, rode hard and fast to get here, and now she falls before the Man of God who prophesied this child to her and finally has Elijah's attention. What of her statement? What was she saying? She was perfectly contented until he gave her this son. And now, the responsibility of the child's well-being and welfare was on him. She had asked him not to mock or deceive her, which would be if, as in this case, the son would be given and then taken away in an untimely way.

Elisha's first attempt was to give his staff to Gehazi and have him carry it immediately to the boy and lay it upon him. "Do not stop for anything," he said. But this is not enough for the afflicted mother, who will not leave the man of God. So he followed them home. Gehazi came out and reported the child has not awakened. When Elijah goes in, the boy is still dead upon his bed. So he goes in and shuts the door and prays, laying upon the boy, face to face, mouth to mouth, eyes to eyes, and hands to hands. Doing all he could in the natural, while turning to the Giver of Life and the Great Physician, he does all he can.

The flesh of the child begins to warm. Elisha leaves the boy and walks to and fro. When he returns, he stretches himself out on the child again. This time the child sneezes seven times, opens his eyes, and his life comes back into him. Amazing! He calls for Gehazi to call the Shunammite woman to come and take up her son. When she came in, she fell, bowing at Elisha's feet, and took up her son. What a combination of drama and suspense! What amazing faith of this mother and the prophet! They did all they could, and God did the rest, bringing resurrection power.

What miracles have we missed? Is it possible the crisis you may be facing is an opportunity for a miracle? Or do we engage our mouth agreeing with whatever comes our way? Maybe your situation is as dead and lifeless as this little boy. Like the Shunamite woman, ask the God who rules and reigns. Doctors, medicine, and counselors have limitations; God does not. Like Elisha, through faith, put all of your being, eyes, lips, hands, body into the Lord, and then turn and minister this to your spouse. Breathe life, see life, speak life, and touch with all your body, covering the death of your loved one with life.

This woman made a way for hope to stay alive by her declaration and corresponding actions. Her statement, "It shall be well," carried in it great implications, not only encouragement for herself and a resistance to anything the evil one could gain, but an avenue for the glory of God. Do you understand now the power that is released in your words? Oh, the world would mock you, but God will honor you. Do not agree with the enemy; agree with the Truth, God's Word. Speak life into your body, your marriage, your family, your wallet, your business, and your church, "It is well!"

"Well" is to be sound, whole, or complete in your body, soul, and spirit. Well, to be in a satisfactory, advantageous condition. Paul understood this and prayed,

> *And may the God of peace Himself sanctify you through and through [separate you from profane things, make you pure and wholly consecrated to God]; and may your spirit and soul and body be preserved sound and complete [and found] blameless at the coming of our Lord Jesus Christ (the Messiah). Faithful is He Who is calling you [to Himself]*

and utterly trustworthy, and He will also do it [fulfill His call by hallowing and keeping you].

1 Thessalonians 5:23, 24 (AMPC)

God is faithful. He will sanctify, purify and preserve us completely, spirit, soul, and body. He is trustworthy. Just like this Shunammite woman, you can dare to put your hope in God's Word and have faith in God. He is God, and He is a rewarder of those who diligently seek Him. May you run well and finish well. May you believe well and hope against hope. When all looks dead, lifeless, and hopeless, you, my dear, sweet one, beloved, keep hope alive. Declare to that which is dead in your life, "It is *well!*"

> *Cast not away therefore your confidence, which hath great recompense of reward. For ye have need of patience, that, after ye have done the will of God, ye might receive the promise. For yet a little while, and he that shall come will come, and will not tarry. Now the just shall live by faith: but if any man draw back, my soul shall have no pleasure in him. But we are not of them who draw back unto perdition; but of them that believe to the saving of the soul.*
>
> Hebrews 10:35-39 (KJV)

This woman demonstrates that a victorious faith walks not by sight! Keep praying, keep believing, and keep your confession of faith. Wait well, watch well, worship well, walk well, work well, and war well. When the day comes to stand before our God, may we hear these words:

> *His lord said unto him, Well done, thou good and faithful servant: thou hast been faithful over a few things, I will make thee ruler over many things: enter thou into the joy of thy lord.*
>
> Matthew 25:21 (KJV)

To be well is to be whole or sound, complete body, soul, and spirit. When I declare this, I agree with God, His Word, and His Spirit that everything concerning me is in a satisfactory, advantageous condition and nothing is lacking. The Lord is my Shepherd, and I shall not lack! Set up this seventh stone with me by declaring over your life, your marriage, your children, your job, "It is well! *It is well.*" I am whole spirit, soul, and body. My marriage is well, my children and family are well in Jesus' name, amen, and amen!

May you be inspired by this tragic yet courageous story of a treasured hymn, "It Is Well with My Soul." Horatio G. Spafford was a successful lawyer and businessman in Chicago with a lovely family—a wife, Anna, and five children. However, they were not strangers to tears and tragedy. Their young son died with pneumonia in 1871, and in that same year, much of their business was lost in the Great Chicago Fire. Yet, God, in His mercy and kindness, allowed the business to flourish once more. Philanthropists engaged in supporting the evangelistic ministry of Dwight L. Moody, the Spaffords looked forward to what God would do in Great Britain while they were there.

On November 21, 1873, the French ocean liner, *Ville du Havre*, was crossing the Atlantic from the US to Europe with 313 passengers on board. Among the passengers were Mrs. Spafford and their four daughters on their way to enjoy a vacation and ministry with the Moody evangelistic team. Although Mr. Spafford had planned to go with his family, he found it necessary to stay in Chicago to help solve an unexpected business problem. He told his wife he would join her and their children in Europe a few days later. His plan was to take another ship.

About four days into the crossing of the Atlantic, the *Ville du Havre* collided with a powerful, iron-hulled Scottish ship, the *Loch Earn*. Suddenly, all of those on board were in danger. Anna hurriedly brought her four children to the deck. She knelt there with Annie, Margaret Lee, Bessie, and Tanetta and prayed that God would spare them if that could be His will or to make them willing to endure whatever awaited them. Within approximately twelve minutes, the *Ville du Havre* slipped beneath the dark waters of the Atlantic, carrying with it 226 of the passengers, including the four Spafford children.

A sailor, rowing a small boat over the spot where the ship went down, spotted Anna floating on a piece of the wreckage, still alive. He pulled her into the boat, and they were picked up by another large vessel which, nine days later, landed them in Cardiff, Wales. From there, she wired her husband a message that began, "Saved alone, what shall I do?" Mr. Spafford later framed the telegram and placed it in his office. One can only imagine Spafford's grief upon receiving the news. It must have been paralyzing. Another of the ship's survivors, Pastor Weiss, later recalled Anna saying, "God gave me four daughters. Now they have been taken from me. Someday I will understand why."

Mr. Spafford booked passage on the next available ship and left to join his grieving wife. With the ship about four days out, the captain called Spafford to his cabin and told him they were over the place where his children went down.

There, according to another daughter born later after the tragedy, Bertha Spafford Vester, he was inspired to write the lyrics for the hymn "It Is Well with My Soul."

Unlike many songs of brokenness, it focuses less on what was lost and more on where hope is found. No doubt, Spafford was shattered by the loss of his daughters, but his heart turned to the faithfulness of God in the midst of loss and the work of Jesus to rescue sinners. The hymn does not diminish the pain and tragedy but rather proclaims that God, present in them, is greater than them. And, though the hymn begins with loss, it ends in hope for the day when "faith shall be sight."

"It Is Well with My Soul"

When peace like a river attendeth my way,
When sorrows like sea billows roll,
Whatever my lot, Thou hast taught me to say,
It is well, it is well with my soul.

Chorus:

It is well with my soul,
It is well, it is well with my soul

When peace like a river, attendeth my way,
When sorrows like sea billows roll;
Whatever my lot, Thou hast taught me to know
It is well, it is well, with my soul.

Refrain
It is well, (it is well),
With my soul, (with my soul)
It is well, it is well, with my soul.

Though Satan should buffet, though trials should come,
Let this blest assurance control,
That Christ has regarded my helpless estate,
And hath shed His own blood for my soul.

My sin, oh, the bliss of this glorious thought!
My sin, not in part but the whole,
Is nailed to the cross, and I bear it no more,
Praise the Lord, praise the Lord, O my soul!

For me, be it Christ, be it Christ hence to live:
If Jordan above me shall roll,
No pang shall be mine, for in death as in life,
Thou wilt whisper Thy peace to my soul.

But Lord, 'tis for Thee, for Thy coming we wait,
The sky, not the grave, is our goal;
Oh, trump of the angel! Oh, voice of the Lord!
Blessed hope, blessed rest of my soul.

And Lord, haste the day when the faith shall be sight,
The clouds be rolled back as a scroll;
The trump shall resound, and the Lord shall descend,
A song in the night, oh my soul!

Horatio Spafford

CHAPTER 11.
MEMORIAL STONE 8
WIN

"Though no one can go back and make a brand new start, Anyone can start from now and make a brand new ending".

(Carl Bard)

"You won!" I love to hear that. What about, "You make it look easy! You are a real winner! Great job, well done!" When your name is called, even your number in a game, you get this "thrill of victory." When it's not, they used to call it on the "Wide World of Sports," the "agony of defeat." How great to see or hear your name called as the winner. Maybe you have never experienced either; you know neither the "thrill" nor the "agony" because you have never attempted anything competitive or challenging. Although, life itself, to live fully, is the call. "You've all been to the stadium and seen the athletes race. Everyone runs; one wins. Run to win" (1 Corinthians 9:24, MSG).

Maybe you have never won a race, or, for that matter, an award, or maybe you have a cabinet full of trophies. If you are competitive, then likely you were raised in a competitive environment. Maybe a sibling or parent spurred you on, challenging you, or a coach or a friend. Somehow you knew you had to find a way either to beat them or just win. And sooner or later, beat them you did. Somehow, it is just not as much fun to play unless you win.

Oh yes, I know, it's good for socializing, team building, and even brain development, etc., but isn't the point still to win? Then if you don't win, you are supposed to be a "good loser!" That's nice, but what is a "good loser" anyway? You smile and shake hands and say, "Good game." Yeah, right! Okay, maybe sometimes. You definitely do not want to be known as a "sore loser." Unfortunately, some may have been called or tagged a "loser." You know, when they hold the big "L" up to their forehead, I never understood why that was so popular. But God holds up a big "W" over you now, and says "you are a Winner; I believe in you!"

Whether it is an "ugly" win or a "pretty" win, a win is still a win. Life teaches us that a "win" is coming up at the end as the last one standing, or crossing the line first, or having the highest score or the lowest (as in golf), or simply just beating out the other competitor(s). Competitors receive rewards like the Emmys, Oscars, Tonys, Gold Medals, Lombardi Trophies, Yellow Jerseys, Green Jackets, Belts, Cups, Crowns, Rings, Plaques; you name it, the list can go on and on. Although now, we see a relatively new phenomenon, a heavily debated issue where players get awards just for participating, not winning. The results of this are beginning to manifest in a generation where motivation to win or even finish is lacking because there is not any real significant prize or accolade, or on the other hand, an entitlement mindset that says, "I should win" just for participating.

Christianity, however, is not influenced by cultural swings or paradigms; although all believers participate, only the believers that press on to win, receive the prize. We each have an individual race, a great amazing race, I call it the "grace race." God has called us to run to win. We run in His grace and, like Paul, testifying of and winning by His grace, the "grace race."

But none of these things move me, neither count I my life dear unto myself, so that I might finish my course with joy, and the ministry, which I have received of the Lord Jesus, to testify the gospel of the grace of God.

Acts 20:24 (KJV)

Actually, this race is an epic journey, the adventure of faith, the journey of life. All those that endure to the end, the ones who do not give up, win and receive the prize. If you know Jesus, you have begun, being quickened or awakened by God Himself, and by His grace, you have been empowered to begin. And yes, along the way, you have experienced some joys and sorrows, some wins and losses, but this is not a sprint; this is a marathon. "And let us not be weary in well doing: for in due season we shall reap, if we faint not" (Galatians 6:9, KJV).

We will reap if we don't give up! Just don't give up! Maybe you have felt like it is just not worth it, like throwing in the proverbial towel, like Rocky. The devil thinks he can win if he gets us to give up, but for the enemy, it is already a loss. Our problem is we don't believe this. We win, God wins, and the devil loses because Jesus already won. The victory is in His name, not mine or yours. We know who the enemy is, and we know he is already defeated. It is that simple, making a short chapter. But why aren't we winning? That will require a few more minutes of your time.

Simply put, our eighth memorial stone, win, is to be successful in a conflict or contest, to take first place, triumph, be victorious, and prevail by effort. We have talked about the conflict between good and evil, the war that is against us. But now we see the real journey; this "epic journey" of life is a race, our "grace race," with battles all along the way. Yes, we war, but the ultimate vision of success is cast, win! We "win the day" because we have been given the victory. You are a "shoe-in," the race is fixed, the deck is stacked, and you have the upper hand!

"For whatsoever is born of God overcometh the world: and this is the victory that overcometh the world, even our faith" (1 John 5:4, KJV).

Faith wins! Again, here John gives further evidence of the power of right believing affecting our victory. When we placed our faith in Christ, we became overcomers, winners. Our faith or belief in God gives birth to victory. The enemy does not want us to know or have this "vision of victory." When beginning with a clear picture or vision of winning, a goal helps to create winning thinking, which instills and fuels winning believing, which then promotes winning.

We have read about the amazing faith, strength, and endurance of some godly women who ran their race with a vision. Hannah received the son for which she prayed, offering him to the Lord; Esther, facing potential death, helped to save her people, the entire Jewish nation; Sarah gave birth to nations and the line of Christ; and Mary conceived the Son of God, raising Him well. We read how Ruth left her homeland, bound herself to Naomi, and brought purpose and restoration to their family, giving birth to Obed, the grandfather of David, and how Deborah spoke on behalf of God, charging the military leader Barak to take the victory. And then, we just saw how the "great woman" of Shunem saw her son raised from the dead.

These were all women of faith—who had a trust and belief in God that manifested in acts of surrender, service, and courage when called upon. They each overcame tremendous obstacles, ridicule, mockery, fear, culture, and poverty. Holding their vision with tremendous passion and fervor, they endured, ran their grace

race, and finally won. Fortunately, their journeys are recorded as our examples. In like manner, God has placed a dream, a passion, and a vision within you.

This dream or vision is usually a strong desire in your heart; some call it your passion. Much like Christ's death on the cross, we refer to it as the "Passion of Christ," meaning His life's purpose was to reveal God's love for His people through living and dying in our place. His "passion," His great love for you, me, and the Father, is what led Him to lay His life willingly done on the cross. We, however, through various reasons, tend to give up on our passions, our dreams, or our visions. The pressures, the schedules, the responsibilities, and even the distractions can squeeze out and empty our hearts, leaving us feeling lifeless and listless. But not anymore; God is coming to say get up and get back in the race; it is not over; it is time to revisit that vision. Awaken thou that sleepeth and arouse thyself! "Where there is no vision, the people perish: but he that keepeth the law, happy is he" (Proverbs29:18, KJV).

If winning is succeeding, then our vision or interpretation of success affects the outcome. Think about how you define or determine success. You might say a lot of money, a big house, a fancy car, fame, happiness, health, good family relations, promotions on the job, etc., is success. Success in the kingdom of God and winning this race though maybe something altogether different. Beauty, brains, and brawn bring many superstar statuses in our society. Talent shows, the silver screen, the arena, the internet, etc., have all provided a venue or platform to create idols propelling literally unknowns into fame and fortune. But without these, can we still "win" in life? The prerequisites or qualifications for winning our race and receiving the rewards are not as the world defines them but as God does. Those who walk the heavenly "Red Carpet" to claim their prize may surprise you. Maybe you think if you do not have this beauty, brains, or brawn, you cannot win. But think about these women of faith; what did they have in common? They are not our example because of their beauty or brains, but because of wisdom. A wisdom that nurtured a great fear of the Lord. A holy fear that stirs faith to arise in their heart to believe God, not man. They trusted God with their heart and, thus, their passions, desires, and vision. "Success is not the key to happiness. Happiness is the key to success. If you love what you are doing, you will be successful" (Albert Schweitzer).

If you have a heart for God and love Him, you will love serving Him right He has you. A vision usually starts out with a desire, or maybe it even feels like a burden. For example, we have been talking about a husband, the desire to be in a close, loving, exclusively intimate relationship. The vision is, "The Lord is my Husband," truly to know Him as the love of my life. My desire, my burden, is to know intimately through experience the depth of what it means to be married to the Lord, knowing His love and passion and sharing it with Him. The win begins internally first, seeing myself as the winner, His bride. Then, the win comes to pass, one step at a time, one battle at a time, winning one day at a time. The dream, the desire, promotes thinking like a winner, which precedes and promotes living like a winner.

> And the Lord answered me, and said, write the vision, and make it plain upon tables, that he may run that readeth it. For the vision is yet for an appointed time, but at the end it shall speak, and not lie: though it tarry, wait for it; because it will surely come, it will not tarry.
>
> Habakkuk 2:2-3 (KJV)

You have a vision, a dream, a desire in your heart. It is time to revisit that vision, write it down so that as you read it, you will remember, focus, and run your race. So go ahead, think about it; what is your dream, your vision? Maybe you receive this challenge and desire to know intimately the Lord as your Husband; write that down for yourself, "The Lord is My Husband." Or whatever dream or vision is pulling on your heart.

My Vision: _____

_____

"This one step—choosing a goal and sticking to it—changes everything" (Scott Reed). In so doing, you give your heart to God. Now enjoy the freedom that comes from trusting God with the vision. Your heart is lifted. Thoughts feed my beliefs, and beliefs determine my direction. What you believe is where you are going. Belief is power. Even the medical community knows and understands the power of belief. They call it the "placebo effect," giving "decoy drugs" like a sugar pill in place of medicine. More times than the medical community care to acknowledge, the placebo has had as good of a result as their expensive drugs and even procedures. "Why?" You might ask; it is the power of believing. These false medicines, treatments, and even surgeries yield positive or negative responses in direct proportion or relation to the positive or negative belief the patient has in them. Even so much that when they take the patients off of the treatment, oftentimes, they will detox or even cause their condition to reverse. "If thou canst believe, all things are possible to him that believeth" (Mark 9:23, KJV).

The possibilities are endless to the believer! They are just proving what God has been saying for thousands of years. Interesting how God allows the scientific community a little at a time to catch up to the scriptures and even support it, as Proverbs 23:7 (KJV) says, "For as he [a man] thinketh in his heart, so is he" (brackets added for clarity). Or, as Jesus said many times, "Be it unto you according to your faith." That is another way of saying that what you say and believe sincerely and wholeheartedly will come to pass. Believing is an essential prerequisite to winning. Jesus told Mary and Martha, "Only believe, and you will see the glory of God." We must believe and then see ourselves as a winner to be a winner, victorious to get the victory, overcoming to be an overcomer, and succeeding to be successful.

Thank God, He took care of that. He gave us His Word, let this drop in your heart, and let faith arise: "O sing unto the Lord a new song; for he hath done marvelous things: his right hand, and his holy arm, hath gotten him the victory" (Psalm 98:1, KJV). "But thanks be to God, which giveth us the victory through our Lord Jesus Christ" (1 Corinthians 15:57, KJV). "Nay, in all these things we are more than conquerors through him that loved us" (Romans 8:37, KJV).

He got the victory and handed that victory to us and made us more than a conqueror, a true champion through Jesus. Good news, we win, so that makes us winners! If we begin to think victory in every area of our life, lining up and agreeing with the Word of God, we will see it! It is simple. Think victory and win every time, everywhere. You are the official "Titleholder" to victory, holding the victory in your heart. You are the Queen, a "D.I.V.A.," a Divinely Inspired Virtuously Anointed woman, and daughter of the King. Now please, do not get all sideways about this; I am not talking about using egotistic sex appeal to lure men and women under a spell. I am talking about the divinely inspired virtue of a truly anointed woman of God who walks in the confident humility of holiness as a woman under authority, not over it! Properly positioned women win every time.

If, by chance, you have grown weary, fainted in your mind, and lost sight of your dream, take encouragement from another tremendous example of how faith coupled with humility inspired a "certain woman" to win her race. Found in Mark 5:25 and following:

> *And a certain woman, which had an issue of blood twelve years, And had suffered many things of many physicians, and had spent all that she had, and was nothing bettered, but rather grew worse,*
>
> Mark 5:25-26 (KJV)

We are not given her name, not even "sweetie" or "honey." Basically, she is unidentified or unknown, just that she is a "certain woman," identified by her problem, "an issue of blood." That is like saying, "You know, that woman." Most likely, she was well known as "that woman." She had been to every doctor in the area and spent all her money. They all knew her and knew her "issue." You may feel like this; everyone looks at you and says, "Oh, it's that woman, you know, the woman with the issue." Well, she is "that" woman, a woman, with a problem; and a serious problem. "An issue of blood" meant that she did not stop bleeding; it was uncontrollable. On that day, this made her "unclean," meaning no one could touch her, nor could she touch anyone, or that would make them unclean.

According to the Levitical law, not only was she unclean but whoever touched her was unclean as well. Likely, she would have been divorced or, at the least, separated from her spouse. She was to be totally separated, cut off from society and religious worship. She could not just walk up to the priest and ask him to lay hands on her and pray for her because she was unclean, but would also defile the priest. Not to mention, this must have been extremely embarrassing and humiliating. She was out of options, having spent all her money, broke and likely alone by now, getting worse. Wow! A tough spot, hopeless and alone, but something happened. "When she had heard of Jesus, came in the press behind, and touched his garment. For she said, If I may touch but his clothes, I shall be whole" (Mark 5:27-28, KJV).

She heard of Jesus. We are not told here specifically what she heard, only that she responded. A response, springing out of restored hope and belief from the message, the gospel message He came preaching that the kingdom of God was at hand. That this kingdom is one of repentance and forgiveness, a message of faith in God. Maybe she heard how Jesus went about casting out devils and healing the sick as demonstration of forgiveness and wholeness. She likely heard that this Jesus was the prophesied Messiah who would bring healing in "His wings," meaning the hem of His prayer shawl. With her hope renewed and revived, she could "hope against hope." We call it getting a second opinion so we can get our hopes up or keep our hopes alive. We want someone, usually a doctor in our case, to tell us better news, tell us something can be done to help us. Good news came, and now, with her hopes up, she said! She confessed out loud her victory, "If I touch Him, I shall be whole." Her self-talk changed into victory, revealing her belief. The message she heard of Jesus inspired faith for wholeness and manifested in a passionate response. Putting herself out there and saying, "This man, if I could just touch the hem of His garment." "And, behold, a woman, which was diseased with an issue of blood twelve years, came behind him, and touched the hem of his garment" (Matthew 9:20, KJV).

What are we saying to ourselves? In order to say that in faith, she had to hear the gospel of grace, a message of wholeness, and believe it. The beauty here is her humility, coupled with persistence. How irresistible to God! She pressed through the crowd in all her uncleanness, likely bowed down on the ground where she would not be noticed in the throng of people or thrown out, just so she could reach out and touch the hem of His garment. The hem or border, known as the "tallit," was significant in that it represented the authority of the priest and the promises of God.

All she wanted was one little touch where her faith could touch His grace. She would not wait to ask or for Him to touch her! She had the kind of faith that reaches out and takes or seizes her victory. Seeing herself with her healing and speaking the victory gave evidence that she believed what she heard about Jesus. She would not be deterred by the crowd, the disciples, or even her own condition; she would be whole. If yielded to, these obstacles would have diluted her faith, inevitably preventing this opportunity. The resulting polluted faith would either delay or possibly deny her healing. Not her! No, she remained focused, denying distractions and pressing into Jesus. She believed with faith that wins! Lord, help our unbelief! Look past the obstacles, speak the truth, press toward the goal, and you will win.

> *And straightway the fountain of her blood was dried up; and she felt in her body that she was healed of that plague. And Jesus, immediately knowing in himself that virtue had gone out of him, turned him about in the press, and said, Who touched my clothes? And his disciples said unto him, Thou seest the multitude thronging*

thee, and sayest thou, Who touched me? And he looked
round about to see her that had done this thing.

Mark 5:29-32 (KJV)

After she heard, she believed, she said, and then touched, instantly she received her healing, so much so she could feel it. Imagine the joy, the relief, the excitement! She had been living with this for twelve long years, looking for a solution, and now, with one touch, she was completely whole! How would she be able to hide her enthusiasm and what she had done? What would happen if they were to find out that she, an unclean woman, had touched the Rabbi, Jesus?

Imagine the crowd and the disciples when Jesus begins to ask who just touched Him. With crowds of people pushing against Him, He still sensed something different, special. Someone had pulled or made a request on the power, the virtue of God, and He felt it! Think about that; He could actually feel the power of God being released through this touch. It is like what happens when a positive and a negative charge make a connection; there is a flow of power that is detectable. Then, Jesus sees her, Jehovah Roi, the God that sees. Now what? Would she confess, and if so, how much should she tell?

> *But the woman fearing and trembling, knowing what*
> *was done in her, came and fell down before him, and*
> *told him all the truth. And he said unto her, Daugh-*
> *ter, thy faith hath made thee whole; go in peace, and be*
> *whole of thy plague.*

Mark 5:33-34 (KJV)

She told Him everything, the whole story! When she went low, He lifted her up. What an amazing confirmation to faith that not only believes but acts. Jesus tells her, "Thy faith has made thee whole," but maybe equally as significant, he changes her name from a "woman" to "Daughter!" Let faith arise in you as you hear these words, "Daughter or Son," there is power in believing God at His Word. He was not going to let her run off in obscurity, and for a good reason. Thank God she had enough fear of God to stay and say. He wanted a confession, a testimony. Her confession sealed her healing! Jesus gave her an opportunity to go away, not only healed but restored in her new identity. In testifying, she gave glory to God and removed all possibility of losing her blessing to fear or condemnation.

Not only did she receive healing, but He sent her away to enjoy her blessing with His gift of peace upon her. Jesus did not make it about His healing power but about her faith. She believed, received, and testified. That is overcoming, more than a conqueror, more than she asked for. Who could touch that or take it away? When she confessed to Him, He confessed her as His "daughter," confirmed her faith, and gave her peace. With the blessing of peace, she is not only restored in her body but in her position in the community as "clean."

What a complete victory! She heard, believed, spoke, pressed, and finally, touched and testified. Faith, a fully persuaded, undivided heart, combined with works, a corresponding action, released the power of God to bear on her "issue." God releases salvation, complete with healing, restoration, and peace. As a great example of winning, she portrayed the winning attitude we need. Her win began internally and then manifested externally. If this winning attitude got the attention of the Almighty God, maybe its light could cast enough glow in our hearts for some honest self-evaluation. She put it all on the line, everything. With nothing left, nowhere to turn, and no one to help, she looked to Jesus. This belief moved her and moved heaven, making her a true overcomer. As John records and explains our victory in Revelation 12:11, she overcame by the blood of the Lamb and the word of her testimony. Her confession or statement of faith in the Lamb of God gave her what doctors and money could not. She overcame disease with a faith that speaks privately and publicly, a consistent faith in Christ alone. As a daughter of the King, pursuing, pressing, and receiving, she left rejoicing in her newfound victory. Maybe she could be reunited with a husband; we are not told. But no doubt, the future looked brighter for her.

I am not saying here that if you do not get your healing, you have lost. What I am saying, though, is that without this passionate believing pursuit, we will not receive all that is ours, whatever that may be. Maybe the joy before her was the desire to be restored to her family. It is hard in our modern culture to understand the separation required for those like her that were considered "unclean." How lonely, and even lost she must have felt. What great inspiration! If God gives you the vision, the dream, pursue it. It is your race, run and run to win. No one else can win for you.

Faith in the salvation of God through the blood of Jesus Christ, believing and confessing Him as Lord, Healer, Redeemer, Husband defeats the devil every time. We overcome today, warring and winning over the enemy by the blood of the Lamb and the word of our testimony. Believe in your heart and confess with your mouth victory! Open your mouth and win with words of faith. Now we have the vision of victory, no excuses! Maybe somehow you want this too, just to reach out and touch His grace and experience His healing power of freedom from lack in any area. Claim now what is yours, the "children's bread," believe and receive. Let your faith touch God's grace.

For a deeper look into this winning attitude and what it yields, let's zoom in a little closer and go back to our "grace race."

> *You've all been to the stadium and seen the athletes race. Everyone runs; one wins. Run to win. All good athletes train hard. They do it for a gold medal that tarnishes and fades. You're after one that's gold eternally. I don't know about you, but I'm running hard for the finish line. I'm giving it everything I've got. No sloppy living for me! I'm staying alert and in top condition. I'm not going to get caught napping, telling everyone else all about it and then missing out myself.*
>
> 1 Corinthians 9:24-27 (MSG) (emphasis added)

"And every man that striveth for the mastery is temperate in all things. Now they do it to obtain a corruptible crown; but we an *incorruptible*" (1 Corinthians 9:25, KJV). This race is as individual as you and I. You may not have an "issue," but, just like the women we have studied, we, too, face battles along the way that include opportunities for love to win, faith to win, peace and joy to win, forgiveness to win, just to name a few. These women fought to lay aside the weights and distractions of fear and doubt, resisting the comforts, and went on, disciplined and enduring to win their grace race. They left their "comfort zone" for the "throne zone." Hannah left the celebration, Esther left the table, Rahab left her home and past, Ruth left family and tradition, Deborah left home for the battlefield, and still, others left anonymity for the Leaving the "comfort zone" of familiarity like families, traditions, games, TV, home, even "my pew" or "seat" in church, to reach out and embrace the unknown, the unpredictable, the unsearchable riches of Jesus Christ found in the "throne zone." This is the adventure, the abundant life, the "grace race."

Upon examination of our present condition, what kind of scouting report would you give yourself? Could you say, "I am ready to compete; I have trained hard, so now I can run hard to the finish?" How well will you compete? God has challenged my spirit, soul, and body to love, learn, and train hard. Some days are better than others, but I see the goal; I know He wants me in top condition, spirit, soul, and body. Feeding our spirit as well as body nutritious daily manna will serve to boost and lift our soul to rise to this challenge and press onward and upward. No more taking it "easy." How is your training going? If we are to give it all we have got, is it possible we may have to make a few adjustments? Open your schedule to God and ask Him to add or delete what He wills.

Rewards

Inspiration for motivation helps us run to win. Aligning ourselves with victory and enduring the pain of pressing, training, and discipline is promoted by knowing and then seeing the rewards God gives. For example, if you want to lose weight, maybe back down to a size you once were, put up a picture somewhere that you can look at regularly that inspires you. Give yourself an opportunity to see yourself once again at that weight. What a great reward to feel good about yourself. God gives us a picture of winning in Christ; His victory is ours. Now it is time to see and seize the win. For the Christian, scripture tells of at least four rewards or prizes we win for finishing our race: Crowns, Calls, Children, and Christ.

This is quite a package of rewards to encourage and inspire us to rise to the challenges of winning. Before David fought the Philistine Goliath, he wanted to hear the list of rewards recited several times. He wanted to know and keep in mind just exactly what the king would give or do for the man who would defeat this Philistine. Not only would the nation of Israel be saved from their enemy as if that was not enough, but personally for David, he would be rewarded. First, he would get the king's daughter to wife, then he would never have to pay taxes, and finally, he would be enriched with great riches. Some nice rewards for a young man! So David, with great courage, fought on behalf of the God of Israel and, with a sling and a stone, defeated the enemy. Reciting our rewards is not often mentioned, yet God said unless we believe "He is and He is a rewarder" of those who diligently seek Him, we cannot please Him. He wants us to know and understand He is a rewarder. Like David, we, too, can stir our spirits to run to win, overcoming tests, trials, tribulations, and temptations, enduring to the end, by fully comprehending the rewards that are at stake and by His empowering grace.

Reward 1 - Crowns

Our wins yield both earthly rewards as well as eternal rewards. Like these many women of faith who, out of barrenness and lack, won children, nations, husbands, provision, safety, and victory, we, too, can receive and win our prizes here and now, as well as in eternity. The first heavenly prize or reward Paul mentions, however, is a crown, eternal, permanent, and incorruptible. Unlike the Laurel wreath, the victor's crown used in Greece and Rome in that day, the winner's heavenly crown will never fade. A golden crown may not feel like the motivation needed to win, especially since you cannot see or touch it until eternity, but that is where the real race is won.

> *Wherefore seeing we also are compassed about with so great a cloud of witnesses, let us lay aside every weight,*

and the sin which doth so easily beset us, and let us run
with patience the race that is set before us,

Hebrews 12:1 (KJV)

With such a great cloud of witnesses, God, Jesus, the angels, and the church cheering us on in the City of God, Mount Zion, the heavenly Jerusalem, we run and win for a kingdom which cannot be moved and never fades away. Paul speaks of the heavenly rewards, the crowns as something to pursue, to desire, a reward that cannot decay, be stolen, or taken away. Several types of crowns will be rewarded at the heavenly Rewards Ceremony: crowns of life, of righteousness, of glory, and of rejoicing. These crowns are prepared specifically for soul winners, enduring saints and martyrs, faithful shepherds, and those watching for His appearance. God rewards the disciplined, the obedient, the enduring, the faithful, the longing, the winners who not only love Him but choose to love others. Those, who, in the midst of intense challenges, will be an example of God's love and grace, will be crowned. Imagine how busy heaven is preparing all these crowns! What a sight that will be, the crown room!

The beauty of these crowns, however, will never obscure or cast a shadow on the glory of the Crown of Thorns Jesus wore so that we could be His crown, His joy. That joy set before Him helped Him to endure His cross and bear the thorny crown, and ultimately, fulfill and complete His joy. Now, with the four and twenty elders, the victorious Church will return to Him the glory He deserves. Upon receiving our crowns, with the symbol of triumph in our hand, we will cast our crowns before His heavenly throne, giving all the honor and glory to our King and Lord.

The four and twenty elders fall down before him that sat on
the throne, and worship him that liveth for ever and ever,

and cast their crowns before the throne, saying, Thou art
worthy, O Lord, to receive glory and honor and power: for
thou hast created all things, and for thy pleasure they are
and were created.

Revelation 4:10-11 (KJV) (emphasis added)

For by His grace, we win souls, endure, obey, teach, and watch to receive the heavenly crown, which we, too, may each have a crown to cast before the Lord! This life is brief, fading and passing quickly; only what is done with eternity in mind and in view yields eternal rewards.

Reward 2 - Calls

Brethren, I count not myself to have apprehended: but this
one thing I do, forgetting those things which are behind,
and reaching forth unto those things which are before, I
press toward the mark for the prize of the high calling of
God in Christ Jesus.

Philippians 3:13-14 (KJV)

Forgetting, reaching, and pressing are the prerequisites for this prize. Forgetting the failures and successes of the past, turning, looking to Jesus, reaching and moving toward Him with all I am, I answer the call. The prize of the "high calling of God" is as unique and individual as you and me. You have a call on your life, it is the upward heavenly calling placed in your spirit, and it is found in Christ. Your calling is the mission God has placed you on, that dream within you, that which does more than motivate you; it inspires you, it calls you.

Much like the divine influence that moved upon men of old, patriarchs, prophets, kings, and apostles to write the Bible, you in like manner are moved upon, inspired to press toward that call. Inspiration, that touch of the Lord upon our heart, a life of passion seeking to please the lover that compels or draws one forward, much like the light at the end of a tunnel. More powerful than motivation, inspiration draws you forward from within to train, to compete, to run hard, and to give everything for the win. Focused to fulfill, accomplish, and achieve the prize of your "high calling," you ignore all the distractions and temptations to get off track. With your vision, the goal, and calling before you, now is the time to get on track and stay there; you will win if you do not quit. Do the next right thing, take the next right step on the right path toward your call. Your calling is your purpose, and your purpose is your prize. Each successive short-term victory encourages long-term success.

Nothing satisfies like fulfilling your purpose. Rather than from without, this inspiration, this call appeals to the highest quality within our spirit, our desire to please God. Through the encouragement of her stepfather Mordecai, Esther wanted to be used by God to save not only her life but the life of her people, for she saw that she might have been "called to the kingdom for such a time as this." Ruth desired to stay with Naomi to serve her God and do what she could to bless and care for Naomi and make a life for them. So too, Rahab feared God for her family, hid the spies, and put the crimson cord in her window to save not only herself but all her family as well. Hannah pulled on God to fulfill the desire to be a mother, Mary and others ran their race from a place of grace. The place we know we would never be had it not been but for the grace of God. Grace, the power of the Holy One in us to focus, to succeed, and to win the fulfillment of the vision.

God's grace that nourishes and satisfies our spirit each day we run toward our "high calling."

Jesus had to stay focused even when His disciples did not understand his mission, his vision, the upward, eternal call. Remember when the disciples wanted to go around Samaria, but Jesus, responding to God's call, went right to the middle of it and met the woman at the well. He brought salvation to this whole region on one visit. If the disciples had had their way, Jesus would never have gone there. But Jesus stayed focus on His call and fulfilled the will of God for eternal purposes. He could "see the seed" and thereby won the prize of the city of Samaria for the kingdom of God. Have you ever asked yourself if what you are currently engaged in clarifies or fulfills your call?

If we know our mission, please the Lord by fulfilling His call on our life to wait, worship, watch, walk, work, war, and win, then all our time, energy, and resources should be employed to this end. This is the prize, fulfilling our call, living a life of purpose. We have an appointment with destiny; as the "called" ones of God, we answer that call. You may be called to the military or the ministry, the White House or the schoolhouse, inside the home or outside the home, but either way, you will know in your inner man, your spirit, if what you are doing fulfills the call of God and ultimately, leads you to your destiny. Your call begins with the people God gives you to honor, your spouse, your children, your church, your neighbors, authority, etc. Pursue and press for the prize of the high calling, the heavenly, holy, eternal call of God. This is true victory, a satisfying reward and victory that honors God.

Reward 3 - Children

Behold, children are a heritage from the Lord, the fruit of the womb a *reward*" (Psalm 127:3, added). This may be a tender topic but stay with me; all throughout scripture from the beginning, God desires seed. He told Adam and Eve to "be fruitful and multiply." In Deuteronomy 28, he promises to bless the children of those who "listen and do His commandments." When the enemy attacks our unborn children, he is stealing the very reward and blessing of God. You can see how abortion is such an affront to God when He is the Creator and Giver of life as a reward. Yes, God forgives and heals and also gloriously restores! What God calls a blessing, a gift, a reward is not a curse. This applies not only to your physical children by birth but also to adopted children like myself, as well as to spiritual children. The next generation is our legacy, our heritage as well. What a beautiful gift. I remember so well the joy and delight as we anticipated the birth of our child. Yes indeed, what a great reward. But my greatest joy is when one of these precious ones gives their heart to the Lord. You may say, "If you knew my kid, you wouldn't say it's a reward." Well, I understand, there are days when you look in the face of your child by faith and have to declare, "God said you are a reward," and begin to thank God that He knows what He is doing. Or, maybe you have been struggling with infertility, desiring a child, but unable, for whatever reason, to bring one to birth. God still has a reward for you, dear one, do not despair. Be open to what His reward looks like. God has a very special word for you:

> *Sing, O barren one, you who did not bear; break forth into singing and cry aloud, you who did not travail with child! For the [spiritual] children of the desolate one will be more than the children of the married wife, says the Lord.*

> Isaiah 54:1 (AMPC)(emphasis added)

Your reward is even greater! God is after "holy seed." Begin now to see and declare your children and children's children, a "double portion" for those who desire a turnaround.

Reward 4~Christ

Yea doubtless, and I count all things but loss for the excellency of the knowledge of Christ Jesus my Lord: for whom I have suffered the loss of all things, and do count them but dung, that I may win Christ,

Philippians 3:8 (KJV) (emphasis added)

"After these things the word of the Lord came unto Abram in a vision, saying, Fear not, Abram: I am thy shield, and thy *exceeding great reward*" (Genesis 15:1, KJV) (emphasis added).

The "I am," the *Lord* Himself, Christ is not just a simple reward; He is our exceeding great reward! Paul goes on to explain that winning Christ is to "gain Him" or to be found in Him, in His righteousness. By faith, when we know and experience His life, death, and resurrection, we win. Because we have been "apprehended" or captured by the love of God, we desire to, in turn, daily capture and apprehend our lover, Jesus Christ. Looking into Him, seeing who He is in His Word, we gain Him by discovering His "unsearchable riches," that He alone is our "pearl of great price." The romance is consummated; we win. To discover all that Christ is and came to give us in Himself, we now enjoy as the victors. Oh, that we may win together as women of God the ultimate beauty of pleasing our Lord with the simple child-like faith of trusting He is good, and He is a rewarder of those who diligently seek Him. Stop pursuing anyone or anything else; it is simply refuse, garbage in comparison to what is waiting for you. Pursue the eternal rewards prepared for you, the crowns, call, children, and Christ. I hope and pray to see you at the finish line where we will join the saints who have gone before in the "Winner's Circle" and receive our rewards.

Now with this renewed vision of victory, you can begin to write the story of your journey. To what or to whom is God calling you? Bring them Jesus. If God be for me, who can be against me? Take heart, my sister, "it is not by strength nor by might, but by my Spirit says the Lord." With the power of His Holy Spirit, we will hear Him say, "Well done thou good and faithful servant, enter thou into the joy of thy Lord." When we refuse the pleasures and comforts of sin for a season and rather, like Moses, choose to endure the discipline and pain of winning our race, following the examples from the "Hall of Fame, of Faith," we win. You will join the company of Esther, Ruth, Mary, Hannah, Deborah, Sarah, and so many others who are standing in the "Winner's Circle."

> By faith Moses, when he was come to years, refused to be called the son of Pharaoh's daughter; Choosing rather to suffer affliction with the people of God, than to enjoy the pleasures of sin for a season; Esteeming the reproach of Christ greater riches than the treasures in Egypt: for he had respect unto the recompense of the reward.
>
> Hebrews 11:24-26 (KJV)

How do we do it? We value these rewards. Moses esteemed reproach and respected the reward. Think of how you learned the "value of a dollar" or how you want to teach your children the "value of a dollar." Why? So we could learn and pass on an appreciation for the cost or price of things. In other words, we come to a place of spiritual maturity where we realize the invisible is more valuable than the visible. Instead of making a nice little comfy spot for the pleasures, refuse them, choose to endure the pain because you esteem or value identifying with Christ, and respect the reward, Jesus Christ.

Put aside the fears and doubts, step out in faith today and do the next right thing. Stop settling and start seeing. See Christ, see the call, see the crowns and let faith arise. Value the true reward that is eternal. Believe, and you will see the glory of the Lord. Let His glory fill your heart and mind right now with the vision of victory. Like Christ, "see the seed." See the souls, the lives that need one touch of the love of God. Value the reward, so like Moses, you esteem the reward of God greater riches than the fleeting passions of the flesh. Don't give in, press in, don't give up, look up. In the next verse, we are told Moses forsook Egypt and endured as "seeing him who is invisible." Raise your sights to new heights, and let faith take you into His glorious presence, where you receive the true rewards. "Cast not away therefore your confidence, which hath great recompense of reward" (Hebrews 10:35, KJV). "And, behold, I come quickly; and my reward is with me, to give every man according as his work shall be" (Revelation 22:12, KJV).

God is a rewarder, and He wants to reward you. Place your value on these heavenly rewards and be the winner He made you to be. You can do all things through Christ, who loves you. Things do change! Wait on God like Hannah, hear His voice and receive the seed of truth. Worship Him with His word like Mary, releasing the seed. Watch for His activity; it could come knocking at your door like Rahab. Walk away from the flesh, the world, the known, and into the unknown by faith like Ruth. Then, work as unto the Lord, the works of God. Stay alert; war a good warfare; you win when you play by the rules, the perfect law of liberty, and the greatest commandment of love. And yes, it is well. God is in control; He is on the throne and coming soon. Look up, long for your lover; He longs to bring us home with Him.

The resistance you endure is required for the win. Resistance brings with it temptations to yield or to quit. Do not get weary in well-doing, for in due season, you will reap *if* you faint not! Through prayer, we endure the temptation to quit or to yield, and in so doing, we position ourselves to receive the victors' crown of life. When you are tempted to give your husband a sermon, and instead you give him silence, you win! Trusting God to deliver him his mail, you have successfully endured temptation and not only won a battle but, more importantly, won your husband. So, save your breath, keep your peace, stay silent and win! These small wins add up to one great victorious life. That is why Peter has to instruct the women to win without a word; otherwise, we would go on thinking if we think it, we are supposed to say it! Instead, we are to pray it! Pray the answer.

We receive when we pray according to God's will. So, find out God's will in His Word and pray that for your husband. We can soon begin to give thanks for the resistance because by overcoming, we are blessed. See the resistance as your blessing and get happy! Begin to take notice of the blessings, and give thanks. God will find a way to bless you. It might be in a small way, but the beauty is, you will know it is God. He will even work through your husband and have him do things he would not have normally done. It is a beautiful thing.

Sometimes we just need to stop it. Just stop, whatever it is that is distracting and deterring you from your victory, friends, associations, TV, books, games, posting, tweeting, chatting, snapping, texting, etc. Focus on the "one thing" to which God has called you. You will most likely have to say "no" to things that are stealing away your time in order to replace it with the right things. Think now, what are some things you need to stop and say "no" to? Do they bless your marriage and others? Oftentimes, we put so many things ahead of intimacy with our spouse. Have you been meeting your husband's needs? Are you putting children, grandchildren, jobs, errands, ball games, school ahead of your husband? If he feels second fiddle to any of these things, you will not experience victory in your marriage.

Lay aside the weights, the encumbrances that prevent you from winning. Learn to say "no." Remove the distractions and replace them with your goals. The victory is won day by day, one step at a time. Then you will receive the victor's crown of the one who endures to the end! You are more than a conqueror! Keep hope alive; on these wings, faith rides and wins. This is the victory that overcomes even our faith. The Lord is your husband! Hope in that, believe it, act and speak as it is so. "Your husband is your maker. His name is the LORD of Armies. Your defender is the Holy One of Israel. He is called the God of the whole earth" (Isaiah 54:5, GW).

Do you believe? Have you confessed Him as the Lord, your Husband? Do you receive that? He is your defender. Will you act in faith and receive your victory in Christ Jesus? Trust His Word and invite Him to be the Lord, your Husband, and then pass the tests, mark the way of your journey, and set up the memorial stones of Wait, Worship, Watch, Walk, Work, War, Well, and Win. Fill your mouth with His word and declare, *the Lord is my husband*!

Not until I repented and came to the cleansing flow of the blood of Christ for speaking and doing things my way and began confessing the Lord as my Husband did I begin to experience change in my marriage. It began in my heart first. I had to believe God. I had to trust not only Him but also His way of winning. I had the victory in my heart first. Through a quiet confidence in the blood and the Word, we see and experience daily victories for the kingdom of God. You may default to your old ways; yes, I know, I did. Recognize it, repent, and return to His way. Get back on track. Guard your heart and mind with your armor and walk in the winning way, loving God in your worship, your work, and your war. Believe, God is at work, especially when you don't see it. God desires to manifest His loving-kindness to you through your husband. This shows the world and manifests the love of Jesus for His bride, the church. No wonder Satan throws everything he has against the institution of marriage.

Oftentimes, we experience defeat because we try to love selfishly or in the flesh. We have not loved God first or ourselves, but we go on trying to use "love" to manipulate people to get our way, to make us look a certain way. That is not the love that wins. Be honest in assessing your own motives. Only the agape, unconditional love of God, shed within our hearts by the Holy Spirit, is irresistible.

Remove the distractions and refocus on the vision, the vision of victory. Love is the victory. Love is looking to win you so you will love God and others. The Lord your Husband, in the person of Jesus Christ through His sinless life, death, and now relentless pursuit, keeps loving. With this agape love in our hearts, we win. In order to have a clear vision, God, throughout the Scriptures, has given us pictures of victory, paradise, Eden. You might say, "That's impossible; you don't know what I live with day in and day out." And to that, I ask, "How big is your God?" Remember what the angel asked Sarah when she laughed? Is there anything too hard for the Lord? With God, all things are possible! After all, He created us.

So let's refocus here and get His vision of victory, love. By reminding ourselves of the amazing, true, passionate, pursuing lover we have as our Husband, we are inspired to win. We find the heart of our lover here:

> *Thou art all fair, my love; there is no spot in thee. Thou has ravished my heart, my sister, my spouse; thou hast ravished my heart with one of thine eyes, with one chain of thy neck. How fair is thy love, my sister, my spouse! How much better is thy love than wine! And the smell of thine ointments than all spices! Thy lips, O my spouse, drop as the honeycomb: honey and milk are under thy tongue; and the smell of thy garments is like the smell of Lebanon. A garden enclosed is my sister, my spouse; a spring shut up, a fountain sealed. Thy plants are an orchard of pomegranates, with pleasant fruits; camphire, with spikenard, my beloved spake, and said unto me, Arise, my love, my fair one, and come away.*

Song of Songs 4:7, 9-13; 2:10 (KJV)(emphasis added)

And our response:

> *Let him kiss me with the kisses of his mouth: for thy love is better than wine. I sat down under his shadow with great delight, and his fruit was sweet to my taste. He brought me to the banqueting house, and his banner over me was love. My beloved is mine, and I am his: he feedeth among the lilies.*

Song of Songs 1:2, 2:3, 4, 16 (KJV)(emphasis added)

The Conclusion

"*I am my beloved's, and his desire is toward me*" (Song of Songs 7:10, KJV) (emphasis added). You are loved; live like you are.

The God of the universe is crazy about you. He has a banner of love placed over you, identifying you as His Beloved Bride. Go to Him, enjoy His kisses, His taste, and His time. He is always there, waiting to enjoy you. He misses you when you are not there. Hear Him call, sense His nearness, smell His aroma, and taste of His goodness.

> *I sleep, but my heart waketh: it is the voice of my beloved that knocketh, saying, Open to me, my sister, my love, my dove, my undefiled: for my head is filled with dew, and my locks with the drops of the night. I have put off my coat; how shall I put it on? I have washed my feet; how shall I defile them?*

> Song of Songs 5:2-3 (KJV)

Open your heart once again and trust the true love of the Lord your Lover, your Husband.

The Creator calls His creature, the Infinite "I *am*," reaches to the finite, the Invisible reveals Himself to the visible, and Divinity has reached down to humanity. Through Jesus the Christ, the Son of God, God pursued you. Through His death, burial, and resurrection, He redeemed you or bought you back from death. He has now vowed Himself to you, revealing Himself and His love, calling you into covenant with Him so that finally, He can bring you to the marriage supper of the Lamb. Until that final day, when the trumpet of the Lord shall sound, and He calls His bride, the church, to come home and live with Him for eternity, He waits for the precious fruit of the earth. He pursues to the end, even that last one to surrender their life to His all-consuming love. We join Him in His vision, in His unyielding pursuit to reveal His love to the objects of His love, His bride. We now, as loved, look to love. Every moment of every day, love.

Our journey is complete; with the memorial stones set marking the way, reminding us of His faithfulness, we arise and shine as His beautiful bride. The challenge is issued. We begin with waiting on Him, we then offer our worship, keep our watch, while walking, working, and warring, declaring "all is well," we finally win our race. One day, one soul, and one battle at a time, we win if we do not quit. This is success, a winning life of love. God manifests Himself through our earthly husband or whoever He chooses. May you and I join the company of these women Esther, Ruth, Rahab, Mary, Hannah, Deborah, Sarah, and so many unknowns who are standing in the "Winner's Circle." Will you trust His power and rest on His Word, His promises? If so, you will hear, "Well done, thou good and faithful servant." Enjoy the rewards of the life of faith, communion with God, now and forever.

Come to the altar; your Bridegroom awaits. Accept His vows today, declare to Him, "My Creator is my Husband, the Lord, and the God of Angel Armies. He has come for me, and now I go with Him to enjoy the unsearchable riches of His treasure." Let the two become one, the Lord and you, His most prized creation, His beloved. He stands ready to shower you with His all-consuming love. The Royal invitation has been given. Take the Royal ring of authority, the Royal gown of His perfection, and your Royal place as you say "yes" and step through the door of hope with a song of rejoicing into a life of love eternal.

I love you and am for you, along with all of heaven. I hope to see you there, seated at the banqueting table of the Marriage Supper of the Lamb where we, His glorious Bride, the church, will live in His love forever. God bless you, beloved of the Lord, hear him as He speaks to you:

Thou hast ravished my heart, my sister, my bride; Thou hast ravœished my heart with one of thine eyes, With one chain of thy neck.

How fair is thy love, my sister, my bride! How much better is thy love than wine!

Song of Songs 4:9-10 (ASV)

The Gospel & Prayer
for Salvation

My prayer for you: Jesus would You make yourself real to my friend now, bless them and do a quick work in their heart. May she/he receive Jesus Christ as her/his Lord and Savior right now.

Did you know God loves you and has wonderful plan for your life?

The Bible says: "For all have sinned and come short of the glory of God." Romans 3:23 (KJV) And, "For the wages of sin is death, but the free gift of God is eternal life in Christ Jesus our Lord." Romans 6:23 (NASB1995)

It also says "Whosoever shall call on the name of the Lord shall be saved."

If you, a whosoever, would like to receive this gift of eternal life, say this simple prayer and believe in your heart:

> *Heavenly Father, I come to you in the name of Jesus and ask that you come into my heart, forgive me of my sin. Wash me and cleanse me, set me free to be what you made me to be. Thank you Jesus that you died for me. I believe that you are risen from the dead and that You are coming back again for me. Fill me now with the Holy Spirit. Give me a passion for the lost, a hunger for the things of God and a holy boldness to preach the Gospel of Jesus Christ. I am now saved, born again, forgiven, and on my to Heaven because I have Jesus in my heart.*

You are now forgiven and saved! Always run to God not away because He loves you so much. Please get in a good Bible preaching church nearby and read your Bible everyday. Please follow the Lord in Baptism, this is an outward expression of an inward commitment, as soon as possible.

Please let me know @ www.Janetlash.com when you prayed this prayer.

God bless you!!

CONNECT WITH

JANET

JANET LASH
—— MINISTRIES ——
A FRIEND WITH FAITH

Visit
www.Janetlash.com

CPSIA information can be obtained
at www.ICGtesting.com
Printed in the USA
JSHW041259170822
29400JS00002B/5